THE TYRANNY OF GOD

Liberating Ourselves
From Our Own Beliefs

By
Marquez Comelab

OrangesAndLime
Publishing

MELBOURNE

Copyright © September 2008 by Marquez W. Comelab.
All Rights Reserved.
Published by Oranges And Lime.

ISBN: 978-0-646-50169-7

YOURS TO HAVE AND TO HOLD, BUT NOT TO COPY

No part of this publication may be reproduced, stored in a retrieval system or transmitted in any form or by any means: electronic, mechanical, photocopying, recording, scanning or otherwise, except in fair use as permitted under copyright laws in Australia, without the prior written permission of the author.

Last Update: 23-11-2008

ACKNOWLEDGEMENTS

This book is dedicated to my wife, Nancy Comelab, who shared with me the surprises, the shocks and the enlightenment I experienced whilst writing and researching for this book. Nancy, with your ceaseless support, encouragement and editing work, this book is your work just as much as it is mine.

Thank you to my family, especially my mother who still believes in God, for supporting me in everything I do and for engaging me in endless discussions on religion.

Mario Astorga, my theist friend, you have helped mould this book. Thank you so much for being my sparring partner, talking and debating with me for hours. I have had so much fun.

Chris Birt, my atheist friend, you have been with me since the start of this project. Thank you for sharing your enthusiasm and excitement during all stages of its progress.

To many of my other friends and colleagues, from varying religious and cultural backgrounds, who have shared their thoughts and ideas with me: I will not mention your names here to avoid complications with your families, friends and relatives, but know that regardless of the length of our conversations, they were all valuable to me and I thank you.

CONTENTS

PREFACE 1
   About This Book 8
   How I Structured This Book 9
   The Readers Of This Book 10

CHAPTER 1: COSMOLOGY 13
   The Big Bang Theory 13
   What happened after the Big Bang? 14

CHAPTER 2: THE ORIGIN OF LIFE 21
   The Replicator 23
   The Anthropic Principle 24

CHAPTER 3: GENETICS 29
   DNA, Chromosomes, Cells And Genes 29
   Sex, Heredity, Alleles And Traits 31
   Children Not Exactly Like Their Parents 32
   Sexual And Asexual Reproduction 34
   Definition Of A 'Gene' 34

CHAPTER 4: EVOLUTION BY NATURAL SELECTION 37
   Natural Selection 38
   Speciation 42
   The Tree Of Life 44

CHAPTER 5: HOW LIFE EVOLVED ON EARTH 47
   Prokaryotes and Eukaryotic Cells 49
   Oxygen And The Ozone Layer 50
   Early Plants And Animals 51
   The Cambrian Explosion 52
   Opisthokonts 52
   Animals (Metazoa) 53

    Bilaterally Symmetrical Organisms (Bilateria) *54*

    Deuterostomes (Deuterostomia) *54*

    Early Life On Land *55*

    Chordates (Chordata) *56*

    Craniates (Craniata) *56*

    Vertebrates (Vertebrata) *57*

    Jawed Vertebrates (Gnathostomata) *57*

    Teleostomi *58*

    Osteichthye *58*

    The Terrestrial Vertebrates *59*

    The Tetrapods (Tetrapoda) *59*

    Plants Evolved Seeds *60*

    Amphibia and Reptiliomorpha *61*

    Synapsids ('Beast Faces') and Sauropsids ('Lizard Faces') *62*

    Therapsids (Therapsida) *63*

    Mammals (Mammalia) *64*

    Placental Mammals (Eutheria) *65*

    Supraprimates (Euarchontoglires) *66*

    Primates *66*

    Simians (Simiiformes) *67*

    Cattarhini (Downward-Pointing Nose) *68*

    Apes / Hominoids (Hominoidea) *68*

    The Great Apes / Hominids (Hominidae) *69*

    The Hominini *69*

    The Hominina *70*

    Humans (Homo Sapiens) *71*

    Conclusion *76*

CHAPTER 6: RESPITE **79**

    Our Definition Of 'God' And 'Religion' *79*

    Introduction To My Thesis On God And Religion *81*

CHAPTER 7: LANGUAGE **85**

CHAPTER 8: MEMES 89
Introduction To Memes.. 89
How Memes Affect Our State.. 90
Memes: The New Replicators 91
Memes Evolved To Religions.. 93

CHAPTER 9: BELIEFS AND DELUSIONS.. 99
The Nature Of Our Beliefs... 99
Our Capacity For Delusions 102

CHAPTER 10: EARLY HUMAN SOCIETIES 107

CHAPTER 11: WHY WE ARE MORAL 113
Violence, Threats and Fear 116
Favours And Acts Of Kindness... 117
Our Desire For Honour And Respect... 118

CHAPTER 12: AN AMORAL WORLD 121
Morality Is Independent From Religion 121
Human Beings Define Their Own Morality.. 122
Believing The Unbelievable... 123

CHAPTER 13: WHY OUR ANCESTORS USED RELIGION.................... 127
Religion Helped Explain Natural Phenomena................................... 127
Religion As A Tool For Controlling And Organising Societies......... 137
Religion As A Tool For Unity And Mobilisation 141

CHAPTER 14: THE NATURE OF RELIGION 147
Religion As An Organism 147
Religion As An Organisation... 148
Successful Religions 149
Conversion Fecundity: Convert Minds Fast...................................... 150
Conversion Longevity – Protecting Minds 153
Accurate Indoctrination (Copying Fidelity) 157
Competition 159

CHAPTER 15: THE TYRANNY OF GOD **161**
   Establish God And His Book As Authorities *162*
   Demand People To Take This God Seriously *164*
   Substitute The Need For Evidence With Faith *164*
   Instil Obedience *165*
   Discourage Doubt and Enquiry *166*
   Enforce Regular Meetings To Keep The Faith *167*
   Protect Beliefs And Silence Contradictory Ideas *168*
   Systematically Acquiring Minds *173*
   Kill People Once They Stop Believing *174*
   Coerce People To Do The 'Will Of God' *176*
   The Cloak Of Morality *180*

CHAPTER 16: ESCAPE FROM RELIGIOUS DESPOTISM **183**
   The Protestant Revolution *183*
   The Age Of Reason, Enlightenment And Beyond *189*
   Life Today Vs Life During Religious Dogmatism *191*
   The Rise of Irreligious, Secular Ideas *196*

CHAPTER 17: GOD'S THREAT TO DEMOCRACY **207**
   Democracy *208*
   Winding Back The Separation of Church And State *210*
   Freedom of Expression *220*
   Indoctrination of Children *227*

CHAPTER 18: THE FALLACY OF RELIGIOUS MODERATION **233**

CHAPTER 19: WHY WE NEED TO JUSTIFY OUR BELIEFS **241**

CHAPTER 20: A WORLD WITHOUT GOD **245**

CHAPTER 21: THE POWER OF REASON **247**
   Prediction And Intelligence *248*
   When Knowledge Stops Working *250*
   What Constitutes Good Information? *251*
   Reasonism *255*

CHAPTER 22: HUMAN NATURE 261
   Controlling Violence 263
   Empower People to Exchange Favours and Acts of Kindness 263
   Empower People With Their Own Ambitions 264

CHAPTER 23: ONE LIFE 267

APPENDICES 273
   (1) What Existed Before The Big Bang? 273
   (2) Explaining Consciousness 278
   (3) The Infant Mind 282

BIBLIOGRAPHY 287

INDEX 289

ENDNOTES 291

"Everything we do is based on what we believe. Our religious beliefs influence where we stand on many important issues like sexuality, abortion, ethics and terrorism, amongst many others. In a democracy, we vote for leaders to whom we abrogate responsibility to make decisions that affect us all. Since all votes are equal, the value of a well thought-out vote is the same as that of a careless one. We owe it to ourselves, to each other and to our children to be well-informed so we can start making more educated decisions today."

– Marquez Comelab

PREFACE

I was born in the Philippines, a country predominantly formed by grouped islands. The north and the middle islands were introduced to Christianity when the Spaniards ruled it for 300 years. The Philippines was Asia's trade centre centuries ago. Indians, Malaysians, Indonesians and Islanders all contributed to its culture, religion and heritage. The religion of the southern groups of islands was, and still is, Islam. I was born in the northern islands of Luzon: a region where people, up until today, believe in 'anitos', the spirits of the dead. Plenty of ancient Chinese superstitions are still lurking in many villages in the islands of the Philippines.

My mother was born a Roman Catholic and my father was baptised in an Anglican church. When I was a young boy, my father worked a lot in faraway places, like Saudi Arabia. Although my parents had humble beginnings, it was my father's profession as a Civil Engineer that gave him the privilege to work. Back then, as it is now, work was hard to find and poverty makes it common for Filipinos to work overseas to support their loved ones back home.

My mother made an effort for our family to attend mass every Sunday. She also encouraged us kids to attend Sunday school, which was usually held after mass. She has always believed in God but to her it did not matter where we praised Him. We attended many Bible study classes, Sunday schools and masses organised by Baptists, Anglicans, Seventh Day Adventists and even Jehovah's Witnesses.

I enjoyed the Bible stories. I loved the stories of Adam and Eve, Samson and Delilah, Moses, Abraham and Jesus Christ, among many others. Living in one of the most religious countries in the world, there was plenty of religious literature around.

My father, on the other hand, did not mention religion much. He once brought a poster from Saudi Arabia on evolution: a picture of apes progressing to a human form. He introduced me to evolution, something I was never taught in elementary school. It is not surprising since the private school I went to was founded by the Episcopals, another denomination of Christianity. Between the 'anitos', Anglicans, Episcopals and Catholics, I grew up with an eclectic mix of religious and supernatural beliefs.

For most of my life, I did not question the existence of God. My wife, most of my family, friends and relatives were all born into Christianity. We can be classified as 'non-practicing' or 'moderate' Christians. We went to church occasionally. When we did, it would be mainly for baptisms, deaths and marriages. The strength of our beliefs varied from believing that God exists to believing that religion is beneficial, regardless of His existence.

Does God exist? Should we believe in God? Having an opinion on such big questions seemed inconsequential. We did not see how our lives would be impacted if we were to have an opinion on the matter. For us, there was no urgency. These questions were not as important as getting good grades, finishing studies, getting jobs or taking care of loved ones. Besides, what did it matter? We just had to be good mothers, fathers, sons, daughters and neighbours. All that mattered was that we were good to other people and that we did not inflict injury, harm, or suffering to another human being. The golden rule of treating others the way we want to be treated was our guiding thought, and to us, that was enough.

My true beliefs are a mix of many influences. A big part of me is an existentialist. I did not believe in the after-life and I lived in an indifferent universe. My human experience is what I make it to be. Everybody must be given freedom of choice but they must be responsible for the consequences of what they do.

A part of me was also an agnostic. There were still too many things we did not know, and cannot know, in our lifetimes, to hold strong convictions about how everything came into being.

A part of me also believed that if there was, and if there is, an all-powerful creator of the universe, He or She would be so complex that we could never understand Him or Her. He would have to be pervasive everywhere in the universe, like energy.

Puzzlingly, I also prayed. Parts of me believed that even if I was an atheist, the act of praying could give me strength and solace. So in moments of pain, trepidation, fear, anguish or loss, I prayed.

How can all these different sets of beliefs exist in one mind? Somehow, unconsciously, I have found, a way to make them all coexist with one another. I picked and chose which belief to use, depending on the circumstances I faced. It is only after I went through a period I call, 'my active search for truth', did I realise the contradictions between these different belief systems.

A month before my thirtieth birthday, I read a book written by an evolutionary biologist, a professor in Oxford University. The author's name was Richard Dawkins. The title of the book was *The God Delusion*. In his book, Dawkins argues the case that God does not exist. His logic overwhelmed me. Even though I did not grasp all the ideas he discussed, my mind was stupefied by what he wrote. He made so much sense that it shook me to the core. Then, the weirdest numbness happened. I began to feel weak, physically, emotionally and mentally. It took a man like Dawkins, to make me realise that, contrary to what I thought, I actually did believe in an all-knowing God. When confronted with the real possibility that He does not exist, I began to react uncontrollably.

Emotionally, I rejected the idea there was no God watching over me and my family. I felt alone and deserted thinking that there was nobody out there who knew, shared or empathised with me in my struggles. Ultimately, we are all alone and there is only the Here and the Now. Once my loved ones die, I will never see them again.

For days, questions raged through my head: How should I live my life? How should anybody live their lives? What could deter people from committing crime and causing others to suffer if they did not believe in a God who punished them for their sins?

What are the things we should value? Should we live life selfishly and enjoy as much of it as we can, while it lasts? Should we subscribe to hedonism and spend most of our lives seeking sensual pleasures and materialistic, superfluous luxuries? In what ways can we be responsible and accountable for what we say and do when there is no judgement at the end of our days?

At the age of thirty, it seemed crucial that I needed to think things through again. There was a sense of emptiness, ultimately transgressing into fear and panic.

I talked this through with my wife. Unlike me, she was not disturbed by the possibility of no God. The book just confirmed what she had long suspected, even as a child. Instead of feeling empty and panicky, she was relieved to know that she was not 'abnormal' for thinking the way she did. The most surprising aspect of this whole experience, for both of us, was the fact that I was affected at all.

I classified myself as an existentialist and yet, when I was challenged to confront the impossibility of a God, I experienced such mental, physical and emotional distress. Imagine what would happen to anyone else who had been indoctrinated just a little bit more than I?

A couple of weeks later, my wife and I attended a funeral. There, amid the sadness and sorrow, I got into a discussion about God and religion with another friend who also read *The God Delusion*. He was a Roman Catholic. Like I, he also found his thinking being transformed after reading the book. As much as he agreed and applauded the arguments against God, his belief in Him remained.

I asked how he could explain the fact that he agrees intellectually with the logical arguments against the existence of a supernatural god, and still be able to believe in one. He said, "I don't know. Perhaps because I have always been religious. It might not be easy to get rid of one's beliefs."

"How do you reconcile the two conflicting ideas?" I asked.

"I am still thinking through it. I feel there must be something useful about religion if it was able to survive so long. I am not sure that I can, or, that I should, let go of it", he replied.

Eventually, I advanced to tell him that I felt physically weak, I felt mentally unsettled and I was emotionally unable to reject what seemed glaringly obvious.

What happened next came completely unexpected. I expected him to take my state of discomposure as a sign that the Creator does exist, and perhaps, I was experiencing what it feels like to reject God and that I was wrong to doubt Him. I expected him to - tell me to repent my sins and ask for God's forgiveness. But my dear friend did not. Instead, he told me about how he tried other forms of religions.

"When I was growing up, my sister was religious", he began. "Because she was the older one, it was natural for me to follow her around different sorts of gatherings. That was how I developed my interest in religion. I tried Catholicism, flirted with Baptist, hovered around El Shadai, considered Sun Myung Moon's Unification Movement, and a couple more".

He continued to explain, "The reason why I tell you this is because I think you are experiencing the same thing I experienced when I first changed religions. My first religion was Roman Catholic. I decided to change to a fellowship called *Jesus Is Lord*. In my first few days, I also could not function as normally as I used to. It was strange. After a while, however, I began to feel better and think clearer again. I eventually got used to living and seeing life through the eyes of my newly-adopted religion. I think what happened to me – and what is happening to you now – is natural."

"Oh I see, we learn to live with a set of beliefs and see everything else in the world through that filter", I asked.

"That's right", he said. "I think that when you take away something which you have lived with for a long time, you start feeling confused, agitated and so on. Eventually, you will learn to live with the new beliefs you choose, and then you will begin to feel your strength and mental clarity come back".

I found him to be one of the most sensible and most unselfish individuals I have ever met. He was very much unlike most religious people I knew, who would not have hesitated to give me a sermon. I also find it ironic, that the strength I gained to let go of my half-baked beliefs in the existence of a supernatural god, came from a man who still believed in one.

The message I took from the conversation was that, I was experiencing some from of withdrawal symptom. I was taking away that part of me on which I had built my entire being. Naturally, I became unstable. If we remove a portion of a building's foundation, for example, that building will naturally shake. If it is taken out too quickly, without replacing it with any form of support or cushion, it will collapse.

With a new understanding of what was happening to me, I reflected on how I once managed to stop smoking. I remember I could not feel anything else but my craving for cigarettes. In my first few days, the urge was so strong that, to stop myself from lighting up, I had to sleep a lot. This made it possible for my body to get used to passing the hours without nicotine. I focussed on getting by without a cigarette, hour by hour, until I did not smoke for three continuous days. It got easier each day. Days turned to weeks, and weeks turned to months.

I used to have a cigarette before and after every task including eating, showering, driving, working and studying. In kicking off the habit, I realised I had to replace it with something else that was not addictive. When it got really bad, I would suck on a straw. I had plenty cups of Milo. I had to drink so much that I only added a teaspoon of the chocolate drink to a big mug of hot water so I would not get sick of it. I ate plenty of apples too. It filled the minutes I used to fill with smoking.

In tackling my latest challenge, I decided I needed a substitute for religious beliefs like I did for cigarettes. I realised that religious beliefs have seeped into every aspect of our being, our thinking and our way of life, regardless of whether we are aware of them. Many people use religion to deal with the pain of losing a loved one. Some of us turn to faith to live through great misfortunes, and to deal with great injustices and indignities.

We live our lives by creating a model of how everything in the universe fits. We create these models consciously or unconsciously. These models are important to help us understand who and what we are; what to do and where to go. Like maps that help us navigate streets, these models help us chart our course through life. With the dominance of religion in our lives, most of us end up with religious maps. When I refused to look at my map, I felt lost.

If there is no God, then how could we account for all the variety of life on this planet? If we evolved from ape-like creatures, and they evolved from something else, then how did life begin on Earth? If life on Earth began on a different planet, how did it start there? If our universe originated from a big explosion called the 'Big Bang', what was there before the Big Bang?

For most of our lives, religion has answered many of these questions for us. It is difficult, therefore, to remove or defuse religious dogmas because they are ingrained into the foundations of the models that you and I have created and adopted for ourselves.

If I were to take out the belief that there is no God from my mind, I also needed to extract everything else that necessitated His existence. When I did, I began to notice gaps in my mind and this resulted in my discomfort. With so many gaps, many of the questions I had previously answered were devoid of answers. And I desperately needed answers.

I no longer felt I could live the best possible life I could if I no longer knew the standard on which to base it. The only way was to fill these newly-created gaps in my mind, with new ideas, new knowledge and new ways of thinking.

I prepared to dedicate most of the thirty-first year of my life to read and research as much as I could. I wanted a new understanding of life, us, morality and God. This book is the result of that pursuit.

About This Book

One of my biggest worries in writing this book was the breadth of topics I had to cover. At times, I wondered whether I was doing the right thing in casting as wide a net as I did. I chose to proceed because, to understand the true nature of religion, we cannot limit our discussions to religious texts. Instead, we need to take a larger, macroscopic view. We need to see how it relates to human nature and to our society. We need to consult our sciences and corroborate our analysis with our history.

In our struggle to broaden our outlook, we need to start from the very beginning. From there, we work progressively. We will learn about cosmology, abiogenesis, genetics, evolution, language, memes, history, current affairs and so on.

The main purpose of this book is not to argue against religion. Rather, it tells our story and how we have come to oppress ourselves with the tyranny of our own beliefs. I wrote this book to include everything I discovered to be relevant in my search for the truth, not just the truth behind God and morality, but also behind us and our existence. Instead of reading this book with the expectation that it is trying to prove the tyranny of God, I would like to recommend you read it as a story book: as a book that tells the story of humanity from the Big Bang.

I wanted to make this book easy to read and simple to understand, to the extent that I can in explaining some complex ideas. I also wanted it, regardless of the extensive amount of information, light enough to carry around whilst keeping important information intact.

Please be aware that in some cases, I had to choose among competing scientific theories. I chose to present the ones I found most convincing. Please use this book as a guide to direct you towards other knowledgeable and often beautiful works written by philosophers, scientists and other experts. The bibliography, therefore, will be valuable to you in expanding your search for knowledge. As science advances, and as I find better ways of expressing my arguments, it is likely I will update this book in the future.

How I Structured This Book

I sought to tell the story of humanity from the beginning to the present. I structured this book so you can read it like a story book, where the earlier chapters are the foundations of later chapters. The following is a quick preview of what we will be discussing.

The Scientific Explanation

- The Big Bang
- How galaxies and our solar system formed.
- How our planet Earth and its moon formed.
- The first life.
- How life replicates.
- How life evolved on Earth.

Understanding How We Think

- Language and consciousness.
- Language as a tool for communication.
- How language is like sex.
- What are memes?
- How memes coalesce to religions.
- The nature of ideas and beliefs.
- How we delude ourselves.

Human Nature and Human Societies

- The three truths of being human.
- The Golden Rule.
- Why we are moral in an amoral world.

Religion

- The three main purposes of religion.
- How religions are like organisms.
- How religions are like any human organisations.

- How we enslave ourselves with our tyrannical beliefs.
- How we escaped the grips of religious oppression.

Us And Religion

- The threat to democracy.
- The threat to freedom of speech, expression and the press.
- The fallacy of religious moderation.
- Why we need to justify our beliefs to one another.

Building Our Future

- The power of reason.
- How to identify intelligent reasons.
- How to identify good information.
- What is Reasonism?
- How we can build a better future by understanding human nature.

The Readers Of This Book

In writing this book, I imagined five groups of readers:

- The irreligious or the atheist
- The agnostic
- The moderately religious
- The religious
- The subject-matter experts

Every one of these readers will have different needs and reasons for wanting to read this book.

The Irreligious And The Atheists

This book can be a handy tool if you need help in clarifying why you may lack belief in God. I hope it helps you argue some of the ideas you have with other people.

The Agnostics

I was an agnostic once. As I found out, much of my agnosticism stemmed from my inability or unwillingness to seek the answers to the big questions of life and our existence. I went to an Episcopalian primary school and I went to a public school in high school. Neither of them taught the theory of evolution, natural selection or how life began.

Science is now at the stage where it is able to provide us all with intellectually-satisfying answers to many of our cosmological questions. Yet, sadly, millions of people remain ignorant of its ability to give us all a sense of wonder and appreciation for the beauty and drama of the world we live in.

The Moderately Religious

I understand that many of you may have doubts about the existence of God. Perhaps you even doubt that religions come from divine sources, however, you still believe that religions could be beneficial in some way. I think many of you will find the scientific explanation behind the origins of life and evolution pleasantly surprising. To many of you, who have not really read your Scriptures, you might be interested to have another look at some of the verses and re-examine what it means to be moderately religious.

Regardless of your religion, I want to appeal to you because I am sure we share the same belief that extremism and the literal interpretation of the scriptures are not conducive to the type of society we want to live in.

The Strongly Religious

Strongly religious people usually get angry, offended, annoyed or dismissive of anybody, or anything, that challenges their beliefs. Sometimes they are even fearful of entertaining any idea that deviates from their beliefs because God might be watching. This book is not to make you doubt your beliefs; rather, to help you understand how people can not be religious like you.

I hope you will finish reading this book. I want to appeal to you by saying that, because we share the same planet, what you choose to believe in, affects everybody else. Likewise, what another person believes, will ultimately affect you. It is therefore very important to continue engaging in dialogue because that is the only way for humanity to overcome its challenges.

The Subject-Matter Experts

I have made every effort to find the latest and most robust theories and ideas to cover in this book. However, I am also aware that ideas are continuously being challenged by other ideas. Such is the reality of our search for truth. But so long as we ground our knowledge and wisdom with reality, we will eventually discover the answers we are looking for.

In writing this book, I largely wrote to communicate with people who have not formally studied your field… people like me. It is difficult to be an expert in all the subjects religion touches. This is why I have resorted to quoting many of you instead of using my own words. I hope I can arouse enough interest for people to learn more about your works, your theories and your ideas.

I welcome any feedback, corrections and invitations for further discussions, should you allow me the privilege. In this book, I have made some observations and postulations of my own. If you have any thoughts, experiments or works that either support or disagree with them, I would be delighted to hear about them.

CHAPTER 1: COSMOLOGY

The Big Bang Theory

The universe began around 13.7 billion years ago.[1] The origin of the universe is explained by the Big Bang Theory.[a] In its standard form, everything in the universe began from what is called a 'singularity', a zone that defies our current understanding of physics. The universe then exploded, or expanded, this 'singularity'.

It was the American astronomer, Edwin Hubble, who made an interesting and important observation in the late 1920s, with the aid of the largest telescope at the time.[b] He saw that distant stars and galaxies are moving away from the Earth in every direction. Every object in the universe seems to be distancing itself from the Earth at an increasing speed. These findings implied the universe is expanding and it was more condensed at a previous time. From this came the suggestion that everything we can observe in the universe as initially an infinitely small, hot mass which exploded and sent matter and energy in all directions.[2]

If the universe came into existence after a big explosion, then, scientists deduced that the temperature in deep space today should be several degrees above absolute zero. Observations showed this to be true. In 1965, radio astronomers Arno Penzias and Robert Wilson discovered a 2.725 degree Kelvin (-454.765 degree

---

[a] Evidences for the Big Bang Theory: Hubble's Law, Cosmic Microwave Background and the abundance of light elements such as hydrogen and helium in the universe.

[b] The largest telescope at the time was the 100-inch Hooker Telescope.

Fahrenheit, -270.425 degree Celsius) Cosmic Microwave Background radiation (CMB) pervading the observable universe.[3] Furthermore, the Cosmic Microwave Background Explorer (COBE) satellite launched in 1991 confirmed that the background radiation field has exactly the spectrum predicted.[4]

Another strong evidence for the Big Bang theory comes from what we know about nucleosynthesis. Nucleosynthesis[5] is the formation of new atomic nuclei by nuclear reactions we think occurs in the interiors of stars, and in the early stages of the universe.

To explain this, we consult the Berkeley Astronomy Department of the University of California. On their web page on Big Bang nucleosynthesis[6], they explain, and I paraphrase:

> If the Universe relied on stellar nuclear reactions from the Big Bang as its only source of production, then around a quarter of its mass must consist of helium. "The fact that helium is nowhere seen to have an abundance below 23% mass is very strong evidence the universe went through an early hot phase." This is one of the corner-stones of the Big Bang model.

What happened after the Big Bang?

After the Big Bang began its expansion, the temperature of the universe was too high for anything to bind. Eventually, however, the temperature of the universe fell to a point where atoms were able to form. About 70,000 years after the initial expansion, small structures began to form due to competition between gravitational attraction and pressure effects.[7] In the hundreds of thousands of years that followed, matter collected into clouds, which condensed. Smaller structures formed and they began forming bigger structures.

Galaxies

"Changes in pressure caused gas and dust to form distinct clouds. Where there was enough mass and the right forces, gravitational attraction caused the cloud to collapse. If the mass of the material in the cloud was sufficiently compressed, nuclear reactions began and a star is born."[8] Stars are grouped in galaxies and we group galaxies in clusters.

We have developed two models which explain how galaxies form: 'top-down' and 'bottom-up'. In the 'top-down' model, galaxies are thought to have formed from huge gas clouds larger than the resulting galaxy. The clouds begin collapsing when their internal gravity is strong enough to overcome the pressure in the cloud.[9] The rotation of the gas cloud, and the rotation of the collapsing gas cloud within, determines whether the resulting galaxy is elliptical or spiral.[c]

A more recent variation of the 'top-down' model suggests that extremely large gas clouds fragment into smaller clouds. This model predicts that it takes a long time for super large clouds to fragment into individual galaxy clouds. If this is true, there should still be galaxies forming today.[d]

In the 'bottom-up' model, galaxies are built from small clumps of matter merging. "These clumps would have started collapsing when the universe was still young. Then galaxies would be drawn into clusters, and clusters into super clusters by their mutual gravity. This model predicts there should be many more small galaxies than large galaxies – that is observed to be true. The dwarf irregular galaxies may be from cloud fragments that did not get incorporated into larger galaxies. Also, the galaxy clusters and super clusters should still be forming – observations suggest this to be true, as well."[10]

---

[c] "If the gas cloud was slowly rotating, then the collapsing gas cloud formed most of its stars before the cloud could flatten into a disk. The result was an elliptical galaxy. If the gas cloud was rotating faster, then the collapsing gas cloud formed a disk before most of the stars were made. The result was a spiral galaxy." - http://www.astronomynotes.com/galaxy/s10.htm.

[d] A galaxy called 'I Zwicky 18' is now being studied because it is through to be a very young galaxy: only 500 million years old.

One model does not quash the other. In fact, galaxies in the universe could be the result of either formation process. Scientists are now exploring models that combine the 'top-down' and the 'bottom-up' models.

In understanding how galaxies are formed, it is also worth noting that galaxies merge and collide with one another because they are so close. The distances between galaxies are only a few tens of times bigger than the galaxies themselves.[11] These collisions take place over long timescales, several tens of millions of years. When they do occur, the stars within them rarely collide.[e] This is because the distances between the stars are hundreds of thousands, even millions, of times larger than the sizes of the stars themselves.

The Milky Way Galaxy

Among the speckles of light in the blackness of the universe, there is a sector of space we call the Local Group. It is a group of two other large galaxies and thirty small ones. The largest of these galaxies are the Andromeda galaxy and the Milky Way.

The Milky Way began forming 530 million years after the Big Bang.[f] It displays a spiral structure and a prominent bulge component in the middle. It is approximately 100,000 light-years[g] in diameter and is believed to be about 1,000 light-years thick.[12] We estimate that it contains anywhere between 200 to 400 billion stars.[13]

---

[e] These are based from the studies done by Astronomers who program all known data – including gravitational data, as well as the masses and sizes of galaxies and stars – into powerful computers to simulate what would happen.

[f] I got this number based on the oldest star in the galaxy, we have discovered so far which is believed to be 13.2 billion years.

[g] Distances in the universe are so vast that we use the speed of light to measure them. In a vacuum, light travels 299,792,458 metres per second. A light year is the distance light travels, in one year. It is equivalent to exactly 9,460,730,472,580.8 kilometres.

The Star Sol

About 5 billion years ago, 8 to 9 billion years after the Big Bang, a young star was born in the outer regions of the Milky Way galaxy. Its name is Sol. Like most stars, Sol formed from the gravitational collapse of a small part of a massive and dense molecular cloud. It took around 100 million years for it to form.[14]

The complex process of star formation always produces a gaseous disk around young stars. For Sol, this was extremely hot but eventually it cooled down, enough for small dust grains of rocks and ice to form. These little particles eventually coagulated with one another like water drops attaching themselves to bigger drops. Together, they formed objects with masses that were large enough to become planets.

The planets that formed closer to the star have solid, earth-like rock surfaces. They are called Terrestrial Planets. Beyond a certain distance away from the sun, called the 'snow line', it is cold enough for hydrogen compounds such as water, ammonia and methane to condense into solid ice grains. Planets further away from this distance are gaseous planets that do no have clear and defined surfaces. Their atmospheres only become denser and denser towards the core. These planets are called gas giants or Jovian planets.

In its solar system today, Sol has 4 terrestrial planets (Mercury, Venus, Earth and Mars), 4 Jovian planets (Jupiter, Saturn, Uranus and Neptune), 3 dwarf planets (Pluto[15], Ceres and Eris) and 166 moons. The third planet from Sol is planet Earth…our only home in this vast universe. The star Sol is our sun.

Planet Earth and Its Moon

Dust and debris accrete together. They form bigger masses of matter, called protoplanets. After further accretion, these protoplanets will eventually grow enough in size to become planets. As their size grows, so does their gravitational force.

With the rest of the planets in our solar system, the Earth began as a disk-shaped mass of dust, gas and debris, left over from the formation of the Sun 4.54 billion years ago, 9.16 billion years after the Big Bang.[16]

The young proto-Earth gradually became bigger and bigger as it pulled more matter from it surroundings with its ever-strengthening gravity. Inferred from observational scientific evidence, another protoplanet[h], named Theia, hit the proto-Earth around 4.533 million years ago. Most of Theia's core sank into the Earth's core. Because it hit it at a slanting angle, the collision caused most of its rocky mantle into space. We can still see the debris when we look up at nights. They have coalesced to form what we now recognise as the moon.[i]

As the Earth grew in size, its gravity became strong enough to retain its own atmosphere.[17] The Earth's surface was originally molten because of extremely hot temperatures in a volcanic landscape. Its primordial atmosphere was made up of carbon dioxide, steam, ammonia and methane. There was no oxygen. Over time, the earth's surface cooled down. The steam in the atmosphere condensed and formed water. Water was also released from hydrous minerals of the Earth's rocks.

Compared with the water-content of earth-like bodies, the unusually large amount of water we have on Earth is unlikely to have come from terrestrial sources alone. We now know that water is more abundant in objects further away from the sun, where the temperature is a lot colder.

The Asteroid belt is the region of the Solar System between the orbits of planet Mars and Jupiter. It is full of asteroids and debris. The water found in carbon-rich meteorites, found in the outer reaches of the Asteroid belt, contained the same proportion of deuterium and protium as the water in our oceans today.

---

[h] Protoplanets are collection of matter, in the process of condensation, from which a planet is formed.
[i] This hypothesis was first proposed by Dr. William K Hartmann and Dr. Donald R Davis. It is consistent with the actual angular momentum of the Earth-Moon system and with the findings from the Apollo Moon landings which shows that unlike rocks from Mars and meteorites, rocks from the moon show oxygen isotopes composition the same as the Earth.

It is likely, therefore, that most of today's water came from protoplanets that formed in the outer Asteroid belt that plunged here on Earth,[18] billions of years ago.[j] With the water being released from the Earth's rocks, the water condensing from steam in the atmosphere and water from protoplanets pulled by the Earth's gravity, the world's first oceans slowly began to take shape.

During the first millions of years that followed, Earth was hazardous to life. The Hadean era – 4.6 million years ago to 3.8 million years ago – was a time when Earth often collided with other large objects from outer space. It was a violent time in the history of our solar system. The impact of this event can still be seen as craters that mar the surfaces of our moon. By inference, the craters seen on the surfaces of Mercury and Mars were created during the same period as well.

---

[j] Based from the studies of three comets – Halley, Hyakutake and Hale-Bopp – it is unlikely that our water came from comets because isotope ratios of Hydrogen were different to what we find here on earth.

CHAPTER 2:
THE ORIGIN OF LIFE

Before anything was alive, the universe was made up of a collection of atoms that can be defined, labelled and named. Atoms in water molecules, rocks, crystals, and galaxies connect to one another, as they naturally do, because it is the most 'stable' configuration possible under existing environmental conditions. What does the word 'stable' mean in this context?

Richard Dawkins explains: "Soap bubbles tend to be spherical because this is a stable arrangement for thin films filled with gas. In a spacecraft, water is also stable in spherical globules, but on earth, where there is gravity, the stable surface for standing water is flat and horizontal. Salt crystals tend to be cubes because this is a stable way of packing sodium and chloride ions together. In the sun the simplest atoms of all, hydrogen atoms, are fusing to form helium atoms, because in the conditions that prevail there, the helium configuration is more stable."[19] Notice how sand and water particles naturally fill every space available, between cracks, nooks and crannies. Nature organises atoms in structures that are the most stable in a particular environment.

Abiogenesis is the study of how life began. How did life come about from a lifeless planet between 4.4 billion and 2.7 billion years ago?[20] Scientists have made discoveries about the origin of molecular and cellular components of life. We understand that the basic chemicals of life are: methane, ammonia, water, hydrogen sulphide, and carbon dioxide. All these chemicals were known to be present on some of the other planets in our solar system.

Based from known facts and evidence gathered from experiments and scientific data, scientists have developed explanations of how life may have started here on Earth. We will discuss only some of them here.

In 1953, Stanley L. Miller and Harold C. Urey conducted an experiment at the University of Chicago.[21] They put water, methane, ammonia and hydrogen inside a sterile array of flasks and glass tubes, connected in a loop. To emulate the hypothetical conditions of the young Earth, they heated the liquid water until it evaporated to another tube, where they fired sparks through the water vapour between two electrodes to simulate lightning strikes through the earth's atmosphere. They allowed the water vapour to cool down so the water could condense and trickle back into the original flask. They repeated this cycle over and over.

After a week, Miller and Urey found that 10-15% of the carbon in the system formed organic compounds. Two percent formed into amino acid, the building block of proteins, one of the two great classes of biological molecules.

This experiment inspired similar experiments by other scientists who were able to produce purines and pyrimidines: the building blocks of the genetic molecule DNA itself. It is, therefore, believed that life began in a similar 'primeval soup' in early seas[k] and along the shorelines where concentrated organic substances combined into larger molecules.[l]

In 1977, scientists discovered, for the first time, that volcanic vents on the floors of deep oceans support strange creatures that thrive in high temperatures without sunlight. It is believed that the origin of life is found under the chemically-rich areas of the seas and rocks underneath. Iron Sulphur Theory was demonstrated by Günter Wächtershäuser and Claudia Huber in 1997, showing that amino acids can form on mineral surfaces near deep hydrothermal vents, where the water is hot from nearby volcanic activity.[m] Deep

---

[k] The Primeval Soup Theory
[l] The Bubble Theory
[m] Günter Wächtershäuser, a Munich chemist and patent lawyer, proposed his Iron-Sulfur Theory and demonstrated that amino acids and peptides can be created in such environments.

Rock Theory is another variation that posits that life may have been supported by the chemicals on, and within, the rocks.[n]

Life could have arisen in one or possibly more of these models. They provide us with ideas of what the Earth must have been like before the coming of life.

For millions of years, molecules of varying characteristics formed, by accident, only to be destroyed later by natural causes. At some point, however, during this mixing and fusing of chemicals, a remarkable molecule was formed: the replicator.[o]

The Replicator

The replicator was distinctly different from the other molecules. It was able to make copies of itself. Like all other molecules, nature came upon the replicator by chance. As improbable as it was, its coming into existence only had to happen once during those millions of years.

I will turn to the expertise of someone more knowledgeable than I am about what this replicator might have been like. In his book, *The Selfish Gene*, Richard Dawkins wrote:

> "Think of the replicator as a mould or template. Imagine it as a large molecule consisting of a complex chain of various sorts of building block molecules. The small building blocks were abundantly available in the soup surrounding the replicator. Now suppose that each building block has an affinity for its own kind. Then whenever a building block from out in the soup lands up next to a part of the replicator for which it has an affinity, it will tend to stick there. The building blocks that attach themselves in this way will automatically be arranged in a sequence that mimics that of the replicator itself. It is easy

---

[n] The Deep Rock Theory
[o] I first found out about the concept of the 'replicator' from Richard Dawkins' gene theory he wrote about in his book *The Selfish Gene*. I urge you to read it for he explains at great length and clarity much of what I cannot cover in this book.

then to think of them joining up to form a stable chain just as in the formation of the original replicator. This process could continue as a progressive stacking-up, layer upon layer. This is how crystals are formed. On the other hand, the two chains might split apart, in which case we have two replicators, each of which can go on to make further copies."

Like crystals, the early replicators multiplied without consciousness.

The Anthropic Principle

It is right at this point where I feel I need to pause. Some of us might find it hard to believe that something like a replicator could have come about from sheer luck without some divine intervention from God. I will now discuss what is commonly referred to as The Anthropic Principle. Failing to understand the implications of this idea will result in any individual surrendering to the easy explanation that God must have started everything.

Let us now do some arithmetic based on what we have discussed so far:

1. It is possible that life started here on Earth after the first water vapour liquefied, 4.4 billion years ago, to when minerals and sediments, as well as photosynthesis are first said to have appeared[22], 2.7 billion years ago. For 170 million years, molecules were formed by accident in a process similar to the Primeval Soup Theory we discussed above.
2. Let us assume at least one molecule was formed every second, all over the entire planet. We include all areas where life could have originated: along the seashores, deep under the oceans or deep under rocks.

3. This means that during the 170 million years, when life was able to begin, 5,361,120,000,000,000[p] molecules have been created by nature, by freak accident.

Is it conceivable that in at least one of those 5 quadrillions of instances, the chemicals that make up life managed to arrange themselves to make a molecule that was able to multiply itself like crystals do?

To assume that only one molecule formed all over the planet might be understating the figures. I am not aware of any estimates made by scientists so for now, we are left to assume. We can multiply 5 quadrillions by the number of molecules we would consider to be a more realistic rate of molecule formation per second during our early history. So, if we assume that, realistically, a trillion molecules have formed on average, per second, across the world, then we can multiply 5 quadrillion by a trillion. This would make 5 octillions[q]. Again, we ask: Is it possible that one of these 5 octillion molecules was able to replicate like crystals do?

Leaving you with that thought, let us consider the possibility that life may have evolved from another planet. Let us divert our attention to our current understanding of life, our planet, our solar system, our galaxy and the universe. According to our observation of other solar systems[23], gathered facts and mathematical calculations and inferences[r], these are what we understand to be true:

1. Life, as we know it, cannot exist if it is too hot or too cold. Therefore, to be hospitable to life, a planet must be at a certain distance away from its star: not too far and not too close.

---

[p] 5,361,120,000,000,000 = 60seconds x 60 minute x 24hours x 365days x 170000000years
[q] This is a 5 with 21 zeros after it.
[r] Including the Drake Equation /The Green Bank Equation / Sagan Equation

2. For life to exist, a planet must have the following ingredients:
   - Methane
   - Ammonia
   - Water
   - Hydrogen sulphide
   - Carbon dioxide or carbon monoxide
   - Phosphate
3. We can already see 70 sextillions of stars in the universe. That is: 70,000,000,000,000,000,000,000[s].
4. Some of these stars have multiple planets and some of them do not. On average, however, each star has 2 planets that are able to support life. This means there are at least 140 sextillion planets that can support life.
5. In each of the 140 sextillion planets that can support life, we assume that they formed similarly to Earth and on average, 5.36120 octillion molecules were also created.
6. In the observable universe therefore, there were 750,568,000,000,000,000,000,000,000,000,000,000,000,000,000,000[t] (read as 750 quindecillion[u]) molecules that could have formed throughout the universe.

Is it conceivable, therefore, that in at least one of these 750 quindecillion molecules, the chemicals that make up life have managed to arrange themselves to make a molecule that was able to replicate itself like crystals do? Again the answer is yes.

A replicator did not necessarily have to be present on a planet either because moons and other celestial satellites would have been able to support life as well.[v] Once formed, these replicators were transported here by one of the comets, protoplanets, asteroids, dust or any other debris that crossed Earth's path during the formation of the solar system.

---

[s] This count was done by a team of astronomers at the Australian National University in 2003.
[t] 5.361120 octillion x 140 sextillion
[u] Any number with 48 zeros following it.
[v] This field of study is called panspermia or exogenesis.

I played with numbers here to expound the probabilities we are working with. Yet I know that playing with numbers still may prove nothing to some people. To many, the likely chance that a replicator formed by chance, is way too small. Therefore, the logic goes, it may not have happened at all.

Here is when the Anthropic Principle kicks in: Even if the formation of a replicator was only one out of a trecentillion[w], we know that it happened at least once in the universe. How can we be sure that replicators were formed? We are sure because we are made up of them. DNA molecules are replicators. You, me, as well as all known plants and animals, are made up of millions and millions of these molecules that have copied themselves over and over, inside every cell of our bodies.

---

[w] That is 1 followed by 903 zeros after it.

CHAPTER 3: GENETICS

We now need to understand how the replicator, after it was formed, was able to make copies of itself.

DNA, Chromosomes, Cells And Genes

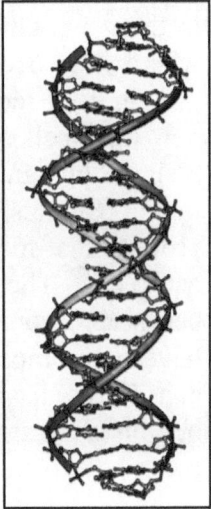

DNA is made of long units of nucleotide chains twisted together in an elegant spiral, called the 'double helix'. A nucleotide is a chemical compound that has a nitrogenous base[x], sugar[y] and one or more phosphate[z] groups.

On the right, you can see a diagram[aa] of a DNA double helix. The two long strands are made of phosphate and sugar residues. Attached to these two strands are the bases.

There are only 4 types of bases in a DNA molecule: Adenine, Cytosine, Guanine and Thymine. Respectively, they are shortened as A, C, G and T. The chemical composition of each of these bases is the same in all known forms of life.

---

[x] a derivative of purine or pyrimidine
[y] made of pentose deoxyribose
[z] Phosphate: Salt of phosphoric acid
[aa] Created by Michael Ströck on February 8, 2006, released under the GFDL

A T-type base found in a worm, for example, is chemically the same as a T-type base found in you and me. The only difference is the way in which these bases, or letters, are arranged.

The letters make a genetic code that scientists have learnt to read since the discovery of DNA.[bb] These letters are the alphabet of life and it is the sequence of these letters that makes words. The words, themselves, make up sentences. These 'sentences' are called genes. Genes tell cells how to make proteins. Our skin cells are different from our muscle cells because they were instructed by our genes to produce proteins that form skin. Our genes instruct our red blood cells to form a protein called 'haemoglobin' which they can use to capture and carry oxygen around our bodies.[24]

"When a cell needs to make a certain type of protein, specialised machinery within the cell's nucleus reads the gene and then uses that information to produce a message in the form of RNA, a molecule similar to DNA. The RNA moves from the nucleus into the cytoplasm of the cell. Once there, the cell's protein-making machinery, the 'ribosome', reads the message and produces a protein that exactly matches the specifications laid out in the gene. Once made, the protein travels to the part of the cell where it is needed and begins to work. Each step in making a protein itself requires the work of highly specialised proteins."[25]

"Each cell contains a lot of DNA. If you pulled the DNA from a single human cell and stretched it out, it would be three meters long!" Strands of DNA molecules are wrapped around some proteins that form a chromosome. These chromosomes exist inside each cell.[26] The DNA double helix is too small to see, however, we can see 'chromosomes' with the aid of microscopes. Mosquitos have 6 chromosomes in each cell of their bodies, onions have 16 and Carps have 104. Each human cell has 46 chromosomes, organised in two sets of 23 chromosomes. The complete set of genes within an organism's genome is called its genotype.[27]

[bb] The structure of the DNA was deciphered by James Watson, Francis Crick, Maurice Wilkins and Rosalind Franklin.

Sex, Heredity, Alleles And Traits

Like letters making sentences, DNA molecules make up genes. Our genes encode instructions that define our traits. We get our genes from our parents. As mentioned above, humans have two complete sets of 23 chromosomes (2 X 23 chromosomes = 46 chromosomes). When a man and a woman produce a child, they each contribute one complete set of chromosomes to the child. This happens when the man's sperm cell joins with the woman's egg cell.

Most cells in our bodies contain two sets of 23 chromosomes, totalling 46. However, a man's sperm cell will only contain 23 of his chromosomes and a woman's egg cell also contains 23 of hers. When the sperm enters the egg cell, they create a single cell called a 'zygote'. This new cell will have 46 chromosomes: half from the man and half from the woman.

You, like me, were once a single 'zygote'. This cell contained your DNA, complete with instructions, made up of a 4-letter alphabet, on how to assemble the chemicals and amino acids in your body to create proteins over time. Soon, that zygote cell would divide in 2, then 4, then 8, 16 and so on... until it was big enough to be identified as a child growing inside your mother's womb. As you grew, your cells continued to divide. A human adult consists of about a 100 trillion cells.

Each child conceived will have a unique combination of chromosomes from their parents. When the child grows up to adulthood and reproduces, he or she will also pass on 23 of his or her chromosomes to the child.

Since we inherit our parents' genes, we also inherit their traits. So, we might have our father's eyes but we have our mother's nose. We also pass on our traits to our children. Physical traits like nose shape, hair colour, eye colour and height are not the only traits that are passed on. We also pass on behavioural traits as well as unhealthy genes that can increase their risk of getting a certain type of disease.

The complete set of traits of an organism – physical and behavioural – is called its phenotype. Phenotype is a result of the interaction between an organism's genotype and its environment.[28]

When two genes compete for the section of a cell's chromosome, they are called alleles of each other. Humans are diploid organisms: we have two copies of each chromosome. Therefore, two alleles make up our genotype: the genetic constitutions of our cells.

A child, who has the gene of the mother's blue eyes and another gene for the father's brown eyes, has two genes that are alleles of each other. What does this child's body do to determine the eye colour? The gene the body chooses is referred to as the dominant gene and the one that gets ignored by the body is the recessive gene.

Generally, the brown eye gene is more dominant than the blue eye gene. If the child's body chooses to manufacture brown eyes, the gene for blue eyes still exists within the child. When it is time for this individual to reproduce, he can still pass on the blue eyes gene to an offspring.

This example is enough to explain the concepts of dominant and recessive genes. However, to explain the many variations of eye colours we see, it is more accurate to remember that other genes exists and they do the choosing, or the compromising, between the two alleles.

Traits can be contained in just one gene called 'single-gene' traits. This is rare. Most of the time, traits are shaped by more than one gene. They are called 'complex traits'.[29]

Children Not Exactly Like Their Parents

Even though children inherit the physical and behavioural traits of their parents, they are not exactly like their parents. Their traits vary from their parents' because of the following reasons:

1. Unique Set of Chromosomes

Each child is unique because the combination of genes he gets is a unique combined set from his parents, who, themselves, have a unique set of chromosomes. Since every sperm and egg cell contain their own unique combination of 23 chromosomes, siblings will have a different set of genes even if they came from the same parents.

2. Genes multiply by division

Nature multiplies by dividing. An organism grows in size by multiplying the number of cells it has in its body. It does this by dividing its cells. When cells divide, genes also get divided.

3. Sex jumbles up everything

During the reproductive process, our body produces and creates sperm cells and egg cells containing chromosomes of bits and pieces of our DNA and mix them with bits and pieces of our partner's DNA. This makes it difficult for a child to be an exact copy of any one of his or her parents.

4. Chromosome Inversion and Misplacement

By rare mistake, a piece of chromosome gets detached from its place. It may then manage to get reattached at an inverted position or in another part of the chromosome. It might even reattach to a different chromosome altogether.

5. Point Mutation

Remember the DNA molecule is like a string on which letters and sentences are printed and read by a cell to produce chemicals in the body. If the molecule is altered in a way that the letters and sentences are misread by the body, then wrong types of chemicals might be produced.

So, even though a child gets one hundred percent of his genes from his parents, the child will undoubtedly be different from either of his parents. The genetic codes of individuals from the same family are more similar to each other, than to the DNA of other individuals belonging to a different family.

Despite all the different variations of height, body shape, skin, eye and hair colours as well as behavioural differences, 99.9 percent of human DNA is identical. It is only the remaining 0.1 percent that creates the diversity we see between people.

Sexual And Asexual Reproduction

Organisms replicate themselves through a process we call reproduction. There are two known methods of reproduction: sexual and asexual. Sexual reproduction, like in humans, requires two individuals: the male and the female. The male is the one who produces sperm or microspores. The female is the one producing ova or megaspores. The male and female combine their genetic material to create a descendant which retains the genes of both individuals.

Asexual reproduction, on the other hand, is possible when an individual is able to create a copy of itself without genetic contributions from another individual. Organisms that are able to reproduce asexually include bacteria, viruses, hydras and yeasts. They reproduce by splitting themselves. Some organisms, such as sea anemones, slime moulds and plant lice, are able to reproduce sexually and asexually.

Definition Of A 'Gene'

To summarise what we have learnt so far, we can imagine a DNA molecule to be a pair of two long strands that have four letters imprinted between them. These letters, or bases, make sentences called genes. These sentences, or genes, instruct the cells how to make chemicals for the body. The DNA string, on which the sentences are printed, is bundled together in a chromosome, inside a cell. A cell could have many chromosomes.

A gene is the basic unit of heredity in living organisms. To make it easier to follow later discussions, lets define our use of the word 'gene' from this point forwards. In classical genetics, from the works of Gregor Mendel, it is acceptable to define genes as hereditary units that can be treated in practice as indivisible and independent particles.

Instead of thinking of genes simply as 'sentences', we can imagine a gene as a piece of DNA strand, or as a particle of a chromosome that gets passed on from one generation to the next, without merging with other genes.

A particular butterfly might have the DNA instructing its body to create brown wings. In reality, many genes are responsible to create the brown wings but for our purpose, we refer to this collective of gene, as a single gene.

Since a gene is made up of DNA molecules, its physical molecules do not last forever. However, a gene has the potential to live forever because copies of it are passed on inside living organisms for millions of years. If the host organism fails to make copies of its genes to the next generation, then its genes will perish.

CHAPTER 4:
EVOLUTION BY NATURAL SELECTION

Now that we have learnt a bit about biology, we should be well-equipped to discuss evolution and natural selection. Without understanding these concepts, we will be left with so many unanswered questions regarding the variety of life we see around us.

Charles Darwin's explanation of how species came into existence was so controversial in its days and often misconstrued. Geneticists had not yet discovered DNA at that time. Through our understanding of DNA today, we are able to explain how the process of evolution through natural selection is possible.

When many of us hear the word 'evolution', we imagine monkeys transforming into human beings. People say things like: 'If humans evolved from apes, then show me an ape that is currently changing into a human being', or 'Show me an ape that is currently giving birth to a human being'.

This is not how evolution works. We did not come from monkeys or apes. Instead, we once shared a common ancestor with them. That statement makes all the difference.

My misunderstanding of evolution and natural selection was hindered because I attributed the word evolution to morphing. I imagined that individuals of a certain species morphed and transformed into something slightly different. I was wrong. When I listen to other people trying to understand evolution, they ask questions that suggest they are under similar misinterpretations.

It has been more than a century since Darwin first wrote about evolution and many people still do not understand it. The papacy took 137 years to support evolution. On the 22nd of October 1996, Pope John Paul II defended the evidence for evolution. Why is it taking so long for such a wonderful and stunningly elegant idea to be understood and embraced?

For the most part, the answer to this question is attributed to the influences of religious beliefs. The theory of evolution through natural selection is in direct conflict with the biblical explanations of our origins. I suspect that it is taking some time for religious believers to find new, or different, ways to interpret their scriptures so they can reconcile it with evidence. We will get to religion later but for now, I will provide the ideas that helped me understand Darwin's theory.

Natural Selection

Charles Darwin observed that if all the individuals of a species reproduced successfully, their population would increase uncontrollably.[30] But populations tended to remain about the same size from year to year. He reasoned that this was because there are limits to the environment's resources to support all life. There is a struggle for these resources. The organisms that are good at acquiring these resources are the ones who will live long enough to reproduce.

The traits of successful individuals get passed on to more individuals of the next generation. Less successful traits will get passed on less. As each generation passes, the more desirable traits become more common among the population.

It is important to remember that it is genes that determine what these traits are. Natural selection, therefore, is how nature selects, or favours, advantageous genes to be passed on to the next generation. Genes that do not help organisms survive or reproduce are not likely to be passed on to an offspring.

I will provide three different examples explaining natural selection.

Example 1: Camouflage

Butterflies with wings and bodies that are able to blend in their natural habitat are harder to see. This reduces the chance of them being eaten by their predators. The next generation of butterflies will, therefore, be more likely to be the descendants of camouflaged butterflies. The butterflies with attractive colours will have been eaten by predators.

Example 2: Predator and Prey

Land predators rely on muscular strength, stealth, speed and agility to hunt and catch prey. Their prey relies on similar physical conditions that allow them to outrun their predators. Predators which are too slow, lacking the muscular strength and physical qualities to approach prey with stealth and speed, will more likely be malnourished. Most will die before they get the opportunity to mature enough and reproduce. Those who manage to reproduce will not have the ability to provide meat for their young regularly. Their young will likely die. If they do survive, they will also lack the genes for superior stealth and speed, and expect to suffer a similar fate as their parents.

Prey with genes that allow them to have more conditioned leg muscles to run at high speeds to outrun predators, tend to live longer. They are more likely to reach the age of sexual maturity and make offspring that will carry copies of their successful genes.

Which genes would be valuable in this case? The genes that allow the animal to have the muscles needed for agility and speed suitable for its natural habitat. In the desert, animals that are better equipped in handling extreme temperatures have a better chance of surviving than ones that are better suited to aquatic environments. So, in this case, it is the environment again which **'selects'** which individuals die or survive.

Example 3: Sexual Selection

In the previous chapter, we have gained a little understanding about how our genes are passed on from generation to generation. Who among us get the opportunity to reproduce? Those with a sexual partner. This means that what we look for in a partner decides which genes are passed on to the future.

In their book titled *Freakonomics*, economist Steven Levitt and journalist Stephen Dubner, wrote about online dating. In a given year, 40 million Americans use Internet dating sites. Currently, these sites are the most successful subscription-based businesses on the Internet. On these websites, people write personal ads about themselves including vital statistics, income, education, likes, dislikes and maybe a photo.

Two economists and a psychologist analysed the data from one of the mainstream dating sites, focussing on more than 20,000 active users in Boston and in San Diego, USA. They were interested in studying the information included in these ads and the responses each ad would get.

What they found fitted snugly with the most common stereotypes about men and women. Men responded to ads of women whom they perceived to be physically attractive while women prioritised the man's income. The richer the man, the more e-mails he received. For men, having red hair, curly hair or a bald head were big disadvantages. So was being short. This is why many men lied about their height. For women, having blond hair was good and being overweight was 'deadly'. This is why women lied about their weight.

Also, 50 percent of the white women and 80 percent of the white men declared that race did not matter to them. But the responses told a different story. The white men who said that race didn't matter to them sent 90 percent of their e-mail queries to white women. The white women, who said race didn't matter, sent 97 percent of their e-mail queries to white men.

The study made many interesting and entertaining findings but for our purpose, this is enough. Assuming the findings of this study represent reality, and everything else being equal, what follows from this study are:

1. Men who are taller and richer will have more likelihood to have a sexual partner, reproduce and pass on their genes to the next generation.

2. Women who are blonde, good-looking and not overweight will have more likelihood to have a sexual partner, reproduce and pass on their genes to the next generation.

In this example, it can be said, therefore, that current culture and attitudes regarding people's perception of choosing ideal sexual partners are the '**natural**' factors that '**select**' which individuals get to pass on their genes to the next generation. These are products of our way of life, determined by the environment we live in.

So long as the prevailing culture and current attitudes persist, future generations of human beings in Boston and San Diego will more likely be endowed with genes that make men taller and women blonder and slimmer. Of course, this statement is subject to the degree in which genetics contribute to these physical traits, as well as the effects of incoming and outgoing human migration in the two cities.

The three examples above illustrate the following aspects of natural selection:

1) The natural selector is the 'environment'. Genes survive if they provide their hosts the abilities and the qualities to adapt to the living conditions of their environments. Genes that do not, or are less efficient and effective in doing so, will get copied less. They will die out. As each new generation is born, individuals with successful traits become more and more common and individuals with disadvantageous traits become rarer. In the perspective of a host organism, genes that provide helpful qualities are considered 'good' genes, those that do not, are 'bad' genes.

2) A team of good genes inside an organism provides that particular organism with the tools that help it survive. Sometimes good genes are teamed up with a few bad genes that are lucky enough to be copied on to another survival machine. Eventually, however, a bad gene will find itself in an organism full of other bad genes. Their team, as a whole, will not be able to provide their host any survival advantages. The host will die without reproducing. Its bad genes will perish with it.

3) Since the environment is not conscious, the process of natural selection is directed 'blindly', without pity or concern for one single gene, individual or species.

Speciation

Speciation is said to occur when one species diverges into two or more genetically-distinct ones. This divergence occurs after members of the same species of organisms become geographically isolated from the others.

For example, consider a population of animals belonging to the same species. They all share common features. They all have snouts, hands and legs. They live in a forest with plenty of four-legged predators.

Imagine if this group of animals separates. Maybe one group decides to migrate to another area where there are no predators. These two groups now live in two different environments.

The group that chooses to stay remains as prey to four-legged predators. Genes for bigger and stronger hands to climb trees would be favourable to ensure the survival of the animals. Only then will they be able to pass on these traits to their offspring. Therefore, many of the animals in the next generation will more likely be suited for climbing.

The second group that chooses to venture out finds itself on top of a food chain. In the new environment, there is plenty food: tiny creatures that live in shallow waters. Not all will be successful in reproducing though. Not all can take care of their young. Those who thrive will be the ones who have the traits to prey on the little aquatic animals. Helpful traits may include a slightly longer snout to make it easier to suck more food out of the water. If this is the case, individuals with the advantage of having slightly longer snouts will be able to feed themselves and their offspring more effectively than those with shorter snouts.

Over time, the two groups will continue to evolve by natural selection. The traits for bigger and stronger hands are further adapted and improved with other complementary traits. Likewise, the trait of longer snouts may be further adapted and aided with other helpful traits, like webbed feet for example.

There will come a time when a descendant of the first group will no longer be able to mate with a descendant of the second group to produce a fertile offspring. Their physical and behavioural traits will have changed so much from each other that reproduction will no longer be possible. When this happens, we now have two separate species and speciation is said to have occurred.

Speciation, Gradation And Language

In the example above, we assume that speciation occurs when two individuals from the same group can no longer reproduce with other individuals from another group. This definition works when we are discussing the cases of species that reproduce sexually. However, other organisms reproduce asexually. Therefore, this method of distinction will not work.

Interesting case studies are hybrid organisms, like mules[cc], hinnies[dd], ligers[ee] and tigons[ff]. They cannot reproduce when they are mated with their own kind (eg: tigon with a tigon) but they can, when they are mated with an individual from one of the parent species (eg: Tigon with a lion).

[cc] offspring of a male donkey and a female horse
[dd] offspring of a female donkey and a male horse
[ee] offspring of a male lion and a female tiger
[ff] offspring of a male tiger and a female lion

In reality, therefore, it is difficult to define the word 'species' in a way that applies to all known organisms. Our inability to use language to define species highlights the challenges of using language to define naturally-occurring phenomena.

To explain this pitfall of using languages further, let us think of colours. Languages can describe black from white but we become challenged when we use it to describe different shades of grey. It is difficult, if not impossible, without creating artificial constructs to distinguish between light grey, medium grey and dark grey. In fact, we can only class the different shades if we use artificial categories by using a mathematical process of dividing the light spectrum in three equal parts, as shown below.

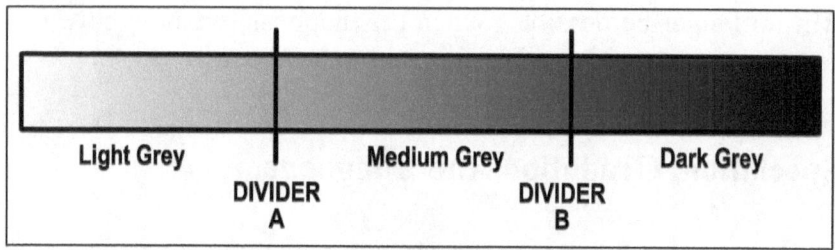

We have divided the spectrum using artificial dividers (marked as A and B on the chart). Language is unable to describe the phenomena. We had to employ a mathematical method to do so. Like colours and shades, there are also smooth and gradual differences between species. We had to make artificial definitions to classify different 'shades' of 'ape-ness' for example. We made dividers that help us distinguish between a chimpanzee and a gorilla.

The Tree Of Life

We have come to understand the origins of different species of life through the works of biologists. As we list all known species of life and connect them to the species they evolved from, we realise the ancestry of all living things resembles a tree. This tree is now referred to as the *Tree Of Life*, complete with branches, twigs and leaves. Biologists from around the world helped plot this *Tree Of*

Life[31] on the Internet. I will use this resource to guide us through species of life-forms on Earth. I will not be discussing all of them; instead, I will take you through a journey that highlights most of the major events in evolution that led to us, human beings.

Instead of drawing this tree vertically from the ground up, like a real tree, we will draw this tree from left to write to adjust for the way we read and write. To show how these diagrams work, consider the following example:

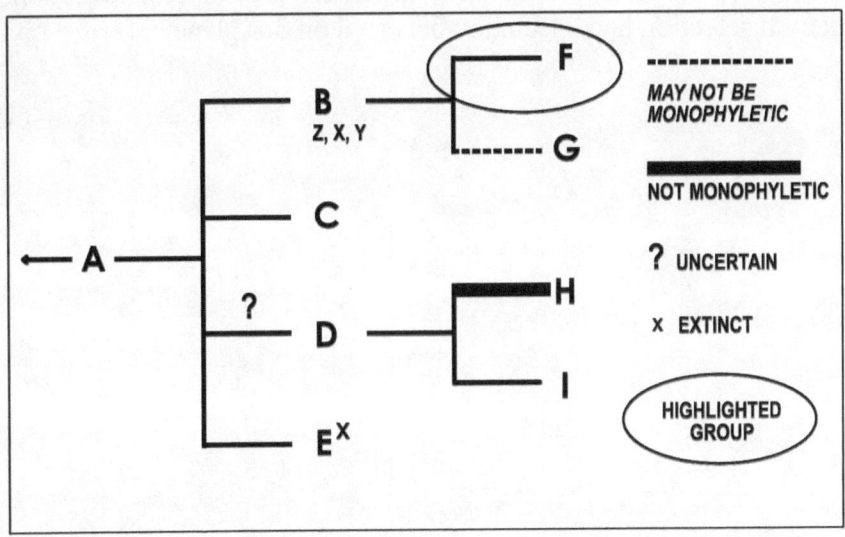

A diagram like above would read the following:

1. The ancestors of Group A came from individuals in another group that preceded it.
2. Some or all members of Group A 'gave birth' to ancestors of Group B, C, D and E.
3. Z, X and Y are examples of Group B.
4. The phylogenetic[gg] position – that is the evolutionary history of a group of organisms – of D is uncertain.
5. Group E is extinct.
6. Group G's subgroup may be more closely related to group F than to other subgroups of Group G.

[gg] Phylogenetic means the evolutionary history of a group of organisms.

7. Group I's closest relative is actually a subgroup of Group H, but we do not know which subgroup.
8. The circles I have drawn highlight the groups we are discussing.

Do not worry if you do not understand the chart above just yet. Later chapters of this book will explain the idea of how evolution, natural selection and speciation occurred on our planet.

CHAPTER 5:
HOW LIFE EVOLVED ON EARTH

At the end of Chapter 2, nature accidentally came upon the very first replicator. I will now take you through how the variety of life we see today evolved from that point.

The replicator was unique because unlike any of the previous molecules that formed before it, it had the ability to copy itself. However, like in any copying process, not all copies are perfect. Mistakes happen. So, as the replicator made copies of itself, and the copies made more copies of themselves, their population grew but they were not all identical.

Think of when you photocopy a document. Take the copy and photocopy that copy again. Keep photocopying the copies of the copies until the latest copy is noticeably different from the original.

"As mis-copyings were made and propagated, the primeval soup became filled by a population not of identical replicas, but of several varieties of replicating molecules, all 'descended' from the same ancestor."[32] Some varieties were more numerous than others, because of one or more of the following reasons:

1. **Longevity**: The group of replicators that existed longer will have more replicas because they had more time to replicate than those who existed for a shorter period of time.
2. **Fecundity**: The replicators that copied themselves faster have more replicas than the slower replicators.
3. **Copying Fidelity**: The replicators that made accurate replicas of themselves will be more numerous than those who kept making mistakes.

4. **Competition**: The replicators that found a way to destroy their rivals, or consume and use the precious organic materials of their rivals, as food, would have made up more of the population by reducing the number of rivals in the pool.

As the replicas multiplied, they began competing for the same chemical resources needed to make more copies of themselves. Smaller building block molecules became scarce and it was harder for any other larger molecules to form.

With the competition for scarce resources and the endless process of copying and miscopying, the ones who eventually survived, were those who competed more effectively and more efficiently. Those who were accidentally endowed with a trait that gave them any advantage would have been more likely to survive.

These advantageous traits were not given to the replicas by their parents. Rather, they acquired them as a result of a copying mistake. These traits are defects, which resulted from an error during the copying process. These 'defects', however, later turned out to be helpful to the replicator.

These traits might have provided a particular replicator with the ability to use chemicals to dismember the molecules of other rivals, and thereafter, reuse the molecules to create more copies of itself. Another advantageous trait might have been one that allowed a replicator to build a physical wall of protein around itself: a wall that turned out to be useful in protecting itself from the harsh environment and from the attacks of rivals.

The replicator in all known life is the DNA. It may have been a descendant of the original replicators that formed billions of years ago. Alternatively, it may have formed similarly but from a different source altogether. We know of another replicator: the RNA (Ribonucleic acid). Unlike the DNA which has two strands, the RNA is a single-stranded molecule.

Starting as single units, Replicators have come a long way from their simple beginnings. Over millions of years through evolution by natural selection, some replicators found themselves joining other replicators and made their beginnings as single-celled organisms.

Prokaryotes and Eukaryotic Cells

About 3.5 billion years ago, the simplest single-celled organisms, called prokaryotes, appeared. For probably another 2 billion years, the only life on Earth came in the form of bacteria, algae and 'their equally simple kin'[33]. Then about 1.4 billion years ago, some of these simple cells were joined with other prokaryotes. Perhaps a smaller cell attempted to parasitize a larger cell, or maybe the larger cell tried to ingest the smaller cell. In any case, two cells joined genetically and over time, the two developed a symbiotic relationship where one needed the other to survive. The larger cell needed energy from the smaller cell, and the smaller cell needed the resources provided by the larger cell.

The two prokaryotes eventually began to function as a single organism called a eukaryote, which has a nucleus[hh]. The cell membrane surrounds the cytoplasm of a cell, serving as a kind of protective skin. These newly-emerged eukaryotic cells have little organs called organelles[ii]. These organelles were the smaller prokaryotes which found themselves inside a larger prokaryote.[jj]

There are many types of organelles. One type is mitochondria, which supplies the cell with a chemical[34] used for energy. It is also involved in other processes, such as coordinating cell activities and helping them specialise in a certain task. It is also involved in the process of cell growth and death. The mitochondria are at present being studied for their contributions to several human diseases, mental illnesses and aging.

Most cells have their DNA contained in their nucleus. What is most surprising about mitochondria, a cell organ, is that, it even has its own independent DNA! We call this the Mitochondrial DNA.

Chloroplasts are other examples of organelles. They are found in plant cells and eukaryotic algae. The purpose of these cell

---

[hh] Famous for his works on Precambrian microfossils, Andrew Knoll from Harvard University suggests that eukaryotic cells developed 1.6 to 2.1 billion years ago.
[ii] A subnunit within a cell that has a specific function and is separately enclosed
[jj] When photosynthetic cyanobacteria enter larger heterotrophic cells, a choloroplasts is formed.

organs is to convert light energy into chemical energy. This is called photosynthesis.

The dictyosome, known as the Golgi apparatus, is another organ found in eukaryotic cells. Its purpose is to help modify, sort and package molecules and send them to the areas of the cell where they are needed.

The flagellum is also another organelle. Eukaryotic cells use this long organ, in a whip-like motion, to propel themselves and travel.

With these new cells being equipped with organs to produce energy, synthesize molecules for food, and provide a mode of transport, the genes are now in a better position to continue replicating.

Oxygen And The Ozone Layer

With their ability to turn light energy into chemical energy, some cells no longer needed to depend on surrounding organic molecules for 'food'. All they needed for energy was the plentiful supply of carbon dioxide in the atmosphere, water and sunlight.

In the process of photosynthesis, the cells 'breathe in' carbon dioxide and later 'exhale' oxygen. So as more and more cells used this new 'technology', the planet became increasingly plentiful with oxygen.

The earliest oxygen ever produced was bound up with limestone, iron and other minerals. We can see this from studying the layer of rocks matching this time period. The coming of oxygen, as a waste product of photosynthesis, also transformed the Earth's atmosphere to its current state.[35] The incoming ultraviolet radiation from the sun reacted with the oxygen and formed what we now know as the ozone layer.

The newly-created ozone layer absorbed ultraviolet rays that damaged exposed cells. As the ultraviolet rays were minimised, the cells below were able to live on the surface of the oceans and eventually, found themselves on land.[36]

Around 1.8 to 1.5 billion years ago, the oldest mass of land was a super continent called Columbia.[37] It was named after the location where the best evidence for its existence was found: the Columbia River region of western North America.[38]

Early Plants And Animals

Around 1 billion years ago, when the super continent Rodinia began assembling, cells continued to survive and diversify in many forms. Some lived and coexisted with other cells in colonies. In some situations, cells did not all share the same realities. The cells inside these colonies were surrounded by other cells. They faced different challenges to the other cells that existed around the perimeter of the colony. The cells there were exposed to harsh elements and the raw materials used for food.

Cells which gained synergy by working together had more chances of survival than those that did not. As this trend continued, colonies began to consist of cells that specialised in particular tasks.[39] Some colonies had, on their surfaces, cells that focused on getting energy from the sunlight or from the chemicals found in contact with the colony. Another group of cells distributed energy to other groups of cells that focussed on other crucial tasks.

As food became increasingly scarce, cells that found a way to work with other cells became crucial. Colonies of cells became more superior at surviving than single, isolated cells. Examples of colonies of eukaryotic cells resulted in what became the early plants, like green algae.[40]

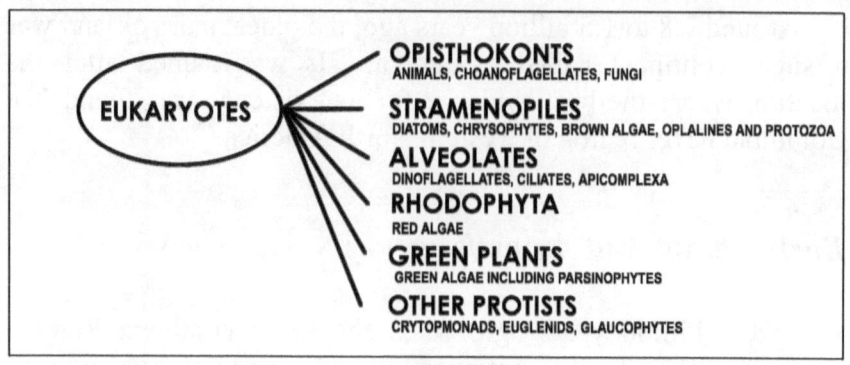

All the while, the super continent Rodinia began breaking up about 750 million years ago.[41] Another super continent, Pannotia, formed after 150 million years and later broke apart after another 50 million years.

The Cambrian Explosion

Early plants and animals reproduced and evolved in the water. Since children are different from their parents, the offspring of plants and animals varied from one another. The variations became distinct from the descendant of one ancestor to another. As generations went by, the differences became great enough for each organism to be classed as a separate species.

Shown by fossil records, the Earth witnessed an explosion of varied forms of life from about 570 to 530 million years ago. This period of time is known as the 'Cambrian Explosion'. All existing life was aquatic. Compared to the animals that exist today, the species then were very small.

Opisthokonts

Descendants of the early eukaryotes branched off to what we can now classify as a group called the opisthokonts. They are the ancestors of all animals, choanoflagellates and fungi like mushrooms, yeasts, moulds and rusts. They were mostly characterised by flagellate cells, such as most animal sperm and spores, which propel themselves with a single whip-like organelle, called a flagellum, behind them. This is unlike the other organisms which had one or more flagella in front of them.

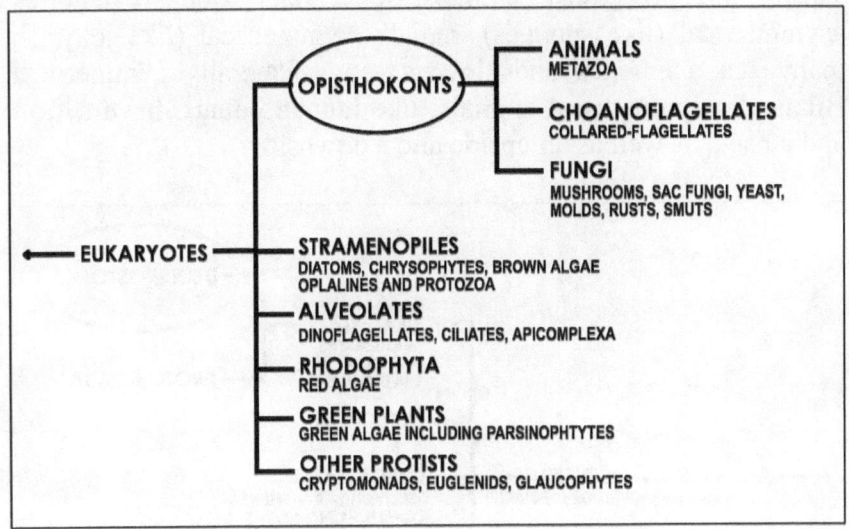

Animals (Metazoa)

Descendants of ancient opisthokonts evolved and gave rise to the early animals. The first animals were distinct from the other opisthokonts:

1) They were heterotrophic: they digested food internally to get the carbon they needed to grow and develop.[42]
2) Their cells were not separated by cell walls like cells in plants, algae and fungi.
3) They were capable of moving spontaneously.
4) Their embryos went through a phase biologists call gastrulation.

Bilaterally Symmetrical Organisms (Bilateria)

The bodies of most animals fell under three categories: asymmetrical (like sponges), radially symmetrical (like jellyfish, many sea anemones and flowers) and bilaterally symmetrical. Bilaterally symmetrical animals, like human beings, have a front and a back, as well as an upside and a downside.

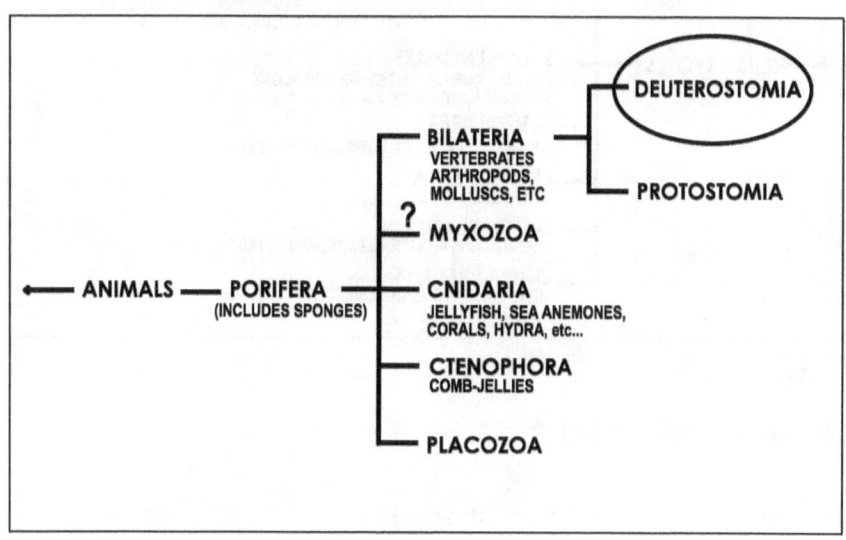

Deuterostomes (Deuterostomia)

Embryos of animals went through a process called gastrulation: 'Typically, before gastrulation, an animal embryo consists of a hollow ball of cells, the blastula, whose wall is one cell thick. During gastrulation the ball indents to form a cup with two layers. The opening of the cup closes in to form a small hole called the blastopore'.[43]

Bilaterally symmetric organisms began to divide between two species: the protostomes and the deuterostomes. They are distinguished from each other by the way they develop as embryos. For protostomes, the blastopore became their mouth. For deutorostomes, the blastopore became their anus. Human beings are deuterostomes.

Early Life On Land

Molecular evidence suggests that descendants of plants and eukaryotic organisms like the fungi began to grow at the edges of the water[44] sometime during 1000 to 700 millions years ago[45].

On the ocean shores and shallow seas of a young planet Earth, organisms began to spend fleetingly short amounts of time on land. Some were born with genes that contributed to physical traits that helped them stay longer on land. As each generation of organisms was 'born', the ability to stay on land longer became more common. With the ozone layer above to protect their fragile cells from the ultraviolet rays, living cells and organisms could finally begin to live directly under the sun.

Arthropods, belonging to the ecdysozoa group of protostomes, were the earliest forms of animals we have evidence to have lived on land, 450 million years ago[46]. So, it seems the protostome animals had beaten the deuterostomes to migrate onto land. They were covered with hard exoskeletons. They had segmented bodies and jointed legs.

Trilobites were among these arthropods. Because of their hard exteriors, shapes of their bodies were easily fossilized over millenniums. They left us with an extensive fossil record with some 17,000 known species. Many species of arthropods have died. However, they remain to make up 83% of all animal species today. They include insects, spiders, crustaceans and myriapods which includes millipedes and centipedes.[47]

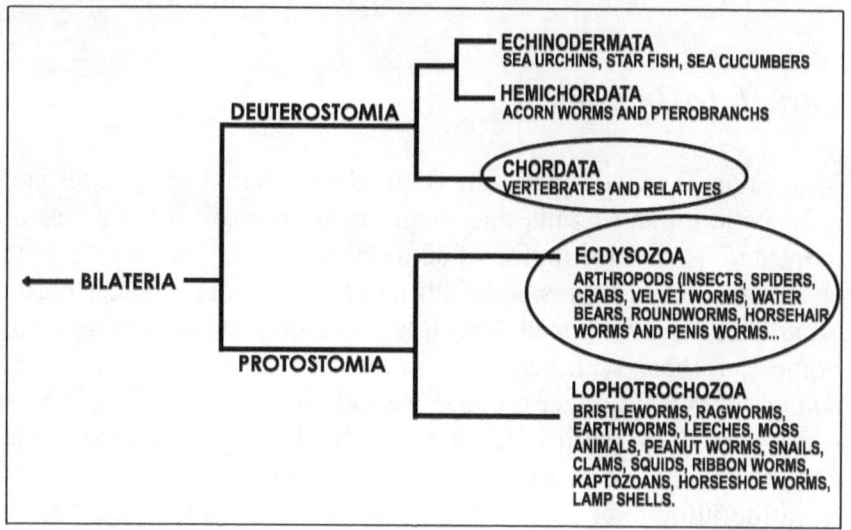

Chordates (Chordata)

The deuterostomes diverged into three main species. First were the echinoderms: marine animals found in ocean depths, including the ancestors of sea urchins, starfish and sea cucumbers. The second group were worm-shaped marine animals called hemichordates. The third group were the chordates. Chordates had their nerve cords running along their back, unlike many of the other deuterostomes which had their nerve cords running along their bellies.

Craniates (Craniata)

A few of the early chordates, the craniates, evolved skulls. Some of the early craniates may have been similar to the hagfish. Hagfish are the only chordates we know of that have a head, but not a backbone. They are however closely related, genetically, to the lamprey eel, a jawless fish that also has a backbone.[48]

Vertebrates (Vertebrata)

Apart from hagfish-like creatures, most chordates had backbones or spinal columns. Vertebrates are the largest group of chordates. Many of them have gone extinct but we have found their fossils. This extinct group include eel-like creatures called conodonts, and groups of jawless fishes called cephalaspidomorphs and pteraspidomorphs.

Jawless fish, called hyperoartia (that include the modern lamprey) and a massive group of vertebrates with jaws, called gnathostomata, survived from this group.

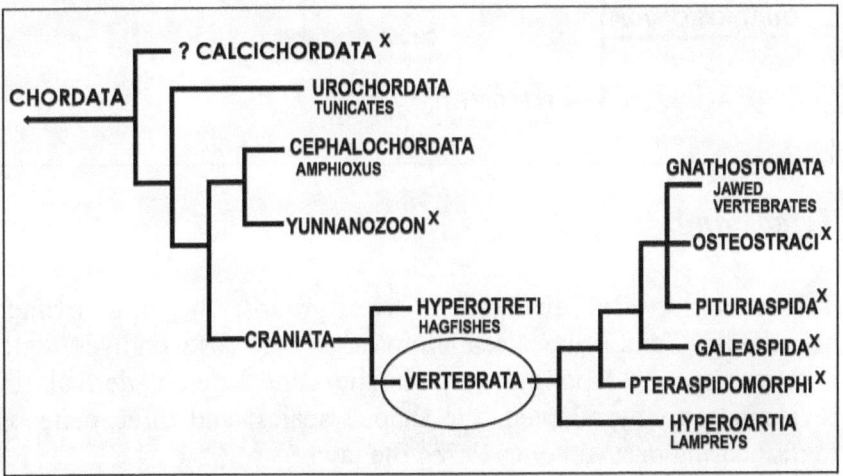

Jawed Vertebrates (Gnathostomata)

Among the jawed vertebrates were a class of armoured prehistoric fish called placodermi. They lived from the late Silurian period (443.7 - 416 mya) and went extinct at the end of the Devonian period (416 - 359.2 mya). Two other groups survived: the cartilaginous fish (chondrichthyes) and the teleostomi.

The jawed cartilaginous fish had skeletons made of cartilage rather than bone. They also had scales, paired fins and nostrils as well as two-chambered hearts. They included the ancestors of today's sharks, rays and chimaera (also known as ghost sharks).

Teleostomi animals, on the other hand, had an operculum (a hard bony flap covering and protecting the gills) and a single pair of respiratory openings, which were lost or adapted in later descendants.

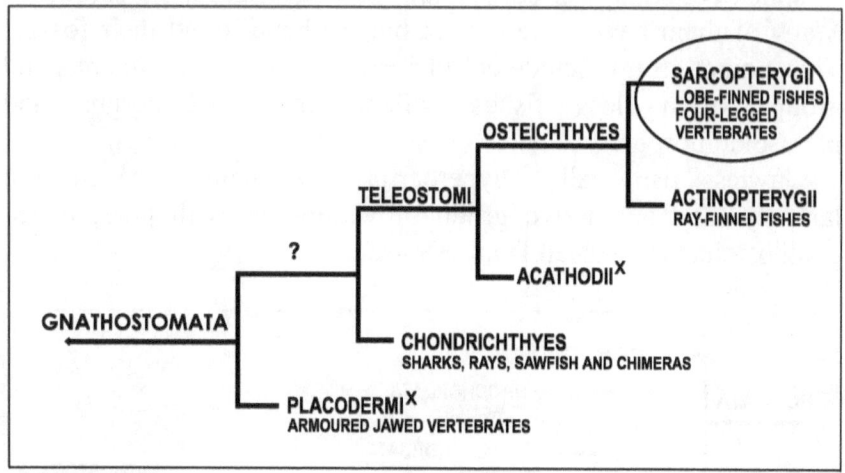

Teleostomi

Teleostomi species diverged in two groups: the now extinct aconthodii, and the osteichthyes. The osteichthyes are characterised by 'spongy' bone in the endoskeleton, dermal fin rays made up by adapted, tile-shaped scales, and three pairs of tooth-bearing dermal bones lining the jaws.[49]

Osteichthye

The osteichthyes split in two main classes: the actinopterygii and the sarcopterygii. The actinopterygii were ray-finned fish. Their fins were webs of skin supported by bony or horny spines. The early sacropterygii, on the other hand, had fleshy lobed fins and included the ancestors of lungfish and coelacanths.

The coelacanths were thought to have gone extinct since the end of the Cretaceous period (145.5 to 65.5 mya). Since 1938, after a specimen was found off the Chalumna River, they were found in other parts of Africa and in Indonesia.[50]

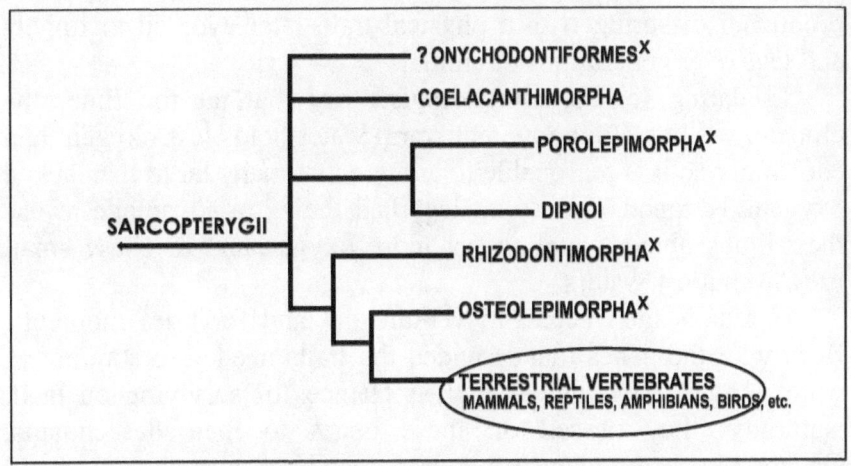

The Terrestrial Vertebrates

Terrestrial vertebrates bear muscular limbs with fingers and toes rather than fins. "The oldest known skeletal remains of terrestrial vertebrates were found in the Upper Devonian of East Greenland."[51]

The Tetrapods (Tetrapoda)

Many fossils of extinct species of early sacropterygii have been found. The only ones who survived were the tetrapods.

Around 416-359 million years ago, during what is now referred to as the Devonian period, land plants had stabilized freshwater habitats. This allowed the first wetland ecosystems to develop. The tetrapods were the earliest deuterostomes to follow the protostomes on land.

There are fossilized tetrapods having fingers.[kk] Published in her Scientific American paper, '*Getting a Leg Up on Land*', Jennifer A. Clack hypothesizes that the environment of shallow and swampy freshwater habitats, advantaged species of fish that began

---

[kk] Earlier species had 8 fingers and later species had 5. It is hypothesized that this is because as the early fishes began to use their legs, having less fingers was more efficient, less difficult and consumed less energy.

producing offspring with a physical trait, later evolved to fingers and legs over generations of animals.

In dating fossils, climatologists say that, at the time, the climate was hot. We know that warm water holds less oxygen than cool water so it is reasonable to assume that many large fish lacked oxygen. Tetrapods born with legs had the extra advantage to use their limbs above water to get more oxygen and to chase small prey in shallow waters.

Tetrapods then began to venture on land for brief moments. Born with the genes that provided the traits needed to stay out of water longer, they increased their chances of surviving on land. Naturally, they passed on these genes to their descendants. Generations later, many of their descendants managed to spend most of their lives on land.

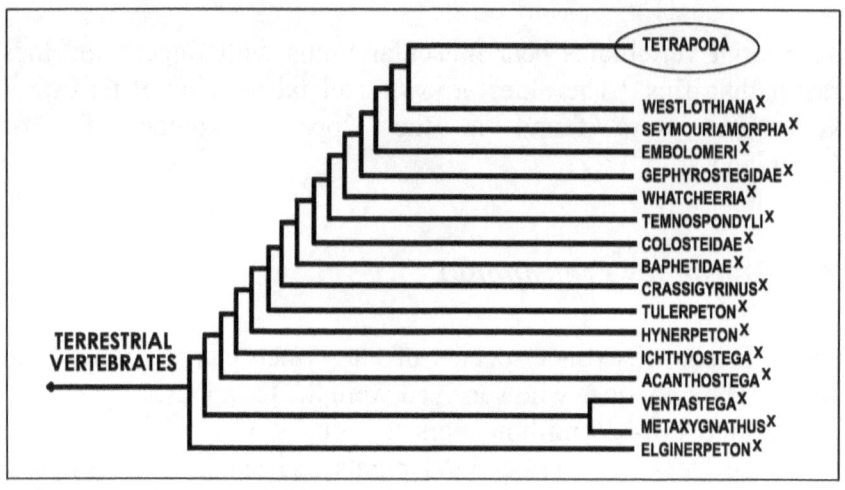

Plants Evolved Seeds

Around 360 million years ago, species of plants also evolved the ability to reproduce using seeds. As their seeds spread all over the Earth, their numbers and variety grew.[52]

Amphibia and Reptiliomorpha

Species of tetrapods began to separate around 340 million years ago.[53] There were two groups: the amphibia and the reptiliomorpha. The amphibia class split into further species including the now extinct adelogyrinidae, aistopoda, and lysorophia. The only ones left out of the entire amphibia class, are the living amphibians we know today: frogs, salamanders and caecilians.

The reptiliomorpha classes also split into other species: amniota, diadectomorpha and solenodonsaurus. Only the amniotes have survived from the three.

Amphibians needed water more than the amniotes. They fed on land and in water, where they could keep their permeable skin moist. Amphibians typically laid their soft eggs in water. When their offspring broke free from their eggs, they entered a feeding larval tadpole stage.

Amniotes, on the other hand, have broken the link with the water.[54] Amniotes did not go through a larval stage after breaking free from their eggs. Unlike the eggs of amphibians, amniotes evolved eggs that were protected by several extensive hard membranes or soft, porous leathery surfaces.

While the other amphibians had to spawn their eggs under water, amniotic eggs emulated underwater conditions by encasing the embryo with a liquid similar to seawater. This new type of eggs evolved new structures to deal with waste problems and gas exchanges between the embryo and the atmosphere, enabling the amniotes to reproduce and lay their eggs on new and much drier habitats.[55] The coming of amniotic eggs, therefore, is a significant moment for many generations of amniotes and the diverging species that will follow.

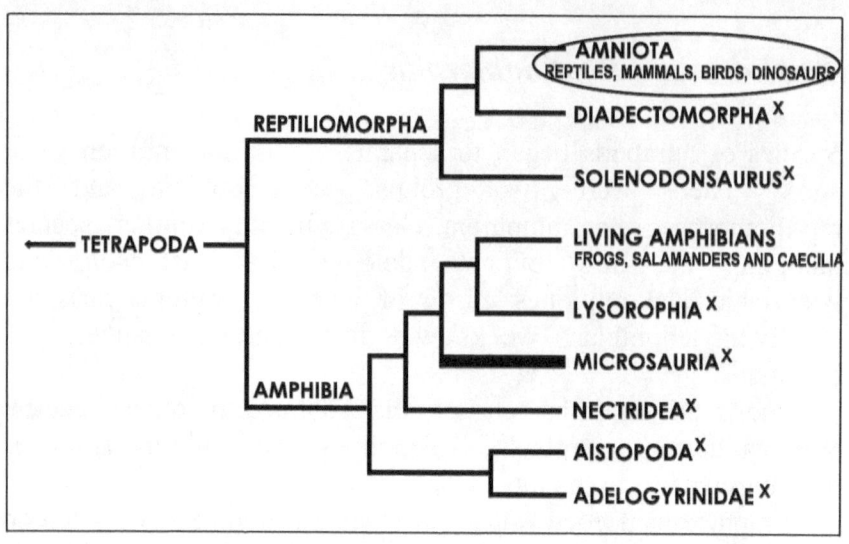

Synapsids ('Beast Faces') and Sauropsids ('Lizard Faces')

After 30 million years (310 mya), species of amniotes became distinguishable from others. They were called the synapsids (beast faces) and the sauropsids (lizard faces). The earliest-known sauropsid, hylonomus, lived about 315 million years ago. The earliest-known synapsids were the archaeothyris and the clepsydrops. They lived during the Pensylvanian period (318 to 299 mya).

Both groups appeared lizard-like. However, descendants of the early synapsids did not have scales like the other lizards. Instead, theirs resembled mammalian hair or avian feathers.[56] They were the first tetrapods to have distinguished teeth, including canines, molars and incisors.

By studying fossils, we know that some animals belonging to either group had a pair of holes in their skulls, behind the eyes. However, the distinguishing feature that evolved differently from the two species was the jaw. For synapsids, their lower jaw evolved to consist of a single bone. The lower jaws of the early reptiles however, consisted of an assembly of smaller bones.

Many species that evolved from the early reptiles have gone extinct. From the many reptiles that once lived on this planet, only two subclasses remained: the testudines and the diapsids. Descendants of testudines include turtles, tortoises and terrapins. Descendants of diapsids include lizards, crocodiles and birds. Like with sauropsids, many synapsids also went extinct. The only ones that survived were the therapsids.

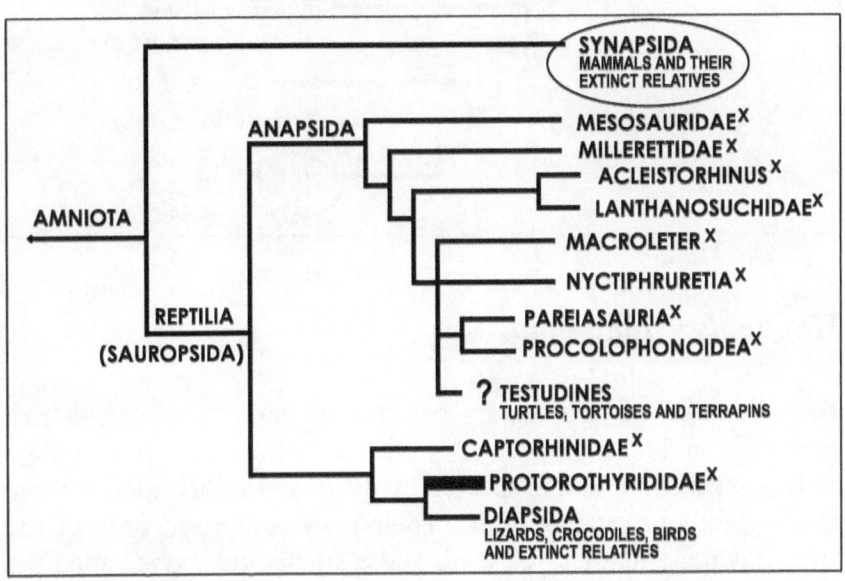

Therapsids (Therapsida)

The therapsids began diverging from the other synapsids during the early Permian period, 299-251 million years ago. They had powerful jaws and their mouths became better evolved for biting and chewing. For example, they evolved teeth called incisors which specialised in nipping. They had large canines beside them for puncturing and tearing. At the back of their mouths, were molars for mashing and grinding food.

Almost all descendants of the early therapsids have gone extinct. Only the mammals survived.

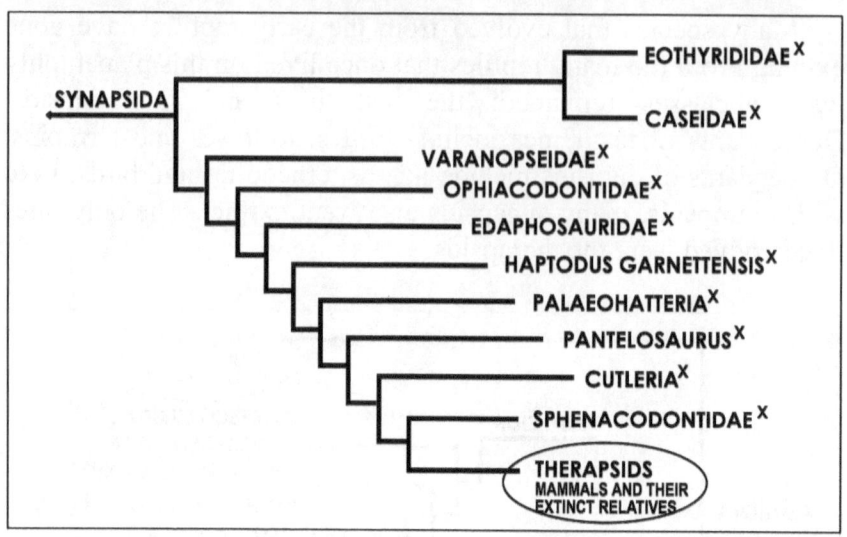

Mammals (Mammalia)

The ancestors of mammals gave rise to early mammals which evolved glands that produced sweat, enabling them to regulate body temperature. Later species evolved the ability to use these sweat glands to produce milk. Their jaws comprised only of the lower jawbone that carried teeth and a small skull bone called the squamosal.

What distinguished the early mammals from their ancestors were the two bones they used for hearing. The same bones were used by their ancestors for eating.

The early mammals also evolved a grey matter as part of their brains called the neocortex. Although the neocortex in some of their rodent descendants is smooth, the neocortex in many larger mammal descendants was able to fold, creating deep grooves and wrinkles. This development allowed some of their descendants later to increase the volume of their brains without taking up too much space.

Six main species evolved from the early mammals. Three are now extinct. They are the triconodonts, multituberculata and palaeoryctoids. The three that survived were the monotremes, the ancestors of platypus and echidnas; the marsupials, the ancestors of possums and kangaroos and the eutherians, the ancestors of placental mammals.

Placental Mammals (Eutheria)

All living species from the infraclass eutheria are placental mammals. During the period of development, foetuses of placental mammals are nourished by a sac-shaped organ that attaches the embryo or foetus to the uterus during pregnancy. This organ is called the placenta. 'Blood flows between mother and foetus through the placenta, supplying oxygen and nutrients to the foetus and carrying away foetal waste products'.[57] Placental animals are viviparous: they carry their offspring inside their uterus until it is fully developed. This made placental mammals different from other mammals. The monotremes laid eggs instead while the marsupials gave birth to underdeveloped young and placed them inside a pouch to complete their development.

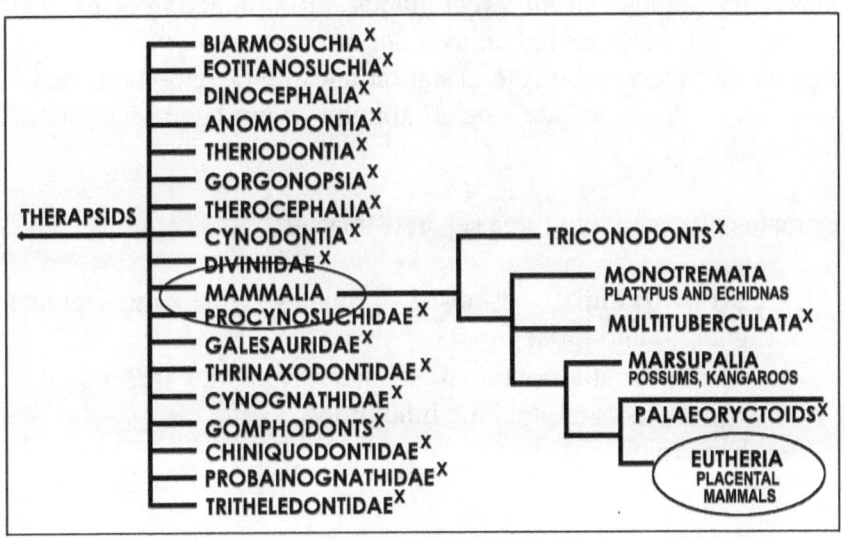

Supraprimates (Euarchontoglires)

From the early placental mammals, a superorder of species called Euarchontoglires ('Supraprimates') began evolving during the Cretaceous period, 145.5 to 65.5 million years ago. Their descendants evolved into two main species: first were the glires, the ancestors of rodents, rabbits, hares and pikas. The second group were the eurchonta. They included the ancestors of treeshrews, flying lemurs, primates and the now extinct order of species, plesiadapiformes.

Primates

Primates evolved in environments where there were plenty of trees or bushes. Herbivorous primates ate plants and the omnivorous primates ate plants as well as other animals. They evolved two mammary glands – from sweat glands – to produce milk for their young. They only carried an average of one to two children when they were pregnant but the gestation and the development period was long. Primates are social animals who have dominance-hierarchies.[58]

Primates diverged into three separate species:

- **Strepsirrhini**: wet-nosed primates, including lemurs, galagos and lorises
- **Tarsii**: small nocturnal primates, like the tarsiers, with enormous eyes and long hind limbs.
- **Simians**.

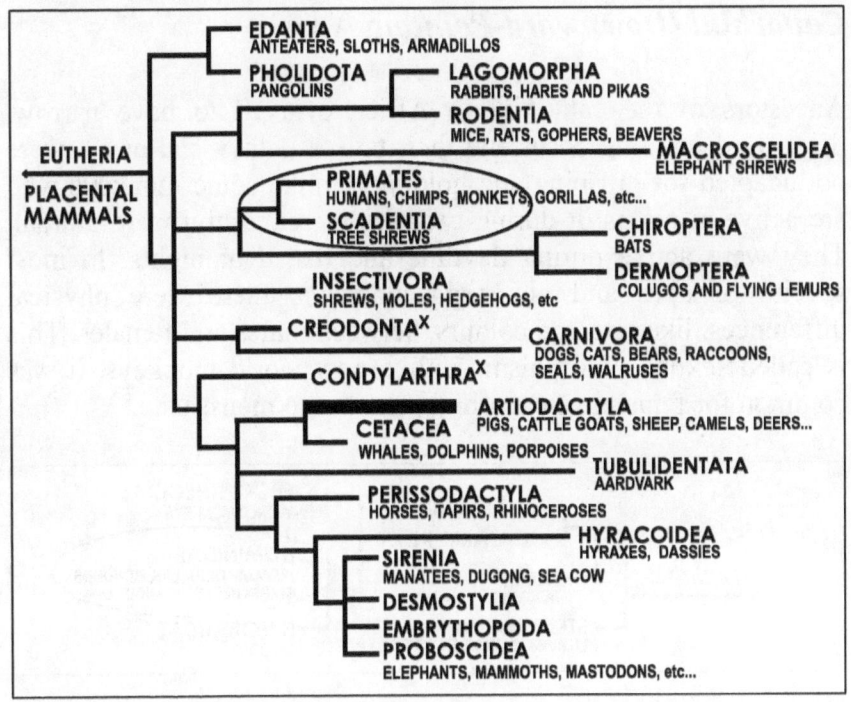

Simians (Simiiformes)

The simians diverged to the platyrrhini (new world monkeys – in South and Central America) and the catarrhini (apes and old-world monkeys – in Africa and Asia).[59] Platyrrhini means 'flat nose', catarrhini means 'down nose'.[60] Platyrrhini primates were different to the catarrhini in the following ways: their noses were flatter[61], they did not have trichromatic vision[62] and they had twelve premolars instead of eight. Many platyrrhini primates had monogamous pair bonds.[63]

Descendants of the first new world monkeys began evolving around 40 million years ago. At the time, Africa and South America were much closer to each other than they are now. Further, the sea level was low. It is likely the early simians made their way from Africa to South Africa to evolve into the new world monkeys we recognise today.[64]

Cattarhini (Downward-Pointing Nose)

Ancestors of the cattarhini in Africa evolved to have narrow, downward-pointing noses and their tails – if they had any – were not adapted for grasping and holding. Unlike some monkeys who are active at nights or during twilight, the cattarhini were diurnal. They were active during daytime and rested at nights. In most species of apes and old-world monkeys, there were physical differences, like size and colours, between males and females. This is called sexual dimorphism. Unlike new world monkeys, it was common for females of cattarhini primates to menstruate.[65]

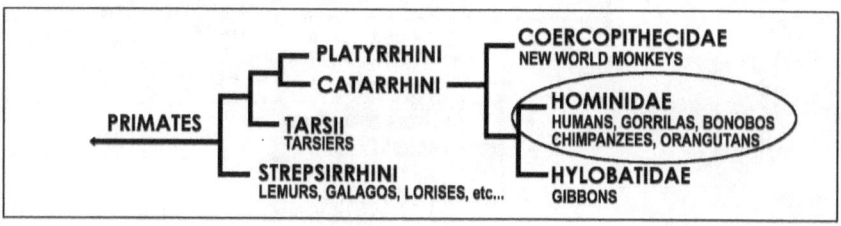

Apes / Hominoids (Hominoidea)

The cattarhini began to diverge into two different species 25 million years ago. They diverged into the cercopithecidae, the old-world monkeys and the apes. The apes had no tails. Apes had more mobile shoulder joints and arms, broad rib cages, were flatter front-to-back, and they had less mobile spines. Apes were omnivorous: they ate fruits and seeds and they also hunted and scavenged for meat. Apes had five molars while old-world monkeys only had four. The early apes gave birth to descendants that began to evolve in two species: the greater apes (hominidae) and the lesser apes (hylobatidae).

The Great Apes / Hominids (Hominidae)

Ancestors of the early hominids, the great apes, separated from the hylobatidae – the gibbons – 18 million years ago.[66] They had no distinct breeding seasons. Gestation in great apes takes between 8 to 9 months. Their mothers must take care of them for long periods of time. It also takes a while for their offspring to stop using milk as food and start eating adult foods instead. Most species become fully mature between 8 to 13 years. Females only give birth every few years.[67] Early great apes gave birth to the ponginae (ancestors of orangutans) and the homininae (ancestors of gorillas and the hominini).

The Hominini

Early hominini gave birth to the ancestors of chimpanzees and bonobos, including the ancestors of the Ardipithecus, now extinct, and our ancestors, the Australopithecus, also extinct. Their descendants included a group of species called homonina.

Among the most recent and exciting findings that provide facts regarding our evolution, has been that of a three-year-old Australopithecus girl who died in present-day Dikika, Ethiopia, 3.3 million years ago. Her remains were found by a research team led by Dr. Zeresenay Alemseged of the Max Planck Institute in Leipzig, Germany.

In a talk given by Dr Alemseged, himself, in a TED conference, he describes the details of the findings and how they arrived at their conclusions. He says that even though this girl looked human in many ways, 'not everything was human'.

Our hyoid bone is a bone that supports the root of our tongue. This bone is supported by the muscles of our neck and it helps us produce noise from our throats. This bone was never in the fossil record but it was found with the 'Dikika girl', as she is known. When an analysis was done on her hyoid bone, it was found to be similar to that of great apes. So, 'if you were there 3.3 million years ago, to hear when this girl was crying out for her mother, she would have sounded more like a chimpanzee than a human.'

She had humanlike features and at the same time, she had apelike features. This tells us that her kind, the Australopithecus, were one of the nearest ancestors we once shared with the other apes.

The Hominina

The hominina did not necessarily live where there were trees and bushes. Their skulls were placed on top of their vertebral column and they walked with their hind legs, standing up. Unlike the rest of the primates, their first toe was aligned with the other four toes, making them less suited to climbing trees and branches than their ancestors'. They also evolved their hands and thumbs in a way that made it easy for them to manipulate objects.

The descendants of early hominina diverged into separate species:

1. Homo habilis
2. Homo rudolfensis
3. Homo ergaster
4. Homo erectus
5. Homo floresiensis
6. Homo antecessor
7. Homo heidelbergensis
8. Homo neanderthalensis
9. Homo rhodesiensis
10. Homo cepranensis
11. Homo georgicus
12. Homo sapiens

The ability to control fire likely began with Homo erectus about 790,000 years ago.[68] Apart from us, Homo sapiens, no descendants of these species survived. However, fossils of their tools and their remains were found in 1829[69], like artefacts letting us know about the existence of our long lost cousins.

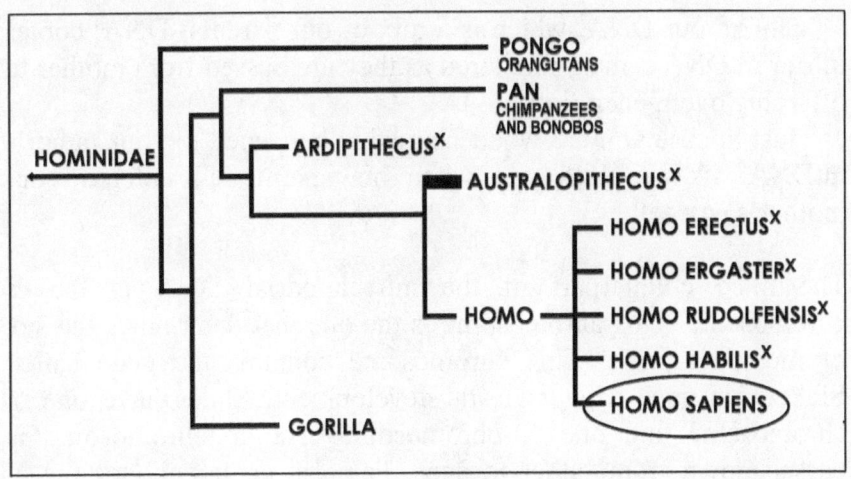

Humans (Homo Sapiens)

We, Homo sapiens, evolved between 400,000 to 250,000 years ago. Homo sapiens originated in the African savanna. We used stone tools, like the Homo habilis, with increasing sophistication. Starting about 50,000 years ago, our technology and culture began to change more rapidly. Later, we developed a larger brain. Our brains are typically 1400 cm^3. That is twice the size of a chimpanzee or a gorilla. We also evolved the larynx and hyoid bone, making it possible to talk.[70]

Y-Chromosomal Adam and Mitochondrial Eve

At the start of this chapter, we have been introduced to the mitochondria: an organelle of a eukaryotic cell. Surprisingly, this little cell organ has its own independent DNA, the Mitochondrial DNA.

In most multicellular organisms, including most animals, the mitochondrial DNA (mtDNA) is inherited from the mother only. The mtDNA inside your cells, whether you are male or female, is inherited from your mother and she inherited it from her mother, who inherited it from your grandmother... all the way up your earlier female ancestors.

Unlike our DNA, which is a mix of our parents' DNA, copies of our mtDNA remain unaltered as they are passed from mother to offspring over generations.

Just in case you are wondering what happened to your father's mtDNA, it was destroyed when his sperm cell entered your mother's egg cell.

The male counterpart of the mitochondrial DNA is the Y chromosome. This chromosome is the one that determines the sex of most mammals. This chromosome contains the gene called SRY. This gene triggers testis development. Males have one Y chromosome and one X chromosome. The Y chromosome is passed down from father to sons. Females do not inherit the Y chromosome from their fathers and they do not pass it down to their sons. A grandson cannot inherit the Y chromosome from his mother's father.[71]

Because the mtDNA and the Y chromosome are copied, largely unaltered, from one generation to the next, we are able to trace our ancestors far back in time. If it was possible to go back in time, we would find that all the mtDNA of every person alive today can be traced back to one woman. This woman would be our matrilineal most recent common ancestor (MRCA). Scientists refer to this ancestor as the Mitochondrial Eve.

We will also find that all the Y chromosomes of every male alive today can be traced back to one man, who is our patrilineal human most recent common ancestor (MRCA). Scientists refer to this ancestor as the Y-chromosomal Adam.

Scientists have in fact tried to find who our most recent common ancestors were by studying the genetic codes of hundreds of individuals from all over the world. From these studies, they believe that Mitochondrial Eve was alive about 140,000 years ago. Y-chromosomal Adam lived about 60,000 years ago.[72]

People who have only heard of the story of Adam and Eve from the Bible, will understandably be confused when they encounter the terms Mitochondrial Eve and Y-chromosomal Adam. So, it is important to point out the following:

1) Mitochondrial Eve ('mt-Eve') and Y-chromosomal Adam ('Y-Adam') were not created by God and they did not live in the Garden of Eden, as described in the book of Genesis. These names were just coined by scientists.
2) 'Mt-Eve' and 'Y-Adam' did not necessarily live during the same era.
3) 'Mt-Eve' and 'Y-Adam' were not necessarily the first Homo sapiens.
4) 'Mt-Eve' and 'Y-Adam' were not a couple. If evidence arises to suggest so, though very unlikely, it would be purely coincidental.
5) 'Mt-Eve' was not the only female of her time, but it is her mitochondrial DNA that her female descendants managed to pass on to their daughters' daughters who are alive today. There may have been many other females during her time which may have had daughters but they left no living female descendants today.
6) 'Y-Adam' was not the only male of his time but it is his Y-chromosome that his male descendants managed to pass on to their sons' sons who are alive today. There may have been many other males during his time which may have had sons, but they left no living male descendant today.

Human Races

Studies on the mitochondrial DNA and the Y-chromosomes provide us with the knowledge that our ancestors originated from Africa. We are all descendants from Africans[73] who lived thousands of years ago. We then wonder how it is that different people look so different from each other.

From our African origins, our ancestors split in groups. Some decided to stay, some decided to venture to other parts of Africa and the world. These groups further split into subgroups. About 40,000 years ago we inhabited Eurasia and Oceania. Our species got to the Americas 14,500 years ago.[74]

These different groups began to evolve independently of one another. Each group was unique because their different geographical locations provided them with different living and environmental conditions. They ate a different mix of food, they hunted and harvested different types of plants and animals and they built different types of homes.

Furthermore, individuals could only reproduce within their own subgroups. Gene flow was therefore restricted because of the distance that existed between these different groups.

Individuals who were endowed with genes that adapted to their way of life and environmental realities, were the ones who managed to have sex and pass on their genes to later generations.

Consider the gene of having dark skin. Dark skin has increased epidermal melanin which provides a natural skin protection factor of about 13 and filters twice as much UV radiation as white skin.[75] In sunny environments, the bodies of individuals who have the gene for darker skin have it easier than those with lighter skin.

This difference would have been enough to provide the extra survival edge needed for this gene to survive and get passed on to the next generation. Even if only one light-skinned person died for every 10,000, for reasons attributable to having light skin, the long-term consequence of this is evident today. Natives of lands along the equator, like the Africans today, have darker skins than those who evolved in countries that receive less exposure to sunlight.

On the other hand, having dark skin is not so important in an environment where the sun does not do much damage to the skin. For example, the people who evolved in the Nordic countries received little exposure to sunlight. Dark skin would have been wasteful to the body's resources. Instead of creating more melanin, their bodies used precious resources for more practical purposes, like storing energy reserves in fat cells during the cold winters, for example.

Gene flow between specific groups was also restricted because of other factors that prevented them from having sexual intercourse. These included varying attitudes, beliefs, religions and cultures that began to evolve in their societies.

Let me give you an idea of how culture impedes gene flow. My mother's friends warned her from marrying my father because he belonged to a different tribe. People in my father's tribe were more dark-skinned, and they were perceived to be aggressive and violent people who loved war and cut their enemies heads. Because of these beliefs, many males and females were prevented from coupling. Mind you, these divisions existed just as recently as the 1960s.

Today, tribalism, racism and sectarianism still persist around the world. Many religions and cultures still prohibit or discourage members of their group to marry outside their circles. Even in western societies – just as recent as 1968 – a kiss between a white male actor and a black female actor, was taboo. The episode of *Star Trek*, containing the kiss between William Shatner and Nichelle Nichols, was not aired in some Southern cities of America.

Geographical and non-geographical factors isolated genes from intermixing with each other for two hundred thousand years. The different pools of genes resulted in the myriad of identifiable physical traits that exist today between people of different 'races'. Surprisingly, however, only 0.1% of our genetic differences account for your appearance and mine. I may have brown skin, brown eyes and black hair while you might have white skin, blue eyes and blonde hair. But, our genetic make up – as well as that of any two people on Earth – are still 99.9% genetically the same.

One wonders what would have happened if we continued to marry within our sub-groups for many more thousands of years. Would we have diverged into different species? This, we will never know. Unlike our grandparents, whose lives were confined to a few kilometres of where they were born, many of us now travel hundreds of kilometres to work, visit friends and meet lovers. Travelling different countries has become so easy. As a result, individuals, who might not have met otherwise, can get married and have children.

When I was growing up it was rare to see inter-racial couples. Now, it is quite common. The shackles of culture, tradition and religion are being shed by individuals who choose to marry individuals of other nationalities, ethnicities and religions. Our gene pool is beginning to inter-mix again, like it did thousands of years ago, when our ancestors belonged to only one, small group.

If and when humanity becomes capable of colonising other planets and moons, some of us will choose to leave Earth and live under different environmental conditions. Humanity will be divided into two groups: those who choose to go and those who choose to stay. If the descendants of the two groups have no way of inter-breeding, might the two groups evolve so radically different, physically and behaviourally, that they can no longer be able to have sex and produce offspring with each other? My guess is yes. Humanity will diverge into different species.

Conclusion

In this chapter, we have summarised the evolution of life as it occurred here on Earth. The history of human evolution, as I have outlined, is based on the works of myriad of scientists all over the world who have dedicated their lives studying palaeontology, biology, physics, chemistry and other related fields. It is thanks to them that we can now look at the very small and to the very far. It is thanks to them that we have studied fossils and DNA. As a result, we have discovered what we are and where we come from.

The process of evolution has taken many paths and in the process, created many different species of life. Unfortunately, the ability of many species to live is limited by the Earth's environment and its scarce resources. Sadly, many of our distant cousins have gone extinct. We will never know what wonderful species they would have evolved into.

What should be most striking to all of us is the fact that, if any of our line of common ancestors had died, none of us would be here. In discovering our origins, I have become very aware that life is much more fragile than I originally thought. I feel extremely lucky that I am here. We should all be. We should all be enormously grateful for the life that we have here on Earth. Let us cherish it and live it the best way we can. In the process, all of us must also respect the lives of other human beings and other creatures. We must recognise that they too, are endowed and entitled to the gift of life, as we are.

So far, we have discovered the latest in explaining our origins and our history. We have gone as far back in time as we could. We discussed the Big Bang. We discussed how the elements in the universe coalesced to form our solar system, the sun, our planet and the moon. We summarised how life evolved here on Earth, from solitary replicators to single-celled life forms. Almost like observing our history from a film, we watched how early life-forms struggled to survive and multiply. As generations went by, the descendants who remained carried the genes favoured by the environment. We have learnt the nature of our 'bloodline' and met many of our great, great, great ancestors. We also met distant cousins who once shared the same ancestors. I am tremendously happy to have known about all this.

I am only sorry that it took me until the age of thirty to become aware and appreciate the beauty of evolution. I am not alone in my predicament. I know that many people have not yet discovered the wonder and the drama they can experience when they seek the truth through knowledge and enquiry.

Many of us are either unwilling or unable to find things out for ourselves. We stop our education as soon as we finish our schooling. We become reluctant to open our minds to such explanations. We may even refuse to accept them. Our tendency and attitude to behave this way is because many of us have been brought up to believe in conflicting ideas. The main sources of these ideas come from religions and superstitions because they too, attempt to answer the same questions. However, the answers they provide are vastly different to the answers we get when we reason with the facts that evidence gives us.

Once believed, many doctrines oppress us and limit our capacity to ask questions that might otherwise lead us to the truths we need. It is because of this, I will now focus on examining religious beliefs because they are, by far, the most influential, most powerful forces that drive the lives of many people today.

CHAPTER 6:
RESPITE

Now that we have come to understand the scientific explanation of how everything came about, we no longer have to confuse our facts with the Book of Genesis to explain how we came to being. Not only that, by understanding how evolution works, we have a framework that we can use to understand beliefs and religions, because like everything else in life, they too, evolve. Before we examine concepts of God, religion and morality, however, I would like to use this chapter as a respite. I want to prepare you for what we will discuss in the rest of this book.

Our Definition Of 'God' And 'Religion'

The words 'religion' and 'God', invoke different meanings to different people. For example, some of us may see spirituality as a belief in God, gods, heaven or hell, but at the same time, the same people may not feel bound to the bureaucratic structure and creeds of a particular organised religion. Some people tailor their individual beliefs to create what they think would be a more tolerant and intuitive form of religion.

Definitions of God can be classified as follows:

1. **Theistic God**

   Theists believe in a supernatural God who created the universe, who watches our every move, listens to our thoughts and punishes or rewards us after we die. Christianity, Islam and Judaism believe in a theistic God. According to Encyclopaedia Britannica, in 2005, 53.57% of people all over the world belong to one of these three major religions.

2. **Deist God**

   Deists' idea of God is a god who created the universe and thereafter left us alone to live our lives. Deists believe that God is either unwilling or unable to keep 24-hour surveillance on every single one of us and our thoughts.

3. **Pantheist God**

   Pantheists are atheists. They do not believe that a supernatural being, created the universe. They use the word 'God' to describe 'nature', 'energy' or the 'universe'.

I grew up with the doctrines of Christianity so in discussing religion, these are the main doctrines I have in mind while writing this book. Much of what I will be discussing, however, will also be relevant to members of other Abrahamic religions including, Islam and Judaism for they all share the following commonalities[76]:

1) They are all monotheisms: They believe in only one God.
2) They all have Semitic origins. Judaism and Islam originated from Semitic people, like the Jews and the Arabs. Christianity originated from Judaism. Because both originated in the same part of the world, they share similar stories like those of Adam, Noah, Abraham and Moses.
3) They recognise and share the same individuals as prophets.
4) They have their bases in divine revelation rather than philosophical speculation or custom.

5) They all have an ethical orientation: they speak of good and evil, of obedience and disobedience to God.
6) They all have an association with the desert, imbuing these religions with a particular ethos.
7) They have a linear concept of history: there is creation and then there is the end of the world when God redeems the world and resurrects the righteous.

I will use the word 'religion' mainly to refer to organised religions, including cults and sects, which believe in theistic gods. It may not be relevant to many Eastern religions including Buddhism or Confucianism because they approach spirituality differently.

Introduction To My Thesis On God And Religion

Since individuals are vulnerable from believing ideas that delude them, how can we distinguish the good ones from the bad? Are the religious beliefs held by hundreds, thousands, or even millions of people better than the beliefs held by a single individual? Many of us believe so. In fact, it is widely believed that without religion, most people would not know right from wrong. Religion is often offered as the sole guide – the sole moral compass – to guide us towards the enlightened path to our salvation... but does it, really? Does it really steer us away from evil? Does it really help us from mistreating one another? I used to believe that this was true but in later chapters, I am going to argue that the nature of religion is more sinister than this.

Religion is ubiquitous. It is complexly interwoven in our culture, our way of life and our thinking. We will inevitably open up many related issues relevant to our society today as well. I will therefore slowly work to present the concepts and ideas relevant to my hypothesis on God and religion.

To tell you a little bit about what I have spent most of my life doing, I trade the financial markets. The financial market is one of the most complex entities one can ever try to understand. That is a bold statement, but many of the world's best scientists and mathematicians have failed to succeed in trading.

In trading, I found that the best way to comprehend complex phenomena is to formulate a model that incorporates everything we believe to be true and relevant to it. We then test our model as many times as possible, in as many situations as possible. If our model helps in making right trading decisions consistently, then we have a viable model. We continue using this model until we have evidence suggesting that our model is no longer in tune with our observations of reality.

As I will discuss later, true knowledge is measured by its ability to provide reliable predictions consistently. I believe that if we truly understand the nature of a phenomenon, then we must be able to create a model that allows us to make reliable predictions about that phenomenon consistently.

Scientists do something similar. They make observations, they formulate a hypothesis, they test it and then they publish it for others to test its validity and usefulness. If it guides enough scientists to make relevant and useful predictions, it becomes a theory. They work with that model until it is not longer viable, or until they arrive at new information that invalidates its truths. When the evidence for the theory becomes so strong, the theory itself is as close to the truth as we can ever get.

Similarly, I am about to put out my personal hypothetical model of God, morality, us and religion. If I am able to provide a model that we can use to make predictions, then I believe it would be worth your consideration.

I want to exercise my freedom to express what I think about God and religion, in the same way as you would discuss your own beliefs with other people. Since you have decided to read this book, you must therefore accept responsibility not to take offence at anything I am about to say. With so many varying religious beliefs that exist, we cannot all expect to agree on everything. Even husbands and wives do not agree on everything. However, now that most of us live and share our cities with people from many religions, it is very important that we can discuss our religious beliefs, or lack of them, openly and maturely.

Our predicament is that, many religious people live among people of other faiths, secretly believing that they belong to the right religion. They will go to heaven, while the rest of the population face annihilation and eternal torture in hell.

With the incompatibility of many religious beliefs and dogma, it is obvious that not all existing religions are right. Either one of them is honest or all of them are deluded. This implies that many of us currently believe in absurdities. This is very dangerous because, like Voltaire once said: **"Those who believe absurdities will commit atrocities"**.

For our sake, and that of future generations, we might as well find out what these absurd ideas are through peaceful and intellectual dialogue and debate, rather than allow our predicament to lead us to fight violent wars and other avoidable disasters in the future.

Arguments and disagreements have helped human society to pinpoint problems. It is through peaceful communication between us to find solutions for our troubles. There is no reason to shrink away from an opportunity to discuss the differences of our ideas and beliefs because only in such enterprises can true wisdom and knowledge be acquired. Like Thomas Paine says:

It is error only, and not truth, that shrinks from inquiry.

American editor and critic, H.L. Mencken adds:

…A superstitious man has certain inalienable rights. He has a right to harbour and indulge his imbecilities as long as he pleases, provided only he does not try to inflict them upon other men by force. He has a right to argue for them as eloquently as he can, in season and out of season. He has a right to teach them to his children. But certainly he has no right to be protected against the free criticism of those who do not hold them. He has no right to demand that they be treated as sacred. He has no right to preach them without challenge.[77]

If you are religious and feel offended by what I am about to say, please consider that perhaps, regardless of how I express myself, you will choose to take offence because you are hard-wired by your religion to close your mind on any information different to its teachings. If you are wiser than I, and if you are as compassionate and understanding as your religion professes you to be, then I am sure you can find it within yourself to demonstrate those qualities.

If you truly believe that God is all-knowing and He created everything, then He must have created me as much as He has created you. He has given me my brain and my own faculty for thinking. Who would you be to question His wisdom and reject the quality of His work?

Galileo Galilei says something similar:

"I do not think it is necessary to believe that the same God who has given us our senses, reason, and intelligence wished us to abandon their use, giving us by some other means the information that we could gain through them".

If you are religious and you believe that your religion has access to universal truths, you should be confident enough and not be afraid of what a book like this, written by a mere mortal, can do. The truth will prevail in the end. If I find that your religion holds the key to truth, then allow me to discover it for myself. If God tells me it is too late to change my mind, then so be it.

Each of us could be wrong. However, when we begin to live our lives based on what others tell us to believe, when we stop using our own capacity to think and reason, then our lives cease to be our own. We become willing puppets, ready to be manipulated by those who claim to know the truth.

CHAPTER 7: LANGUAGE

In this chapter, we will discuss the next important stage in our evolution: the development of our capacity and ability to communicate and cooperate with one another. Unlike bones, languages do not fossilise. It is therefore difficult to theorise about the origin of language because evidence is rare. We can only speculate about how language may have evolved.[ll]

So far, we know of the following:

1) We have learnt about the discovery of the remains of an Australopithecus girl, who lived 3.3 million years ago. The finding indicated that our ancestors were unable to talk as we can today because their hyoid bone was still ape-like.
2) There is a gene called $FOXP_2$ which is linked to our ability to use language, as well as control our face and mouth. A similar, but altered, gene is also found in apes. This gene seemed to have evolved to its present form between 200,000 and 100,000 years ago.
3) We know that humans are not the only species who can communicate. Animals make distinct calls to express immediate concerns regarding food, dangers and threats. The great apes are also able to communicate and cooperate

---

[ll] My description of how language emerged came from a piece written by Ray Jackendoff from the Linguistic Society of America, entitled '*How did language begin?*'

with one another. Dolphins are relatively more sophisticated because they call each other by name.[78]

Once the apparatus required for speech was developed, our ancestors were able to make vocal noises that proved valuable for survival. Fossil evidence suggests that the size of our ancestors' brains increased, thus, allowing them to process more information and perform more complicated tasks. Some of these tasks led to our ancestors' ability to control their hyoid bone, tongue, lips and other speech organs to make sounds. As generations of hominids went by, the ability to mimic sounds vocally and the ability to memorise improved and developed as our early ancestors forced themselves to communicate and cooperate with others in their group.

Eventually, their vocabulary grew. Looking at two-year-old children learning to talk, our ancestors may have begun replacing grunts and calls with sounds to name objects and actions. In making use of their vocabulary, a 'protolanguage' emerged in much the same way it emerges when we try to learn a new language. We mix words with other words and we aid our expressions with hand gestures. Likewise, our ancestors began structuring and inventing ways to improve this protolanguage. They began adding grammatical devices to suggest tenses, plurality and so forth. From all our earlier ancestors, only the Homo sapiens have managed to develop language that evolved into the complex and sophisticated form we recognise today.

Speaking a language came first. Writing came much later. The oldest historical record of linguistics dates from 500 years BC. In a place called Gandhara, found somewhere between northern Pakistan and eastern Afghanistan, a grammarian named Pāṇini, formulated 3,959 rules of the Sanskrit language.[79] Findings also suggest the Tamil language began classifying nouns, verbs, vowels and consonants. In the Middle East, Al-kitab Fi Al-nahw revolutionised language, with his book, *The Book On Grammar*, published in 760 AD.

Today, there are 6,912 known human languages in use.[80] Like species of organisms, they also evolve gradually as they are moved and used from one geographical location to another. There exists a continuum of languages and again, it becomes difficult to draw the line between two languages. For example, a few dialects of German are similar to some dialects of Dutch. Specifically, the Venlo dialect, a Dutch dialect, has more features in common with the German dialect of Krefeld (which is close to Venlo) than, another Dutch dialect of the Zaan area. Yet, the Venlo dialect is still Dutch.[81]

After our ancestors developed their early languages, it was a lot easier, faster and more efficient for them to coordinate their efforts to survive in groups.

There is more to language than communication. An expert in cognitive behaviour and the President of the Institute of Cognitive Behaviour Management, Gerome R. Gardner writes:

> Mental processing [thinking] is activated through symbols which have been developed to identify and describe the sensations caused by the integration of various stimuli impacting upon the senses. Such sensations help the individual to organize these various sense perceptions into a single comprehension [intuition, hunch]. These comprehensions are then subject to the development or adoption of symbolic representations [language] which not only allow us to consciously comprehend the idea caused by the sensation, but to communicate it as well.[82]

Language gave us the tool and the capability to arrange, set priorities, analyse and understand our thoughts, feelings, perceptions and observations within our minds. It allowed us to create mental narratives and beliefs about ourselves and about everything we know and understand about the world. "Human beings have developed consciousness through the use of language."[83] Most importantly, it allowed us to develop and ask questions. For the very first time, our ancestors were able to wonder and mutter, in their words: Who am I?

CHAPTER 8:
MEMES

Equipped with language, people were empowered to ask questions. In the search for the answers, they gained knowledge. Ideas developed and beliefs were formed. Another replicator – the meme – began to shape our destiny.

Introduction To Memes

The Greek word 'mimeme' refers to anything that can be mimicked. In his book, *The Selfish Gene*, Richard Dawkins coined, and used, the word 'meme' instead. It is sometimes defined as the unit of imitation and is the smallest unit of cultural transmission.

Many people are confused with the word meme and its definition. In fact, since its introduction, a new branch of study called 'Memetics' has arisen. It is devoted to the study of memes as a way to understand cultural evolution in the same way genes made it easy for biologists to understand the evolution of organisms.

For this book, however, let us not complicate or confuse matters more than we need to. A meme is not a newly-discovered phenomenon. It is simply a word that we use to refer to anything that can be imitated. It could be as simple as a thought, an idea, a theory, a poem, a dance move, a recipe, a napkin fold, a design, a phrase and so forth.

Let me provide a personal example of an action meme. I sometimes slap my forehead with my right palm when I realise that I have forgotten to bring something important. An action, as simple as that, is a meme. It can be imitated by another person. I first mimicked it from my father, in fact.

Phrases are also memes. Think of famous phrases from your favourite songs and films. In the film, *A Few Good Men*, Jack Nicholson's famously says, "You can't handle the truth".

In the film, *Sudden Impact*, Clint Eastwood also says a famous phrase: "Go ahead, make my day". It remains to be a popular meme and in fact, in certain states of the USA, the '*Make My Day Law*'[mm] has since been instated.

How Memes Affect Our State

Once a copy of a meme is created in another person's mind, that person will act and behave according to that meme. Memes change our states and our emotions. If you listen to sad music, you feel sad. If you listen to energetic music, you feel energetic.

A joke is a meme. When we hear a joke, it is imprinted in our minds and we either react to it by laughing, by shrugging our shoulders or by getting angry.

Consider the following joke about people with blonde hair:

> *Question: What do smart blondes and UFOs have in common?*
> *Answer: You always hear about them but you never see them.*

The underlying meme in this joke is "blondes are NOT smart". I would most likely laugh if I had other memes in my mind saying "all the blondes I know are dumb". Alternatively, I might shrug my shoulders if I do not agree with the joke. Perhaps, I have a meme in my mind that says 'intelligence is not a function of hair colour'. Finally, I may even get angry if I have a meme in my head that

---

[mm] The law, just in case you are interested, gave a person the legal right to use deadly force to defend his or her place of residence from illegal trespassers and attackers.

says 'it is cruel to make fun of people because of their physical traits'.

People may have found a joke funny because it once reflected their culture. However, as culture evolves, people's sense of humour also evolves. Suddenly, a joke that once triggered laughter on many occasions, may no longer receive a chuckle. Even worse, it might even invite angry responses.

Other examples are racist jokes. They are no longer funny in the culturally-diversified societies we live in today. Many of us have beliefs and ideas we have gained from living, working and marrying individuals belonging to other races, nationalities and ethnicities. We can say that people's minds are now filled with non-racist memes. Therefore when a racist meme tries to infiltrate itself a person's brain, it is rendered useless or ineffective by the other memes that already exist in that brain. These genes reject or cancel memes that are incongruent to their nature. So, racist jokes now attract disagreement and hostility, providing jokers with no benefit. As a result, fewer jokers will tell racist jokes. Eventually, racist jokes will stop becoming a major part of culture.

Now, let us consider the fate of good jokes. As soon as you hear a good joke, it provides you with the pleasurable sensation of laughter. If it is good enough, you memorise it so you can share it with someone. Nowadays, people even pay money to hear good jokes by attending live, stand-up comedy shows. Good memes that have initially formed inside the comedian's head are replicated inside the minds of all attendees who then go away and tell the same jokes to their relatives at home or their colleagues at work.

Memes: The New Replicators

Memes are interesting because they are so much like genes. They are replicators. Instead of travelling within bodies of organisms through the reproductive process, memes are transmitted through communication. Those who can hear us can copy what we say orally. Anybody who can see us can imitate any of our gestures and body language.

We can replicate the memes we have in our minds to the minds of other people, who may not necessarily be in the same room as us. We can also send memes through radio, television channels and now, the Internet.

Genes spread and multiply inside the cells of organisms. Memes also spread and multiply inside the minds of people. Organisms, with genes that happen to complement one another, benefit from the synergy created by such relationships. Minds that have memes that complement one another, also benefit a person. The person will think, act and behave more congruently. This person becomes more decisive than a conflicted person who has opposing ideas inside his mind.

The population growth of genes is limited by the abundance of natural resources offered by the environment. The food supply provided to us by our planet, can only feed so many people. Similarly, the population growth of memes is limited by the number of minds in which they can replicate.

If I am an atheist living in the Middle East, where large portions of the population are practising Muslims, then there are only so few minds in which my atheistic memes can hope to replicate. In this sense, there is competition among memes. Atheistic memes will be repelled by memes that already exist in a religious mind.

Like genes, memes that are successful are memes with the following characteristics:

1) **Longevity**: The memes that exist longer will have more replicas because they have more time to reproduce than those that existed in a shorter amount of time.
2) **Fecundity**: The memes which are copied in the minds of other people faster will have more replicas than the memes that are copied with less frequency.
3) **Copying Fidelity**: The memes that are copied more accurately will be more numerous than those having flawed copies.
4) **Compete**: The memes that find a way to destroy their rivals would make up more of the population by reducing the number of rivals in the meme pool.

Conversely, this means that memes which have the following characteristics: (i) short life, (ii) copied less frequently, (iii) copied inaccurately and (iv) easily destroyed or cannot destroy its competition, are more likely to perish. Their numbers will dwindle as fewer people mimic or communicate them to other people.

Richard Dawkins writes in *The Selfish Gene (p192)*:

> Memes should be regarded as living structures, not just metaphorically but technically. When you plant a fertile meme in my mind you literally parasitize my brain, turning it into a vehicle for the meme's propagation in just the way that a virus may parasitize the genetic mechanism of a host cell. And this isn't just a way of talking-the meme, for say, 'belief in life after death' is actually realized physically, millions of times over, as a structure in the nervous systems of individuals the world over."

Introducing memes allows us to discuss religious beliefs because they, too, are memes.

Memes Evolved To Religions

It is unlikely that a single religion – with all its beliefs, rituals, songs and chants – was formed by one person, or group of individuals, in one generation. Religions, as we recognise them today, are filled with complex ideas. It would be more accurate to assume that the first religions began forming without any conscious design.

God and religion began as memes: memes that formed independently in the minds of many different people who do not necessarily know one another. These memes began to evolve and, over generations, people joined them with other memes.

Some examples of these memes:

1) Living beings have souls.
2) The soul lives after the body dies.
3) There is life after death.
4) Heaven is a place where the soul finds happiness.
5) The souls of good people go to Heaven.
6) Hell is a place of torture, suffering and pain.
7) The souls of bad people go to Hell.
8) The Devil is the anti-God.
9) The idea of transubstantiation.
10) Violence need to be contained.
11) People need to be organised.
12) Someone created everything.
13) People can pray to communicate to the Creator.
14) Kneeling or genuflecting is a good position to pray because it symbolises humbleness.

These memes then went through a process of evolution through natural selection as they are replicated in many minds. People passed on the ones they found appealing to their children and to other people. People began to incorporate these ideas into short parables and short stories. After a few generations, they became part of a moral code or a protoreligion. Eventually, these memes coalesced with other memes that made up ideas, rituals, dances and songs into elaborate belief systems we call religions. Let us get into how this happened with the world's major religions today.

Judaism

The reliability and accuracy of many purported historical facts in the Bible are unverified by archaeologists. Regardless, we will refer to the Bible and try to reconstruct the history of Abrahamic religions.

The origins of the first monotheistic religion, the beginnings of Judaism, can be traced back to sometime during 2000 to 1000 BC.[nn] King Solomon (also known as Sulayman, Suleiman or Sulaimaan to Muslims) built the first temple of the ancient religion of the biblical Israelites in Jerusalem[oo]. It was a focal point for worship and sacrifices, known as the *korbanot,* in ancient Judaism. King Solomon codified early proto-Judaism according to Jewish tradition. King Solomon wrote three books of the Bible:

1) Mishlei (Book of Proverbs): a collection of fables and wisdom of life.
2) Kohelet (Ecclesiastes): a book of contemplation and his self-reflection.
3) Shir ha-Shirim (Song of Songs): a chronicle of erotic love for a woman or God.

Monotheism – the belief in only one god – began with a man named Abraham in the Bible. He is hailed as the first Hebrew and the father of the Jewish people. During his time, people were mainly pagans who believed in many gods. There were different gods for different areas of domain and responsibility. For example, there was a god for death, another for war and another for fertility.

Karen Armstrong, a former nun, wrote a book based on her extensive research called *A History of God.* She explains that Abraham arrived in Canaan and chose to worship the local god, El. El was effective in that part of the world at the time. The prevailing pagan ritual involved sacrificing animals to the gods. They would then eat the animal and this made it seem as though they were sharing a meal with their gods. Sometimes humans, including children, were also sacrificed. Abraham used this idea and he is

---

[nn] Various sources have varying estimates.

[oo] http://www.jewishencyclopedia.com/view.jsp?artid=129&letter=T&search=solomon#0 (23 July 2008). Lack of archaeological evidence for such a temple or a Jerusalem large enough to support it has caused some modern scholars to doubt its existence. The First Temple was destroyed by the Babylonians in 586 BCE. The Second Temple was reconstructed in Jerusalem between 516 BCE and 70 CE.

now especially known for the story of offering his son as a 'burnt offering' to God (Genesis 22:1).

"Judaism begins with the Covenant (a contract, oath or bond) between God and Abraham (ca. 2000 BCE). Throughout the ages, Judaism has adhered to several religious principles, the most important being the belief in a single, omniscient, omnipotent, benevolent, transcendent god, who created the universe and continues to govern it. According to Jewish tradition, the god who created the world established a covenant with the Israelites and their descendants, and revealed his laws and commandments to Moses on Mount Sinai in the form of both the Written and Oral Torah (law or tradition). Judaism has traditionally valued Torah study and the observance of The Commandments recorded in the Torah and as expounded in the Talmud."[84] "The Talmud is a record of rabbinic discussions pertaining to Jewish law, ethics, customs, and history. It is a central text of Rabbinic Judaism, second only to the Hebrew Bible in importance."[85]

In his early ideas of God, Abraham could physically see him (Genesis 18:1). He was a friendly, accessible God with whom Abraham had the privilege to share meals. Sometimes, they had lively arguments too. This god was someone with whom you could wrestle. Abraham's grandson, Jacob, had the opportunity to wrestle with God all-night. Realising that He was being overpowered by Jacob, God asked Jacob to let Him go, for the dawn was breaking. God said to Jacob: "Your name will no longer be Jacob, but Israel, because you have struggled with God and with men and have overcome" (Genesis 32:24-28).

Christianity

Christianity arose after the death of Jesus of Nazareth sometime during 6 BC to 27 AD. Early Christians believed that Jesus was the son of God and the Messiah prophesied in the Hebrew Bible, the Tanakh. It began as a Jewish sect in the eastern Mediterranean[86]. The term Christianity first appeared around 100 AD.

"The Christian Church traces its history to Jesus and the Twelve Apostles, and saw the early bishops of the Church as the successors of the Apostles in general. Central to the doctrines of the Roman Catholic, Orthodox and Anglican Churches is Apostolic Succession, the belief that bishops are the spiritual successors of the original twelve apostles, through the historically unbroken chain of consecration.

"From the beginning, Christians were subject to various persecutions. This involved even death for Christians such as Stephen (Acts 7:59) and James, son of Zebedee (Acts 12:2). Larger-scale persecutions followed at the hands of the authorities of the Roman Empire, beginning with the year 64, when, as reported by the Roman historian Tacitus, the Emperor Nero blamed them for that year's great Fire of Rome. According to Church tradition, it was under Nero's persecution that early Church leaders – Peter and Paul – were martyred in Rome.

"Further widespread persecutions of the Church occurred under nine subsequent Roman emperors including Domitian, Decius and Diocletian. From the year 150, Christian teachers began to produce theological and 'apologetic' works aimed at defending the faith. These authors are known as the Church Fathers, and the study of them is called Patristics. Notable early Fathers include Ignatius of Antioch, Polycarp, Justin Martyr, Irenaeus, Tertullian, Clement of Alexandria and Origen.

"Christianity was legalised in the fourth century, when Constantine I issued the Edict of Milan in 313. Constantine was instrumental in the convocation of the First Council of Nicaea in 325. He sought to address the Arian heresy and formulated the Nicene Creed, which is still used by the Roman Catholic Church, Eastern Orthodoxy, Anglican Communion, and many Protestant churches.[87]

"The purpose of a creed is to act as a yardstick of correct belief. The creeds of Christianity have been drawn up at times of conflict about doctrine: acceptance or rejection of a creed served to distinguish believers and deniers of a particular doctrine or set of doctrines.[88]

"On 27 February 380, Emperor Theodosius I enacted a law establishing Catholic Christianity as the official religion of the Roman Empire.[89] This period of history was also marked by the inauguration of a series of Ecumenical (worldwide) Christological Councils establishing and formally codifying critical elements of the theology of the Church. In 382, the Council of Rome set the

Canon of the Bible, listing the accepted books of the Old Testament and the New Testament.

Also, the Council of Ephesus in 431 declared that Jesus existed both as fully man and fully God simultaneously, clarifying his status in the Trinity. The meaning of the Nicene Creed was also declared a permanent doctrine of the Church."[90]

Islam

Muhammad (c.570 – June 8, 632) was an "Arab religious, political and military leader who founded the religion of Islam as a historical phenomenon".[91] Muslims do not regard Muhammad as the founder of a new religion, but as the restorer of the original monotheistic faith of Abraham, Moses, Jesus, and other prophets. Islamic tradition holds that Jews and Christians distorted the revelations God gave to these prophets by either altering the text, introducing a false interpretation, or both.[92] Muslims believe that God revealed the Qur'an to Muhammad, God's final prophet, and regard the Qur'an and the Sunnah – the words and deeds of Muhammad – as the fundamental sources of Islam.

CHAPTER 9:
BELIEFS AND DELUSIONS

The Nature Of Our Beliefs

The most powerful types of memes are beliefs. What is a belief? Anthony Robbins, the motivator and author of the book, *Awaken The Giant Within*, writes the following (p78):

> Most people treat a belief as if it's a thing, when really all it is, is a feeling of certainty about something. If you say you believe you are intelligent, all you are saying is, 'I feel certain that I'm intelligent'.

He goes on to say the building blocks of beliefs are ideas. There are several ideas you may think about but do not really believe.

> Let's take, for example, the idea that you're sexy. Stop for a second and say to yourself, "I'm sexy". Now, whether it is an idea or a belief will come down to the level of certainty you feel about this phrase as you say it. If you think, "Well, I'm not really sexy," what you're really saying is, "I don't feel very certain that I'm sexy".

How do we turn an idea into a belief? We collect references that support our idea. These references are gathered from our life experiences. Robbins uses a metaphor showing a belief as being the top of a table. It is then supported by ideas, collected from the references we have in our lives:

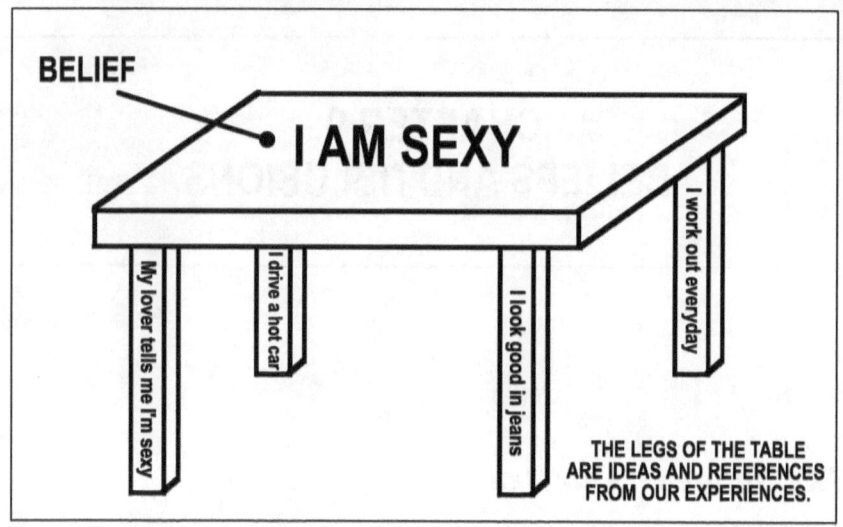

In the example above, the idea of being sexy would not be a strong enough belief if it had no 'legs' to stand on. The more ideas and references you can think of, the more certain you become that you are sexy. The more legs/references you add to support your table/belief, the stronger your table/belief becomes.

Quoting Anthony Robbins:

> Do your references have to be accurate for you to be willing to use them? No, they can be real or imaginary, accurate or inaccurate – even our personal experiences, as solidly as we feel about them, are distorted by our own perspective.
> Because human beings are capable of such distortions and invention, the reference legs we can use to assemble our beliefs are virtually unlimited. The downside of this is that, regardless of where our references come from, we begin to accept them as real and thus no longer question them! This can have powerful negative consequences depending on the beliefs we adopt.

The most powerful force acting on a human being's behaviour and attitude towards himself and others, are the beliefs he holds about what will bring him pain and pleasure. What you do in your life, and how you treat other people, is determined by your beliefs.

Consider what will happen if you come to believe any of the following:

1) You have cancer and you only have one week to live.
2) You won the lottery prize of ten million dollars.
3) Your spouse is having an affair.

Believing any of the propositions above will definitely affect your state of mind. Depending on what belief you adopt, what you will do next and how you will behave will be in accordance to that belief.

Given that our beliefs are merely feelings of certainties about things, which beliefs are true? The most common response to this question is something similar to the following:

> There is no absolute truth. Truth is relative. What is true for you may not be true for me. Believe whatever you want to believe so long as it empowers you or strengthens you to do what you think is right.

To a degree, I agree. We need to be reasonably certain about a few things before we are able to make decisions we are comfortable with. If you believe that you are sexy and this belief enables you to be confident in your line of work, then, enforce the belief that you are sexy. After all, we need to have a strong belief in our capability before we can do anything confidently. Believing in ourselves and hoping for a brighter future, despite the limitations of our realities, is primordial if we want to succeed.

However, are there truly no grounds on which we can criticize our beliefs and someone else's? Should we allow everybody and anybody, including ourselves, to believe in whatever we want as long as it gives us strength and it empowers us to do what we need to do?

Our Capacity For Delusions

Let us consider a few cases when certain individuals believed what they wanted to allow themselves to do what they wanted.

Case 1 – The Pop Idol Contestants

Talent-search shows are where thousands of aspiring singers, models and dancers join to compete on television programs, aired across the country. The most popular shows today originated from a reality program called *Pop Idol* in the United Kingdom, created by Simon Fuller.

The show was a talent contest to decide the best new young pop singer in the country. The first show was aired on October 5, 2001. It was such a success that it became an international franchise and soon after, it was exported to twenty four other countries. In the United States, it gave birth to *American Idol*. Even the Middle-East Asian countries adopted it as *Super Star*.

Ever so often, a young singer, under the impression he or she has exceptional talent, goes to audition and tells everybody that he or she is the next *Idol*, the title given to the winner of the entire competition. Yet, it is almost always those same singers who get told by one of the judges: "Who told you that you could sing?", "You take singing lessons? Do you have a lawyer? Get a lawyer and sue your teacher."

When these 'not-so-good' singers encounter such harsh and unexpected feedback, we witness their confusion, as expressed on their faces. Some of them cry because they have been told by their friends and relatives that they had talent. They were even encouraged to join singing competitions. Because of prior encouragements, some of these singers reject the feedback they get from the judges. Their belief in their ability to sing well is so strong that, according to them, the judges must be wrong and they become angry. There are many other talent-search shows apart from *Pop Idol* where you can witness this drama as it unfolds.

Obviously, in some of these cases, the parents, friends and relatives of these singers failed to give their most honest feedback, fearing the 'truth' might hurt their beloved. One judge said that she felt sorry for some of these contestants because according to her, none of their loved ones cared enough to have the courage to give honest feedback.

This case example is not so much about the harshness of some of the judges' comments or the hilarity of some of these performances. Rather, the point I wish to make is this: Each of those aspiring singers deserved honest feedback from their friends and relatives. The purpose is not so much to stop the singer from competing, but rather, to provide them with useful information to assess theirs skills and then, decide whether they still should compete or not.

Case 2 – The Professionals' Duty To Give Facts

I know someone who was diagnosed with prostate cancer. When he first found out, he did not believe his doctor. He felt great and he believed he was too young to get cancer. He went back to his doctor a couple of weeks later and told his doctor that he regretted the day he came into the clinic for a check-up. He would have been better off not knowing. He was crying as he told his doctor how suicidal and mentally unstable he had become.

Understanding his pain, the doctor hugged him, like he would his son, and told him that it was good that he came. The cancer was still at its early stages, and because they discovered it when they did, there was still enough time to remove it.

This story highlights for me that, what we want to believe may not be what is necessarily best for us. Unlike the friends and relatives of wannabe singers who are afraid of hurting their loved ones' feelings, professionals, on the other hand, have a duty to their clients to give truthful feedback. This is true regardless of what their clients want to hear. If you are operating a business, you want your accountant to tell you if you are being reckless with your company's finances, even if it attacks your sense of business competence. If you are hiring lawyers you want them to tell you, honestly, your chances of winning a case so you can make informed decisions.

People who pay professionals to give them advice sometimes ignore the advice they are paying for because it contradicts or attacks what they want to believe. If you are a business owner and you reject the advice of your lawyers and accountants, you do so at your own peril. More importantly, if you listen only to what you want to hear, you become incapable of knowing what is best for you.

Case 3 – The Secrets Of The Cellar

On August 24, 1984, Josef Fritzl drugged and handcuffed his 18 year-old daughter Elizabeth, locking her in a cellar at the family home in Amsteten, northwest Austria. There, he sexually abused her for the next twenty-four years. During that time, Elisabeth bore her father seven children. One of them died shortly after birth and Fritzl burned the body of the newborn in an incinerator. This story shocked the world when Fritzl was finally arrested in April 2008 for his crimes.

Televised on the Australian show, *60 minutes*, journalist Peter Harvey sought to understand the motivation behind acts like these. He asked Dr Paul Britton, one of Europe's leading forensic psychologists.

Dr Britton believes that Fritzl planned to imprison his daughter when she was still young. He says:

> Men who offend against their children, their daughters, they don't begin when she is a young woman of eighteen, they begin when she is a child. They blame her for arousing in them illicit feelings. So what they are able to do - they are able to push away from themselves responsibility and they put it onto someone else... but what you really have is a straightforward, predatory lust.

In other words, Fritzl believed that it was not his fault that he was sexually aroused by his daughter. Instead he believed that it was his daughter's fault for arousing in him, 'illicit feelings'. Fritzl has permitted himself to believe in ideas that allowed him to rationalise his behaviour. "From his jail cell, Josef Fritzl, 73 years old, is said to be so deluded that he can't see that what he has done is wrong." In interviews done with him, he considers himself somewhat noble. He said he kidnapped the teenage Elizabeth to 'rescue' her from alcohol and bad company.[93]

How deluded can one be? This case highlights for me that beliefs – if kept unchecked – are dangerous and harmful to other beings. We ask ourselves, is Fritzl the only one capable of grossly misleading his mind to justify and rationalise his actions?

In his popular book *How To Win Friends And Influence People*, Dale Carnegie suggests everybody is capable of self-delusion. Let me paraphrase:

> Al Capone, one of America's most notorious Public Enemy, the most sinister gang who ever shot up Chicago, once said: "I have spent the best years of my life giving people the lighter pleasures, helping them have a good time and all I get is abuse... the existence of a hunted man".
>
> Lewis Lawes, who was warden of New York's infamous Sing Sing prison for many years, declared that "few of the criminals in Sing Sing regard themselves as bad men. They are just as human as you and I. So, they rationalise, they explain. They can tell you why they had to crack a safe or be quick on the trigger finger. Most of them attempt by a form of reasoning – fallacious or logical – to justify their antisocial acts even to themselves, consequently stoutly maintaining that they should never have been imprisoned at all".
>
> "If Al Capone, 'Two-Gun' Crowley, Dutch Schutlz and the desperate men and women behind prison walls do not blame themselves for anything – what about the people that you and I come in contact?" [94]

I wish to point out that in each of these cases, the beliefs of the individuals involved, impacted on their world-view, their behaviour and how they treated other people.

We can all find something or someone to back up our belief and make us feel more solid about it. All we need is to find enough supporting references.

As human beings, this is very empowering... but it can also be very dangerous. The beliefs that allow an individual to achieve his or her goals are not necessarily the same beliefs we should encourage if we want our society to survive and progress to the future. Individuals can maintain beliefs that are irrational, delusional and destructive. Just because we believe in something, does not make it true.

How, then, can we be certain that we do not choose our beliefs simply to delude ourselves in justifying and rationalising our thoughts, emotions, behaviour, attitude and actions?

Many of us suppose that because religious beliefs are adopted by many, they are assumed to be wiser, less deceiving and less misleading. Many of us claim that religion is the metaphorical light that guides people to live wise, moral and satisfactory lives.

CHAPTER 10:
EARLY HUMAN SOCIETIES

In the next few chapters, we will try to imagine what it must have been like for early human societies, thousands of years ago. Allow me to paint a picture of a different way of life that is alien to most 'westerners'. It is based on my father's account of his experiences, growing up as a member of the Bugang tribe of the Igorot people, who live in the mountain provinces of the Philippines.

The Igorot people encountered Christian doctrines when the Spaniards colonised the Philippines in 1521.[95] As a result, my father heard stories similar to Noah's flood as well as Adam and Eve. However, since they could not read nor write at the time, the stories were passed down orally generation after generation. As a result, the versions my father heard were strange convolutions of the original Christian stories. For example, as one story goes, there was a great big flood and after the water subsided, Adam was on top of one mountain and Eve on another. They met and had children. Igorots also have deities named Kabunian or Lumawig. However, according to my father, these concepts may have been simply the effect of Christian ideas mixing with their much more ancient spiritual belief system.

Many Igorots think of themselves as pagans. Ms. Philian Louis C. Weygan[96], however, describes their belief system more accurately as a form of animism.[97] Animism comes from the Latin word 'anima', meaning soul or life. It refers to the belief systems that assign souls or spirits to humans, plants, animals and other entities.[98]

Although the belief in souls is common in many religions, animism, itself, is not a religion. In *Primitive Culture* (1871), British anthropologist Sir Edward Burnett Tylor argues that animism is merely an early kernel of religion.

We will not discuss the religion of the Igorot people in this book. I simply want to use my father's account of what he experienced to help us imagine what life must have been like for ancient tribal people who lived hundreds, or even thousands, of years ago.

- The village of the Bugang people was isolated and was the only one among the many villages to sit on the slopes of the Cordillera Mountains. The village contained small houses, just big enough for a space in which to cook and a bed for a couple to sleep in.

- If the couple had small children, they would have a bed for them too. After the children reached a certain age, between the ages of seven to ten, they stopped sleeping in the house. Instead, they went to the dap-ay or the eb-gan.

- The dap-ay and the eb-gan served as sleeping quarters. Young boys and old men slept in the dap-ay. The girls shared the eb-gan with the more mature women of the village.

- The dap-ay and eb-gan also served the role of educational institutions. It was there, where young boys and girls learnt about life, survival and the nature of the world from the village elders.

- The dap-ay served as a storage house for the villages' weapons, including spears, swords, knives and shields. They were used when conflict with other tribes escalated to violence.

- During the day, the dap-ay and the eb-gan became village centres. It was there, where people would get together, mingle, talk about life's frustrations and share a few laughs.

In modern western societies, people go to pubs, clubs and restaurants in the city to achieve the same goals. But before modernity, life for most people was limited to one small geographical area, only a few kilometres across.

- To survive, people relied mainly on planting crops as well as breeding or hunting animals. Physical work, therefore, occupied most of their days. Kids began helping their parents in their tasks as soon as they were big enough to do so.

- Food and other resources for survival were scarce. People lived mainly from corn and sweet potatoes. The decision to kill one of your chickens, or butcher one of your pigs to have meat for dinner, was considered good fortune. So, it was custom for a couple to not just selfishly prepare such meals only for themselves and their children. There was a sense of obligation and gratitude towards the whole village which led them to invite everybody else, like one big family. Even if there was not enough to go around, the small amount of meat had to be shared so everyone could have a taste. Because living conditions were lean, my father explained that during those harsh years, it was such a pleasure and rare experience to have the taste of oil and fat in your mouth, turning an otherwise mundane event in a big occasion. One that was then passed on by another family the following week, and so on.

- I asked my father what happened when selfish individuals never invited others, even if they were fortunate enough to eat meat. My father said people would plainly stop inviting those selfish individuals.

In such an environment where individuals are reliant on the goodwill of other people, being ostracised by your 'extended family' leaves you vulnerable to face your troubles alone. If you were selfish enough not to share your good fortune with others, you will be treated in kind. When you would need food in times of famine, you might be left to fend on your own.

- To answer my question on how they dealt with criminal behaviour, my father replied: If someone was found to have wronged another member of the village, and if the crime was significant enough, everybody gathered to decide what needed to be done. Punishments varied depending on the nature and motivation of the crime. Fines were an option. An offender sometimes gave property, like livestock, to the victim. Or, the offender offered his or her physical services to work for the victim.

- Then how did such a society deal with a violent crime, like rape? The answer I got was interesting. We have to remember that in such a small village, everyone knew everybody. Every woman is someone's daughter, someone's girlfriend or someone's sister and violating her rights as a person can anger her father, her boyfriend or her brothers enough to beat you up or even kill you. Not only was raping wrong, it was fatal. However, in a case where a man raped a woman and the man was not killed as a result, he was obliged marry her and take care of her, should she accept him.

My father, therefore, added that it was highly likely for such a system to have been abused, as a risky strategy for males to get the wives they wanted. It may have been grossly unfair for a woman but there were not many alternatives. Running away to another place, away from the protection and support of her bloodline, was unthinkable and unlikely. There was no police to protect her rights. If she was impregnated, she ran the risk of raising the baby on her own. There was no social welfare funded by taxpayers. If she did not get pregnant, there was a stigma that prevented men from marrying her because she would have been considered as, 'second-hand'. As unjust as it was, women were more likely to concede to marrying the man.

- With the scarcity of food, and in a world without money, many people transacted using the barter system. It was common custom to help a neighbour build his house, till his land or perform any work for him or her and expect nothing in return but the courtesy of being fed. Of course, the Igorot people did not see economics as we do today.

  Today, we see everything in monetary terms. An hour of service, for example, amounts to $20, whereas a meal costs $10. To these ancient peoples, however, the transaction between hours of work and a meal or two, were not measured by some utilitarian concept like money. Rather, they had built an economy that uses the currency of goodwill, gratitude, relationships and reputations.

  If you helped me build my house today and I had only given you two meals for it, the monetary value of a meal versus its value in hours of service would be irrelevant. What matters is that we have built a relationship. If you become hungry in the future, I will feed you. If you need someone to help you, I will be there.

  It is as if human beings have an internal accounting system. We take into account the goodwill and generosity we receive from a person and we balance this account with the animosity and the selfishness that we have been shown by that same person. If, in general, someone had been friendly, kind and generous to us in the past, we are likely to reciprocate. If, however, someone had treated us harshly, we may even avoid having to deal with him or her in the future. We become indifferent and we stop caring for that person.

- The Bugang people had two days in a year which they considered holidays. The day before planting season and the day before harvesting. During these days, no one was allowed to come in, or go out off, the village. They set up surrounding signs – like flowers tied to sticks or trees – advising outsiders to respect their holiday. Any outsiders approaching would be met by a couple of men from the village to inform them of the holiday and welcome them to visit another day.

- During these holidays, everybody enjoyed a restful day. The men walked over to each other's houses, visiting, drinking rice wine and talking, while the women stayed at the eb-gan, mingling and frying peanuts. The men eventually found their way there before the festivities were over.

My father belonged to the last generation of boys who got to experience what it was like to grow up in the dap-ay. As the world modernised, it became easier for young people to go to the cities and explore more of the world. The old ways of living faded out. The last time I saw a dap-ay was when I was a young boy, when my father took me to visit his village. I would have appreciated it back then had I known what I know now. It is such a pity that unlike the Europeans, who learnt to read and write early, tribes in the mountain provinces of the Philippines did not keep written records we can use to learn more about their lives.

My main objective in this chapter is for us to think about how ancient enclaves of people may have organised their societies, without specific guidance from any holy scripture being purported to be written by God. Even though this account is only from the perspective of one person and the reality of other ancient cultures may have been slightly different, it gives us specific examples regarding human behaviour that will be useful to our discussion.

CHAPTER 11: WHY WE ARE MORAL

Most people recognise *The Golden Rule*: **Do unto others what you want them do unto you**. This idea is prevalent and common in almost all cultures, past and present.

Here are a few examples from different sources around different parts of the world iterating *The Golden Rule*:

1. "Never impose on others what you would not choose for yourself."[99] *(Confucius 551-479 BC. China.)*

2. "Do not to your neighbour what you would take ill from him."[100] *(Pittacus of Mytilene 640-568 BC. Greece.)*

3. "Avoid doing what you would blame others for doing."[101] *(Thales of Miletus 624-546 BC. Greece.)*

4. "Do not do to others what would anger you if done to you by others."[102] *(Isocrates 436-338 BC. Greece.)*

5. "What thou avoidest suffering thyself seek not to impose on others."[103] *(Epictetus 55-135 AD)*

6. "Regard your neighbour's gain as your own gain, and your neighbour's loss as your own loss." *(T'ai Shang Kan Ying P'ien. Taoism)*

7. "Do for one who may do for you, that you may cause him thus to do." (*'The Tale Of The Eloquent Peasant', Ancient Egypt.*)

8. "Respect for all life is the foundation." (*'The Great Law of Peace', Native American Indian*)

9. "All things are our relatives; what we do to everything, we do to ourselves. All is really One." (*'Black Elk', Native American Indian*)

10. "This is the sum of duty; do naught onto others what you would not have them do unto you." (*Mahabharata 5,1517. Hinduism*)

The Golden Rule is the ethical foundation of most cultures. I would like to make a point that the Golden Rule is not a product of religion; however, many people seem to think so. In this chapter, I discuss how we are moral beings, with or without religion, and why I feel that religion is getting undue credit for something that is naturally human.

Much of human nature can be explained by the following:

1. Human beings want to be happy.
2. Human beings are **social** animals. We need other people to be happy. Because of this, we have to live with other people. We want to live in **peace and harmony** with one another.
3. Human beings **respond** in kind: We treat other people as we are treated, and they treat us the way we treat them.

To expand:

1) The ambition of every human being is to be happy.
2) For most of us, life seems unnaturally spent isolated in an island or up on a mountain. We evolved to be social beings. Because of this, none of us are willing to live alone. If we think about it, we need other people in order to experience the joys of sharing, working together and living life together. Everything

we value in life, all the pleasures we seek – laughter, joy, compliments, praise, gratitude, admiration, esteem and respect – require us to be with other people.
3) Out of this necessity to live with other human beings, each of us will inevitably come upon *The Golden Rule*. We do not need anybody else telling us about it. Even without any formalised moral code, religion or law, it is inevitable for us to discover it for ourselves.
4) Living by *The Golden Rule* is not an intellectual or a moral choice. We choose to live by *The Golden Rule*, not because Jesus, Confucius or ancient Egyptians have told us; but rather, because we are penalised if we do not practice it. If we want to live peaceful, harmonious lives, we really have no choice. If we continuously mistreat other people, we will suffer pain, isolation and rejection from the rest of our kind.
5) In our discussion of the ancient tribe of the Bugang people, I proposed that people have some form of accounting mechanism that accounts for the goodwill and generosity we receive from other people. We then balance this account with the hostility and selfishness we receive from other people. Let us call this mechanism, ***The Mechanism for Reciprocity***.

Human nature predisposes us to be moral. There are three main forces, acting on us, that help explain how this happens:

1. People are capable of reciprocating threats and violent acts.
2. People are compelled to reciprocate favours and acts of kindness.
3. We have a desire to be honoured and respected to realise our own happiness through the fulfilment of our ambitions... whatever they may be.

I will now elaborate on these.

Violence, Threats and Fear

Without religion, law and law-enforcement, human beings seek to control the behaviour of other individuals by using the most primal tools at their disposal: violence, fear and coercion. In a state of lawlessness, human beings deter people from mistreating them by using threats such as: "Steal my property or mistreat any member of my family and I will do such and such to you".

We terrorise and compel one another into behaving because we have the capacity to inflict violence for revenge and recrimination. Because of this, we have a lot more sense than going around hitting people because we know that they can – and they will – hit us back. We cannot break into someone else's property and steal because if they catch us, they will do everything in their power to teach us a lesson.

When we mistreat other people, they will mistreat us back. So, even without God, we have it in us to police one another. We set our expectations, we tell people how we want to be treated and we warn them about what will happen if they cross the boundaries we set.

Eventually, as human societies evolve, humans establish rules for people to follow. Before we play games, we first set the rules. We do the same thing in every aspect of our lives. There are rules and etiquette in the office, in school, at construction sites, in shopping centres and at home. Individuals, who do not follow these rules and abide by their expectations, will be penalised by the rest of us.

My father's tribe asked offenders to give property or provide their services to compensate and remedy their victims. In modern societies, we do something similar. We fine people for misdemeanours. We send them to doctors or psychologists if their criminal behaviour is correctable. We jail people for serious transgressions. Sometimes, we even execute them.

We might think that using violence, threats and coercion as methods to influence our world equates as being backward and primitive. But, is it really? We need to look no further than politics to realise that violence, fear and coercion are still used by Governments. This is because they are playing a game where the rules are still being set. It must be said, however, that we have made progress by establishing organisations such as the United Nations, NATO and the European Union. They provide structures where national leaders can apply diplomatic pressures on governments who are behaving unfairly or dangerously. Even at this level though, fear and threat of economic sanctions and military actions are still being used.

Favours And Acts Of Kindness

People do no necessarily resort to violence to get what they want because they know other people have the same capacity to be just as brutal. So, without religion, law and police, people will continue to do favours and perform acts of kindness to one another, in exchange for benefits, to serve their interests.

In a sense, moral acts are being used as currency. The idea is simple: "I'll be nice to you and I expect you to be nice to me".

Here are some examples of how we use moral acts as currencies of exchange:

1) Scratch my back and I'll scratch yours.
2) I'll stay up and watch guard for enemies or predators, while you sleep. Afterwards, when you wake up, I'll sleep and you look out for us.
3) I'll share my food today because you do not have any, but when I have no food tomorrow, I expect you to return the favour.
4) You tell me what you know and I'll tell you what I know.
5) Fix my car and I will do your taxes.

The act of giving someone your hard-earned money can be considered a moral act which we exchange for another benefit:

1. You work for me and I will give you $20 per hour.
2. You give me your $100 and this pair of shoes is yours.
3. I'll give you four of my residential houses for your big hotel.

The distinctive feature with all the statements above is that they all offer to make deals. They need the other person to accept before the good deed is carried out. When agreements are done fairly, the outcome of any transaction will be fair, equitable and favourable to both parties.

Using favours as a form of currency works best when there are established rules, laws and regulations that people abide by. Today, we no longer rely on brute force to get what we want because we, and our ancestors, have built a world that is able to support commerce to meet people's needs.

The weakness of such a system of exchange is that people will have no motivation to be kind when there is nothing in it for them. A society built purely on this form of morality encourages selfish and opportunistic behaviour.

There is another class of favours and acts of kindness that can be reciprocated: people doing others a favour, without expecting anything back from the receiver. These acts of kindness foster honour and respect from other people who become inclined to reciprocate them.

Our Desire For Honour And Respect

The most powerful force that drives our behaviour is our ambition. When people hear the word 'ambition' they think of money or career. That is not what I mean by ambition. Ambitions might vary from person to person. Each of us, to whatever degree, is yearning or longing to realise the achievement, or the attainment, of happiness in our lives. This desire is what compels us to do what we need to do, to have what we need to have and to be what we want to be.

Many women strive to be the best mother to their children by supporting them and caring for them. Many men strive to be the best husband to their wife and father to their children by becoming a good provider to their needs.

Our ambitions depend on what we each value most in our lives. Some people strive for emotional and mental peace and tranquillity. Others seek power. Others crave for meaningful friendships and relationships. Others strive to achieve financial freedom.

Regardless of what our individual ambitions are, we will learn that the only way to get what we want is not through terrorising and extorting people. We will never achieve anything if we have made everybody our enemies. We will never live in peace to enjoy anything when we are constantly watching our backs, twisting and turning, in a world where we trust no one and we have no one to love.

We will also learn that when we rely solely on the utilitarian power of doing 'favours' for 'favours', all our achievements and accomplishments will be meaningless and empty. We will realise that people who are there, celebrating with us, are selfish people who are only by our side for their own interests.

Many of us will come to realise that we will never come close to achieving our ambitions if people do not trust, believe or respect us. We want to be honoured and respected. We want and need our wives, husbands, relatives, friends, acquaintances and even strangers to honour and respect us. Most importantly, we want self-respect.

We will eventually come to understand that the best way to achieve our ambitions, to determine our fate and seek fulfilment, is to treat other people as we want them to treat us. In fulfilling this need, we understand that people will never respect us if we steal, kill or destroy their property. We cannot make it by threatening people. We cannot buy respect from people in exchange for favours.

Respect is earned first, before people will honour us. There are no shortcuts. The only way to be respected is to be respectable. The only way to be honoured is to be honourable.

What is honour? To honour is to have great respect. When we are worthy of great respect, it is because people believe in us. They believe in us because they trust us. They trust us because we are credible. We are credible because we treat others with dignity and we continuously prove our capacity to behave and act with utmost honesty and personal integrity. We take responsibility for what we say and we have the courage to say the truth and do what is right. Only then, will people honour us. Only then, may we have true respect from others and from ourselves.

In this chapter, I sought to explain why we are naturally moral. I hope to have explained that our capacity to treat others with kindness and respect comes from our nature: we are social creatures inclined to reciprocate acts of kindness or brutality.

I have used examples that are relevant for us today to make the point that, even when humanity is stripped off its laws and religions, the human race will be guided by its nature to discover *The Golden Rule*.

Our ancestors also arrived to the same conclusions. After all, they were also human, social animals, whom, like us, were predisposed to treat others the way they have been treated. They would have arrived to *The Golden Rule,* on their own. Morality, therefore, predates religion. We explore this further in the next chapter.

CHAPTER 12:
AN AMORAL WORLD

Morality Is Independent From Religion

Morality predates Christianity, Judaism and Islam. In the Middle Ages, European Christians who travelled to the Far East for the first time, had to reconcile the fact that so many people managed to be civil and moral to one another without having heard of Jesus, Moses or Yahweh. Christians, Muslims or Jews cannot argue that, because of their religions, they are more moral than other cultures in the world. They cannot claim that they were, and they are, more morally superior to the Chinese, Japanese, Aborigines, American Indians and the Pacific Islanders.

It has also long been held, by the religious, that because we are God's chosen species, humankind is the only creation capable of being moral. From the studies of animals, however, we now know that such claims were premature. We are now discovering that many animals, including apes, display altruistic behaviour.

> Chimpanzees that cannot swim have drowned in zoo moats trying to save others. Rhesus monkeys are willing to starve themselves for several days to avoid the suffering of another monkey. They were given the chance to get food by pulling a chain but they avoided doing so after they realised that it also delivered an electric shock to their companions.[104]

Another example comes from the works of Gerald S. Wilkinson from the University of California in San Diego, published in 1984, about the behaviour of vampire bats:

> On any given night for vampire bats, some individuals will have been fortunately lucky and manage to consume a surplus of blood while others return empty and hungry. Bats that have been successful, regurgitate part of their blood meal to save another bat from starvation.[105]

Human Beings Define Their Own Morality

Moral behaviour is observed in the animal world and in ours. We witness animals share food, groom one another and warn others from danger. When we see such behaviour, we are pleased. From our experiences, we recognise the feelings of gratitude we had when we were the recipients of someone else's love, kindness and generosity. We see these things as 'good' because we want to live in a world where we can be at peace, where we can trust other beings to treat us with respect and thoughtfulness. We think of such acts as 'moral', 'good', 'common sense' or 'right conduct'.

On the other hand, cannibalism, vampirism and killing, for example, all exist in the natural world. However, we are less disturbed about such acts when we see them done in the animal kingdom. For example, we do not go out of our way to punish female praying mantises for eating their partners after mating.

However, when we witness, or read about, the similar acts done by people to other people, we cower in fear and disgust. We recognise that these acts, if done to us, will cause our death. This disturbs us. Because of the 'negative' feelings we experience towards such acts, we want to discourage other people from committing them. We see them as bad because we do not want to live in a world where we are afraid of being eaten or killed by a stranger, a friend or a relative. So, we learned to label such acts as 'immoral', 'sinful' or simply 'bad'.

In reality, everything in the world is amoral. It is us who decide what is moral or immoral. The morality of anything is only a consensus we make among ourselves, not something mandated by any god or gods we invent. To inspire people to be more moral and discourage them to be immoral, we created an ethereal policeman: God. So, even when we think there is no one else around to witness us steal, kill or mistreat another being, God is there, watching us. He knows what we are feeling and he knows what we are thinking. When the Day of Judgment comes, and we have been good, He will reward us. When we are bad, He will punish us.

People do not normally believe anything they do not see, hear or touch. They need evidence. Because God does not really exist, it is very difficult for people to believe in Him. To believe the unbelievable, people need to be indoctrinated. They need to be coerced into believing that He exists. They need to be threatened with the idea that if they do not believe, the most terrible thing imaginable, will happen. For this to be possible, our ancient leaders needed religions.

Believing The Unbelievable

Why is it, that when you hear or learn about the religious beliefs and practices of other cultures, you get the feeling that they are made up? Why is it that you do not believe in a god, named Kamui, the Japanese god who is supposed to be ruling us all here on Earth, including six Heavens and six Hells? If he does exist, then we, in the west, should have come to know about him.

Yahweh, Kamui, Zeus, Thor and Poseidon are only evident to people who want to believe in them. Muslims, who are atheists with respect to Zeus and his thunderbolt, never experienced Zeus. Australian Aborigines who are atheists with respect to Jehovah, never experienced Jehovah either.

Why is it that people who believe in one god are atheistic to the god of another culture, and religions contradict and blaspheme the beliefs of another religion? Could it be because gods can only exist in our minds when we forcefully indoctrinate ourselves to believe in them? Could it be that people from different cultures are forcing themselves to believe in falsehoods, and, when they finally confront each other, they recognise, with rational minds, the absurdity of each other's beliefs? Well, this is in fact, what I think is going on.

For as long as we can discern, human beings have believed in gods. They believed that these gods told us, and continue to tell us, how we should live morally through religion. Gods, religions, morality and us, are separate and distinct from one another.

I argue, however, among the four, the only thing real in the universe is us. Gods, morality and religions are just concepts and ideas we have created as products of our cultures. They exist only in our heads, nothing more than mere thoughts that spark in the circuitry of our brains. When our brains die, these sparks also subside and die.

If gods exist, they must be evident and observable everywhere, regardless of whether we believe in them or not. This is the case with everything else we know to be true. We can choose to deny the existence of gravity but it affirms itself and we fall. We can choose to deny the truth of electricity but it electrocutes us if we are careless. We may even choose to deny that humans reciprocate but when we hit other people, they will hit us back. Gods, on the other hand, are not like this. They are only evident to the minds who believe in them.

With our imagination, we skilfully craft our gods to our own image. We attribute to them what we attribute to ourselves. We give them the capacity to be loving, caring, angry and vengeful. We believe them to be powerful beings but in reality, it is us who give them all the powers we believe they should have.

Gods exist only in our heads, kept alive by our willingness to believe in them. In our willingness to believe, we permit them to influence our lives. But when our cultures end, when there is nobody left to believe in the gods we have fashioned, the truth becomes obvious. The gods remain as lifeless as they have always been.

If, and when, our civilisation dies, and beings of a more advanced civilisation come in contact with the remains of what we leave behind, they might come to know about our gods. They might even come to know the names and the qualities we attribute to these gods. They may admire or laugh at our ideas, but they will never believe in them in the way many of us believe in our gods today. These aliens will never see or hear from Jehovah, Allah, Zeus or Thor, much like they will never see little blue Smurfs and fairies.

We do not have to wait for aliens to come here to conjecture that this is true. We only need to reflect on the myriad of dead gods that now lay dormant in the graveyard we call mythology. People no longer believe in these gods. To this day, there is no evidence of ancient gods, like Zeus or Thor, ever coming back to punish us for having stopped believing in them. Yet, people once arranged their lives according to the gods they believed in. Our ancestors prayed to them, made sacrifices to them and even killed for them.

Aztec priests, for example, used to cut out the still-beating hearts of their victims and offered them to their ancient sun god: Quetzalcoatl. Children and teenagers were sacrificed to ensure the sun would rise again the next day.[106] Their god, their religion and their sense of morality existed as mere products of their Aztec culture. It is a pity that they are not here today to see it is obvious that the sun continues to rise day after day, without anybody sacrificing children. Furthermore, no evidence of Quetzalcoatl demanding to offer children's hearts has ever been found. We look at rituals and beliefs like these and we realise how many lives have been wasted because of our ancestors' preoccupation with worshipping gods.

CHAPTER 13:
WHY OUR ANCESTORS USED RELIGION

In primitive societies when little or no progress was made in the fields of science, law and order, economics, governance and philosophy, our ancestors used religions to…

1. **Understand** and explain natural phenomena.
2. **Control** and organise individuals within their societies.
3. **Inspire** the masses to achieve a common goal.

Religion Helped Explain Natural Phenomena

In their efforts to understand the meaning of their lives and their existence, our ancestors had to find a way to explain to themselves the phenomenon of the universe. Equipped with the power of language, consciousness and communication, our ancestors asked themselves many questions about life, death, cruelty, suffering, sadness, despair, justice, happiness and good fortune. They were compelled to seek for answers.

Without telescopes, how could they have known that the world was a planet among other planets that also revolved around the Sun; and that the Sun was just one star, among many other stars, in the vast darkness of the universe? Without microscopes, how would they have known that many of their brothers and sisters died because of small germs and viruses they could not see? Before the discovery of DNA, how were they able to explain that their children looked like them? They had no way of knowing because the technology they needed to answer these questions came thousands of years later.

Without modern technologies, our ancestors invented their own answers to deep and thoughtful questions, in their efforts to make sense of their world. As separate enclaves of humanity lived and migrated to different parts of the world, our ancestors formed beliefs and ideas that helped them comprehend their existence.

As bits and pieces of ideas and beliefs were incorporated in parables and stories, our ancestors organised them into myths that explained natural events, humanity and the universe.

Creation Stories

Let us now consider many of the alternative explanations our ancestors devised to explain their origins.

Bakuba

The Bakuba people of Zaire believed the Earth was nothing but water and darkness. Mbombo – 'a white giant' who ruled over the chaos – felt a terrible pain in his stomach and vomited the sun, the moon and the stars. The sun caused the water to evaporate in clouds. The dry hills appeared gradually. Mbombo also vomited the trees, the animals and people.[107]

Maasai

The Maasai people of Kenya explained their way of life, contrasted with neighbouring tribes', as having come from the same origins. In the beginning, the 'Creator' gave the forefathers of the different tribes, three dissimilar items: a stick to the Maasai people, a hoe to the Kikuyu people and finally, a bow and arrow to the Kamba people. Thereafter, the Maasai people used their stick to herd animals, the Kikuyo used their hoe to cultivate the ground and the Kamba people used their bows and arrows to hunt.[108]

Mandinka

The Mandingue people of southern Mali in Africa call their creator, Mangala, who failed in creating the world the first time. In his first try, Mangala compiled time, matter and space into a seed that exploded. Not losing hope, he tried again. This time, he planted two sets of twin seeds in an egg-shaped womb where they gestated. He continued to put more seeds in the womb until he had eight sets of seeds. The seeds transformed into fish. Fish, is the symbol of fertility in their culture.[109]

Voodoo

Damballah, a wise sky-serpent, created water. In the form of a serpent, his movement formed the stars and the planets in the cosmos, including the hills and valleys on Earth. He forged metals from heat and sent lightning bolts to form rocks and stones.[110]

Yoruba

The Yoruba is called Olorun or Olodumare and is helped by a 'lesser god' named Obatala. When there was only water and chaos, Obatala descended from the sky to create land. He descended with a rooster, iron and a palm kernel. He put the metal on earth and the rooster on top of it. The rooster scratched the metal and it spread out to create land. He then planted the palm seed. From it, came Earth's vegetation. He created humans out of the Earth and Olorun blew life into them.

Ainu

"The Ainu people of Japan believed in a universe that consisted of six heavens and six hells, where gods, demons and animals lived. The demons lived in the lower heavens and the lesser gods lived among the stars and the clouds. In the highest heaven, protected by a metal wall and an iron gate, lived Kamui, the creator.

Kamui created our world as a vast round ocean on the backbone of an enormous trout, which sucks in the ocean and spits it out again to make the tides. When the trout moves, it causes earthquakes.

One day Kamui looked down on the watery world and decided to make something of it. He sent down a water wagtail to do the work. By fluttering over the waters with its wings and by trampling the sand with its feet and beating it with its tail, the wagtail created patches of dry land. This way, islands were raised to float in the ocean.

When the animals that lived up in the heavens saw how beautiful the world was, they begged Kamui to let them live on it. And he did. Kamui also made many other creatures for the world. The first people, the Ainu, had bodies of earth, hair of chickweed, and spines made from sticks of willow. Kamui sent Aioina, the divine man, down from heaven to teach the Ainu how to hunt and cook.

Hmong

The creation story of the Hmong tradition began when rivers and oceans covered the Earth. Only a brother and sister, locked inside a yellow wooden drum, were alive. Beings from the sky punched holes in the Earth to drain the water away and exposed the land. They allowed the brother and sister to come out from the drum. The brother and sister realised that it was up to them to populate the Earth with people. They got married and bore children.

Korea

In Korea, they believed that a long time ago, a bear and a tiger wished to become humans. The Supreme Being gave them cloves of garlic and a handful of mugwort, and directed the bear and the tiger to live in a dark cave for one hundred days. Living on garlic and mugwort, the tiger could not stand the life in the cave. So he ran out. The patient bear persevered. Because of her character, she was granted her wish and she became a woman. The woman wanted to have a child and so Dangun, the son of the Supreme Being, married her and established the Kingdom of Korea.[111]

Orok

Sometimes, people think they are seeing three suns in the sky. The real sun is in the middle and there are two other bright objects beside it. They are called sundogs. Sundogs appear during sunrises and sunsets, when the sun is low, and the atmosphere is filled with ice crystals. The light from the real sun is reflected or refracted by the ice crystals. This creates the illusion of there being three suns.

To explain sundogs, the Orok people of Sakhali, Russia, had a story. In the beginning, there were three suns above the sky. The Earth was covered with water. Most of the water diminished and land appeared. 'Under the heat, cliffs and stones boiled.' The only living creatures who existed were the family members of Hadau.

Hadau shot arrows at the two suns, to the left and to the right of the middle sun. The two suns left imprint of themselves on the sky. Today, the Orok people believe that these imprints became the sundogs.[112]

P'an Ku ('Pangu') of Taoism

In one version of the myths of Taoism, the universe began as a cosmic egg and P'an Ku was born within. He was a man in a bearskin and he had two horns. He broke the egg in half. He separated Yin and Yang, and turned them into heaven and earth. "P'an Ku was the centre, standing on earth, supporting heaven. With a chisel and a hammer, he worked. As he worked, he grew in stature, gaining six feet in height every day.

When he finally finished his work 18,000 years later, he got very big. During that time, he formed the Earth, the moon, the sun and the stars. He had to die so his works would live.

His head became the mountains; his breath became the wind and the clouds; his voice became the thunder; his limbs became the four quarters of the earth; his blood became the rivers; his flesh became the soil; his beard became the constellations; his skin and hair became the herbs and the trees; his teeth, bones, and marrow became the metals, rocks, and precious stones and his sweat, became the rain. Today, the insects creeping over his body are us, human beings.[113]

Greek Mythology

The Greeks had many gods, goddesses and heroes. Hesiod was a poet who lived in Greece 700 BC. He describes the genealogy of the gods of Greek mythology as follows:

> "Chaos existed in the beginning, and then gave birth to Gaia (the Earth), Tartarus (the Underworld), Eros (desire), Nyx (the darkness of the night) and Erebus (the darkness of the Underworld). Gaia brought forth Ouranos, the starry sky, her equal, to cover her, the hills, and the fruitless deep of the Sea, Pontus, 'without sweet union of love', out of her own self. But afterwards, Hesiod tells, she lay with Heaven and bore the World-Ocean Oceanus, Coeus and Crius and the Titans Hyperion and Iapetus, Theia and Rhea, Themis and Mnemosyne and Phoebe of the golden crown, and lovely Tethys.
>
> "After them was born Cronos the wily, youngest and most terrible of her children, and he hated his lusty sire.' Cronos, at Gaia's urging, castrates Uranus. He marries Rhea who bears him Hestia, Demeter, Hera, Hades, Poseidon, and Zeus. Zeus and his brothers overthrew Cronos and the other Titans, and then drew lots to determine what each of them would rule. Zeus drew the sky, Poseidon drew the sea, and Hades drew the underworld. The Earth was contested and none of them had absolute sovereignty, as shown by Poseidon's anger when Zeus forced him to leave the battlefield in the Iliad."[114]

Norse/Viking Mythology

Norse, or Viking, mythology belongs to the people of Scandinavian countries. In this set of beliefs and legends, nothing existed except for the ice of Niflheim ('mist world'), to the north, and the fire of Muspelheim ('flame land'), to the south. Between them was a gap, referred to as the Ginnungagap, where a few pieces of ice met a few sparks of fire. The ice melted to form eiter: a mythical substance that is the origin of all living things.

The eiter formed the bodies of a giant named Ymir and the cow whose milk fed Ymir. The story continues:

> "Ymir's foot bred a son, and a man and a woman emerged from his armpits, making Ymir the progenitor of the Jotun, or giants. Whilst Ymir slept, the intense heat from Muspelheim made him sweat, and he sweated out Surtr, a giant of fire. Later Ymir woke and drank Audhumbla's milk. Whilst he drank, the cow, Audhumbla, licked on a salt stone. On the first day of doing this, a man's hair appeared on the stone. On the second day the head became exposed, and on the third day, an entire man emerged from the stone. His name was Búri. With an unknown giantess he fathered Bor, the father of the three gods Odin, Vili and Ve.
>
> When the gods felt strong enough, they killed Ymir. His blood flooded the world and drowned all the giants, except two. The giants grew again in numbers and soon there were as many as before Ymir's death. Then the gods created seven more worlds using Ymir's flesh for dirt; his blood for the oceans, rivers and lakes; his bones for stone; his brain as the clouds; and his skull for the heaven. Sparks from Muspelheim flew up and became stars.
>
> One day when the gods were walking, they found two tree trunks. They transformed them into shapes of humans. Odin gave them life, Vili gave them mind, and Ve gave them the ability to hear, see, and speak. The gods named them Ask and Embla and built the kingdom of Middle-earth for them. To keep the giants out, the gods placed a gigantic fence made of Ymir's eyelashes around Middle-earth."[115]

Egyptian Mythology

Egyptian mythology split into three main versions, corresponding to three separate groups of worshipers[116]:

1) "The Ennead worshippers believed that Atum, a deity, arose from the primordial waters (Neith), and masturbated to relieve his loneliness. His semen and breath became Tefnut (moisture) and Shu (dryness), respectively. From Shu and Tefnut, were born Geb (earth), and Nut (sky), who were born in permanent copulation. Shu separated them, and their children were Ausare (Osiris; death), Set (desert), Aset (Isis; life), and Nebet Het (Nephthys; fertile land). Osiris and Isis were a couple, as were Nephtys and Set."

2) "The Ogdoad Worshippers believed that Ra, a deity, arose, either in an egg, or a blue lotus, as a result of the creative interaction, between the primordial forces of Nu/Naunet (water), Amun/Amunet (air), Kuk/Kauket (darkness), and Huh/Hauhet (eternity). Ra then created Hathor, his wife, with whom he had a son, Hor (Horus; in the form known as Horus, the Elder), who was married to Isis. This cosmogony also includes Anupu (Anubis) as Lord of the dead, amongst others."

3) The third group believed in a deity who was eternal and everlasting. "He created the universe by talking everything to existence, much like Yahweh, the god in the Book of Genesis did."

Aztec Religion

The Aztec religion was polytheistic: it had many gods. "These gods were adopted from the religions of the people the Aztecs conquered. The Aztec religion is one in which the practitioners were constantly trying to win the favour of the gods, to influence the gods to look favourably upon them (Bray 1968: 152). This was done through offerings to the gods—human and otherwise."

"The Aztecs believed that it took four attempts at creating the earth and mankind, before the gods finally got everything right with the fifth attempt." "... The final creation occurred when the gods met and decided one among them had to sacrifice himself to become the new sun. One poor, humble god did this and became the sun. However, the sun hung in the sky and didn't move. In order for the sun to move, it was necessary for all of the gods to sacrifice themselves. Once the sun was moving across the sky, it was Quetzalcoatl, the sky and creator god, who took on the responsibility of creating mankind. He did this by going to the underworld to bring back to earth the bones of past generations. While fleeing the god of the underworld with his bag of bones, he slipped and fell, breaking the bones. He sprinkled the pieces of one with his blood and turned them into men. Because the pieces of bone were all different sizes, the men and women he created were all different sizes, too (Bray 1968: 154)."[117]

Maya Mythology

"In Maya mythology, Tepeu and Gukumatz (also known as Kukulcan, and as the Aztec's Quetzalcoatl) are referred to as the Creators, the Makers, and the Forefathers. They were two of the first beings to exist. They were said to be as wise as sages. Huracan, or the Heart of Heaven, also existed and was given less personification.

Tepeu and Gucumatz held a conference and decided that, to preserve their legacy, they must create a race of beings who could worship them. Huracan did the creating while Tepeu and Gucumatz guided the process. Earth was created, but the gods made several false starts in setting humanity on the earth.

Animals were created first. However, with all of their howling and squawking they did not worship their creators and were thus banished forever to the forest. Man was created first of mud, but just dissolved and crumbled away.

Other gods were summoned and man is next created of wood but they had no soul and soon forgot their makers. The gods turned all of their possessions against them and brought a black resinous rain down on their heads.

Finally man is formed of masa, or corn dough, by even more gods and their work is complete. As such, the Maya believed that maize [corn] was not just the cornerstone of their diet, but they were also made out of it."[118]

Abrahamic Religions: Judaism, Christianity and Islam

According to Jewish and Christian scriptures, the Earth was without form and there was darkness. In the Book of Genesis, God (named Yahweh or Jehovah) created everything in heaven and the earth in six days.

On the first day, God said, 'Let there be light', and there was light and after that, he divided the light, day, from the dark, night. On the second day, he created the sky. On the third day, he made dry land appear and he separated this from the water he called 'seas'. He then created vegetation. On the fourth day, he created the sun, the moon and the stars. On the fifth day, he created the living creatures that lived under water, and the birds that flew across the skies. On the sixth day, he created living creatures that lived on the ground. He created the first human beings, Adam and Eve, and told them to reproduce so their descendants could fill the Earth. God told them to subdue the Earth and "have dominion over the fish of the sea, over the fowl of the air, and over every living thing that 'moveth' upon the Earth".[119] On the seventh day, God rested.

Like in Judaism and Christianity, Islamic scriptures also suggest that God created Adam and Eve (Hawa), who lived in paradise. However, unlike the creator in the Book of Genesis, the creator, in Islam, does not need to rest (Koran 2:255). The creation narrative of Islam is split among many verses in the Koran. The process of creation began with the skies and the earth being separated. God then created the entire universe, and all the creatures in it, with water. (Koran 21:30)

Man Made God

Because our ancestors saw that swords and spears did not exist without blacksmiths, and shoes did not exist without shoemakers, they assumed that the mountains, the trees, the oceans, the birds and us, were also created by an even greater being. So, in their myths and stories, it was gods who created people. Paradoxically, it was our ancestors who were creating their gods.

Once our ancestors invented the concept of gods who worked in 'mysterious ways', who were all-powerful and all-knowing, it became a very potent tool which allowed them to explain anything and everything about life and the universe. Stories and myths were concocted to fill the need for knowledge and information.

Religion As A Tool For Controlling And Organising Societies

The invention of God can arguably have been the most important and most influential tool for our ancestors. This is not only because it helped them form their world-view, the idea of God was also a powerful tool to control behaviour.

We have to remember that the laws we have put into effect, and the law-enforcement organisations we have devised to keep individuals of our societies in check, are modern constructions of humanity.

Controlling Violence

Violence – the use of physical force – is one of the most significant aspects of human societies. The quickest way to get something you want is to take it, physically, from somebody. A hungry man can probably take the money in your wallet faster if he threatened you with a gun, instead of persuading you to give him your money.

In our societies, the ability to inflict violence, and the threat of it, are great sources of power and importance. An award-winning film that illustrates this clearly is *The Seven Samurai*, by Japanese filmmaker Akira Kurosawa. The story was set in the seventeenth century and tells the story of a poor village being constantly attacked by well-armed bandits for its harvests. Unable to fight and defend themselves, the villagers searched for samurais to fend off the bandits. Recognising that they have nothing to offer but food, the village elder recommended that they look for hungry, but honest, samurais to help them.

Clearly, the villagers rejected violence as a way of life. Instead of breeding and training their young to fight, these villagers decided to build self-sustaining farming societies. The irony of their situation was highlighted when they, as peaceful as they were, were eventually forced to use violence. It became unavoidable to seek the help of samurais who were just as capable of viciousness as the bandits who threatened their well-being. This point makes for an interesting discussion about how this village resembles much of our world today.

The systems we have created in our world are designed to control and suppress our capability and our potential to use violence against one another. Can we seriously believe that our nations can remain peaceful if our governments do not have the capacity to oppose organised criminals and insurgents violently? A government needs to be strong. Its military and its law-enforcement agencies need to have more resources than can be mustered by any well-organised group of criminals who seek to benefit solely themselves.

We recognise the importance of controlling violence. It is not so difficult to suppose that our ancestors recognised it too. They must have understood suffering and what it feels like to suffer. They must have recognised injustice when they saw it. Our ancestors knew that a society could not work if they allowed violence to continue unabated. But without sophisticated law enforcement organisations, ancient leaders used religion to stop their people from raping, killing and thieving.

Discipline And Organising Societies

Let us consider what adults do to discipline children. Throughout the ages, many parents used Santa Claus to get their children to behave favourably. Many versions of Santa Claus exist in many cultures. In the UK and in Europe, they have Saint Nicholas, Father Christmas and Kris Kringle. The general idea of Santa Claus for children is this: If you have been good during the year, Santa will bring you your most desired gifts. If you have been naughty, Santa will punish you by giving you coals or sticks for Christmas. The formula is clear: you are rewarded if you have been good and you are punished when you have been bad.

I suppose the same logic applied when ancient leaders began to use religion as a tool to ensure that individuals lived more harmoniously with the rest of their group. Keeping in line with the formula of reward and punishment, they advanced the idea that there is life after death. God would reward those who had been good in this life and punish those who had been bad.

Instead of using sweets to motivate people, ancient leaders devised salvation and damnation instead. If you have been good in your lifetime, you go to Heaven. There, you will be in a state of supreme happiness. For some males, being eagerly greeted by seventy-two female virgins, works as well.

If you have been bad, however, you will burn and rot in the hottest flames of Hell, or whatever you fear most. There, you will experience pain, suffering and guilt without respite, forever and ever.

With the idea of God, Heaven and Hell all set in place, there was finally something to deter people from lying, stealing and killing. Ancient leaders could now say that there was a God who was watching everything and everybody. Do-gooders would be rewarded and evildoers would be punished. The fear of God's wrath and the desire for his goodwill was used by the elites and leaders of ancient societies in the Middle East to keep their majority from running amuck. Like parents of noisy children, they could only be productive when their children had become calm, disciplined and pacified. Like Napoleon Bonaparte said: "Religion is excellent stuff for keeping common people quiet."

The best example I can cite of religion being used as a tool to discipline and organise societies is the way Islam requires Muslims to observe the Five Pillars. These are five duties that unite Muslims into a community,[120] and they are[121]:

- Shahadah: "The basic creed or tenet of Islam says: "I pray that there is no god but Allah, and I testify that Muhammad is a messenger". "Ideally, it is the first words a newborn will hear, and children are taught as soon as they are able to understand it and it will be recited when they die. Muslims must repeat this in prayer."[122]
- Salat: "The second pillar of Islam is *Salat*, the requirement to pray five times a day at fixed times.[123] The times to pray are at dawn, noon, mid-afternoon, sunset, and night fall. According to the Qur'an, the benefit of praying 'restrains [one] from shameful and evil deeds'."
- Zakah: "*Zakah*, or alms-giving, is the practice of charitable giving by Muslims based on accumulated wealth, and is obligatory for all who are able to do so. It is considered to be a personal responsibility for Muslims to ease economic hardship for others and eliminate inequality.[124] The charity consists of spending a fixed portion of one's wealth for the benefit of the poor or needy, including slaves, debtors and travellers. A Muslim may also donate more as an act of voluntary charity (*sadaqah*), in order to achieve additional divine reward."[125]
- Sawm: "Ritual fasting is an obligatory act during the month of Ramadan. Muslims must abstain from food, drink, and sexual intercourse from dawn to dusk during this month, and are to be especially mindful of other sins.[126] The fast is meant to allow Muslims to seek nearness to Allah, to express their gratitude to, and dependence on him, to atone for their past sins, and to remind them of the needy.[127] During Ramadan, Muslims are also expected to put more effort into following the teachings of Islam by refraining from violence, anger, envy, greed, lust, harsh language, gossip and to try to get along with each other better than normal. In addition, all

obscene, irreligious sights and sounds are to be avoided."[128]
- Hajj: "Every able-bodied Muslim is obliged to make the pilgrimage to Mecca at least once in their lifetime if they can afford it."[129]

"In addition to the Five Pillars, Islamic law (*sharia*) has developed a tradition of rulings that touch all aspects of life and society. This tradition encompasses everything from practical matters like dietary laws and banking to warfare and welfare[130]."[131]

Religion As A Tool For Unity And Mobilisation

Apart from being used as a way to control the behaviour of individuals within their tribes, religion was a potent tool for ancient leaders to unite and motivate their constituents to take action for their people.

In harsh times, for example, leaders of the past may have considered it necessary to attack another group of people to loot their harvest and steal their property. With God and religion, this is easily achieved. The formula is simple: Tell your people they are God's people and God is on their side. This simple idea can drive an entire population to believe that, because they are God's people, they are granted the permission to do whatever they think is necessary.

Religious and political history is peppered with gods who favour one people over another. Religion has been used as a tool by one group of people to advance their self-interest and to oppress others. God and religion are still being used this way today. Think of recent political speeches you can remember. In times of war, politicians and war propaganda motivate and inspire young men and women to sacrifice their lives and kill foreigners as their duty to God and their country.

According to a story I found in the Bible, there is nothing wrong with this.

Moses And The Midianites

God incited Moses to attack the Midianites:

> The Lord said to Moses, "Take vengeance on the Midianites for the Israelites. After that, you will be gathered to your people." So Moses said to the people, "Arm some of your men to go to war against the Midianites and to carry out the Lord's vengeance against them. Send into battle a thousand men from each of the tribes of Israel." So twelve thousand men armed for battle, a thousand from each tribe, were supplied from the clans of Israel.
>
> **- Numbers 31:1-5**

> They fought against Midian, as the Lord commanded Moses, and killed every man.
>
> **-Numbers 31:7**

> The Israelites captured the Midianite women and children and took all the Midianite herds, flocks and goods as plunder. They burned all the towns where the Midianites had settled, as well as all their camps. They took all the plunder and spoils, including the people and animals, and brought the captives, spoils and plunder to Moses and Eleazar the priest and the Israelite assembly at their camp on the plains of Moab, by the Jordan across from Jericho.
>
> **- Numbers 31:9-12**

Moses was angry at his men for sparing the women and the boys:

> Now kill all the boys. And kill every woman who has slept with a man, but save for yourselves every girl who has never slept with a man.
>
> **-Numbers 31:17-18**

'...Save for yourselves every girl who has never slept with a man'? What do you propose they had in mind for those virgins?

Then God helped Moses divide their spoils:

> The Lord said to Moses, "You and Eleazar the priest and the family heads of the community are to count all the people and animals that were captured. Divide the spoils between the soldiers who took part in the battle and the rest of the community. From the soldiers who fought in the battle, set apart as tribute for the Lord one out of every five hundred, whether persons, cattle, donkeys, sheep or goats. Take this tribute from their half share and give it to Eleazar the priest as the Lord's part. From the Israelites' half, select one out of every fifty, whether persons, cattle, donkeys, sheep, goats or other animals. Give them to the Levites, who are responsible for the care of the Lord's tabernacle." So Moses and Eleazar, the priest, did as the Lord commanded Moses.
> **- Numbers 31:25-54**

The plunder remaining from the spoils the soldiers took was

- 675,000 sheep
- 72,000 cattle
- 61,000 donkeys
- 32,000 women who had never slept with a man

The half share of those who fought in the battle was:

- 337,500 sheep, of which the tribute for the Lord was 675
- 36,000 cattle, of which the tribute for the Lord was 72
- 30,500 donkeys, of which the tribute for the Lord was 61
- 16,000 people, of which the tribute for the Lord was 32

Notice how God also had a share in the loot?

Moses gave the tribute to Eleazar the priest as the Lord's part, as the Lord commanded Moses.

The half belonging to the Israelites, which Moses set apart from that of the fighting men- the community's half—was

- 337,500 sheep
- 36,000 cattle
- 30,500 donkeys
- 16,000 people

From the Israelites' half, Moses selected one out of every fifty persons and animals, as the Lord commanded him, and gave them to the Levites, who were responsible for the care of the Lord's tabernacle.

Then the officers who were over the units of the army—the commanders of thousands and commanders of hundreds—went to Moses and said to him, "Your servants have counted the soldiers under our command, and not one is missing. So we have brought as an offering to the Lord the gold articles each of us acquired—armlets, bracelets, signet rings, earrings and necklaces—to make atonement for ourselves before the Lord."

Moses and Eleazar the priest accepted from them the gold—all the crafted articles. All the gold from the commanders of thousands and commanders of hundreds that Moses and Eleazar presented as a gift to the Lord weighed 16,750 shekels. Each soldier had taken plunder for himself. Moses and Eleazar the priest accepted the gold from the commanders of thousands and commanders of hundreds and brought it into the Tent of Meeting as a memorial for the Israelites before the Lord.

I included this portion of the Bible to point out that the holy book of God, which is being revered as a foundation for morality, is filled with details of how to divide plunder, and how God, himself, had a share too.

The Fight Against Global Warming

Religions' power to mobilise people is not limited to war and conquest. One recent example of religions' power to mobilise people involves our environmental awareness. For years, scientists have been warning us about the hazards we are imposing on our planet for decades. They have been largely ignored by leaders and the public. In his efforts to get people into action, former US Vice President, Al Gore, used the power of film to bring the issue of global warming to our attention with *An Inconvenient Truth*.

According to Dr Philip Freier, the Anglican Archbishop of Melbourne, much of our society's reluctance to believe the scientists' call for action comes from the book of Genesis giving human beings "the authority to exploit and dominate the earth for their own benefit, regardless of the consequences". "They saw the earth and everything in it as there for the sake of human beings only, who could treat it just as they pleased. This understanding - not entirely restricted to Christians - has had tragic consequences".[132]

Now, when you get the support of a major religion like that of the International Anglican Church; rest assured your message will be heard by millions of people in churches all over the world. The churches were probably right to persuade people to take care of the Earth because it was God's creation,[133] rather than use scientific arguments to do the job. Religious leaders seem to understand that the biggest motivations for people's actions lie behind their fears and their desires, not necessarily in the details of issues.

CHAPTER 14:
THE NATURE OF RELIGION

To help us understand the complex, often conflicting, nature of religions, we can think of them in two ways:

1) We can think of them as organisms made of memes, like biological organisms are made of genes.
2) We can think of them as organisations.

Religion As An Organism

In chapter 8, we said that memes are anything that could be imitated. Ideas are memes. The memes in my mind can be replicated in your mind if I communicate them to you. I tell you a sentence and you can instantly repeat it to me.

In chapter 9, we said that beliefs are simply ideas for which we are certain. We assume that an idea is true if we have many references to support it. Beliefs are memes. The most powerful beliefs influencing our society today are religious beliefs.

In his book, *Breaking The Spell*, philosopher Daniel Dennett writes about the extraordinary power of a lancet fluke to commandeer the brain of a tiny ant. The lancet fluke, in its desire to get inside the stomach of a sheep or a cow to complete its reproductive cycle, parasitizes the brain of an ant. The ant then laboriously climbs up a blade of grass, higher and higher until it falls and it will keep doing this over and over until it gets eaten. The little brain worm is driving the ant into position to benefit its progeny...not the ants'.[134]

We, humans, are like the ants. Religious beliefs are like lancet flukes that drive us to behave in a way that benefits their propagation. Religious beliefs that survived are active in people's minds today because they have been successful in making themselves copied in the past. Beliefs that were ineffective in getting copied went extinct.

In a documentary produced by the BBC, called *Religion: The Root Of All Evil*, Richard Dawkins explains how religion can be likened to a virus in its transmission. Religion is a virus of the mind. "A child is genetically-programmed to believe without questioning the word of authority figures, especially parents – the evolutionary imperative being that no child would survive by adopting a sceptical attitude towards everything their elders said. But this same imperative leaves children open to 'infection' by religion."[135]

Religion As An Organisation

Religions are like any human organisations. Unlike commercial enterprises looking to accumulate money, however, religions are in the business of converting minds.

The products on offer are:

      a.   Salvation of the soul.
      b.   Life after death.
      c.   Emotional comfort and peace of mind.

In exchange for these benefits, it will cost you your mind…and your children's. You submit and devote your mind to religion. Indeed, the word 'Islam' means submission.

Almost anybody can start a religion. Whatever your motivations may be, the only requirement is that you have a congregation. You do not have to come up with proofs or evidence to prove your claims are true.

According to Adherents.Com, a website that compiles statistics on world religions, there are 22 major religions around the world.

In total, there are already 4200 religions in the world. Even just half of that, 2100, is an astounding number. Each of these religions has varying beliefs that distinguishes them from the others. In marketing terminology, it is called their USP, their Unique Selling Proposition.

Here are a few examples of what these distinguishing beliefs could be:

1) Seventh Day Adventists: Recognises the Sabbath day as Saturday, not Sunday.
2) Jehovah's Witnesses: They refuse to take blood transfusions.[136]
3) Calvinism: Believe in 'Predestination' – God has already chosen which people are destined to go to Heaven, and which are doomed to Hell.
4) Roman Catholicism: They believe that, by action of the Holy Spirit, the Pope is 'Infallible'.[137]

Successful Religions

Successful religions depend on their memes being replicated in other people's minds, more so than their rivals. 'Spreading the word of God', as it is often called, can be done orally. With radio and television, you can now listen and watch religious leaders preach. With the Internet, you can also download or stream sermons and masses.

Religions that survive do so because they are good at one or more of the following:

- CONVERTING FECUNDITY

Religions that encourage or force its believers to spread its beliefs will increase the chances of its survival. Religious doctrines place recruiting and converting people as two of the most important duties for a true believer.

- CONVERSION LONGEVITY

Once copied, the more successful religious beliefs stay in the convert's mind longer. This gives them the chance to be shared and copied to another mind.

- COPYING FIDELITY

Any copying process is bound to make mistakes. When religious beliefs mutate or change, when they are interpreted differently, the religion can split into a different sect or cult. Therefore, religions that copy their ideas more accurately to the minds of new converts are more likely to dominate the meme pool. Rarely will they split into other variations. This reduces fragmentation.

- NEUTRALISING THE COMPETITION

Religions that allow their members to organise themselves and eliminate and suppress ideas contrary to their beliefs strengthen their chances for dominance.

I will now expand on each of these qualities.

Conversion Fecundity: Convert Minds Fast

The survival of a religion depends on its ability to make its believers spread its ideas to as many minds as possible, in the shortest amount of time. For a religion, there is nothing more primordial. It is the duty of a believer to 'spread the word of God'. Converted minds are to any religion what customers are to a business. Like a start-up business failing to attract customers, a new religion will fail to grow into a major religion if it fails to imprint its memes in the minds of people.

Religions encourage their members to knock on your door, talk to you and give you information, printed on small pamphlets and brochures, all designed to arouse your curiosity. Many times, I have seen and witnessed how recruitment is done.

While I was growing up in the Philippines, agents from many different Christian groups would talk to my mother. My siblings and I would listen. In Australia, during my teens, I have invited similar agents, wanting to talk to me about their religion, into our home.

Having witnessed door-to-door salespeople do their work, selling goods and services to customers is similar to the process of selling religious ideas and beliefs to a potential convert. The product being sold is a membership and its benefits are peace of mind and emotional comfort and consolation.

Like any good salespeople, religious recruiters and their publications must speak to the person's level of interest. I classify recruiters of religions under one of the following classes:

(1) The Hard Seller
(2) The Solution Seller
(3) The Friendly Agent

The Hard Seller

The Hard Seller demonstrates how and why their religions are good or better than everybody else's and why you should join. Hard sellers dump you with information, citing lists, statistics and facts, to impress upon you why their religion is right and the other religions are wrong. The message usually goes something like this: "We are the one true religion because of so-and-so".

Hard Sellers warn you that the world is ending soon. It will get really bad and you need to be in the right religion to be saved by God when the Earth is consumed by fire and destruction. Coincidentally, of course, their religion happens to be that right religion.

Some agents get right into the converting process immediately after you have invited them in. They usually come in pairs. They read to you verses upon verses of text from the Bible, as if trying to imprint their beliefs into your head straight away. They make it interactive too by asking you to read some of the verses yourself. If, during this process, any of the text you have read rang true for you, then you might get interested enough to allow them to come for another visit.

The Solution Seller

The Solution Sellers identify your needs and concerns before they show you how their religion can fill that need. To achieve their goal, recruiters will engage you in a friendly conversation. The main point of it, of course, is to pinpoint your concerns and priorities in life. If you happen to be grieving or if one of your family members is sick, then they might produce an article about how best to handle the sadness, the grief and the anxiety you feel. Often, these articles will entice you to find out more about the religion.

If you happen to be concerned with the 'violence' and the 'lawlessness' in the world today, they might tell you that it is society's faltering faith in God that is causing our 'moral deterioration'. The 'cure', they say, is to strengthen your faith.

Conversation topics need not be so dramatic. For example, it could be about how to raise children. It could be how the Internet is changing the world. It could even be about insurance. I read an article detailing the story of a man whose carpentry shop burnt down. It defined what insurance was and where it originated. Very quickly, it began introducing the Bible. By the fourth paragraph, it was writing about how, 3500 years ago, Moses instructed the nation of Israel to contribute a portion of their produce periodically for 'the alien resident and the fatherless boy and the widow' in Deuteronomy 14:28, 29.[138]

The objective of all this, of course, is to show you how relevant the Bible remains to be, in today's societies and how you should consider it as an alternative guide for your life.

The Friendly Agent

These agents become our friends because they are genuinely friendly and they have a likeable personality. Often, these are the types of people that most of us would probably develop friendships with. Because of them, we find ourselves visiting places of worship.

The entire process might not happen in one meeting. It can be done in a series of meetings. Once you become interested enough, things start off with a small invitation to attend a church or an organised weekend barbeque. You meet enough interesting and likeable people and you return for the next event. In the next coming events, you make friends.

You start visiting each other's homes, inviting one another for kids' birthday parties, home warming parties, attending weddings and funerals. Weeks turn to months and months turn to years. One day, you realise that your social circle is now composed of individuals who share the same religion.

Conversion Longevity – Protecting Minds

Once the 'imprinting' of beliefs has occurred in the minds of new converts, it is very important to keep those beliefs active for as long as possible. By keeping religious beliefs in a person's mind long enough, that person is bound to 'infect' another mind. For a religion, converts must remain focussed on their teachings. They must stay away from distractions.

The Master Mind

In his book, *The Law Of Success*, Napoleon Hill discusses the power and the importance of keeping all members of a team or an organisation to be in tune with what he referred to as, *The Master Mind*.

To be effective, teams and organisations must be in sync with one another to ensure that they are thinking similarly all the time. The idea is to make many minds begin to think as one master mind.

Team leaders and managers of commercial organisations have team briefs and meetings regularly so their team members can be in tune with their company's goals.

A friend of mine told me about one of the jobs she took, when she was travelling overseas. The job involved talking to strangers in London, getting them to buy little toys, worth a couple of pounds.

Her team started their day forming a circle, dancing and clapping to lively music. They pepped themselves up and motivated one another for the long day ahead.

At the end of every shift, they made their way back to the office. Again, the entire team formed a circle. With loud energetic music blaring, they congratulated the best sellers of the day and rewarded them with claps. The best performer got the opportunity to ring a massive bell, an action that was made out to be somewhat of a privilege. Promises of fast promotions into managerial positions gave them hope to persevere for a brighter future.

She remembered going home by nine or ten at night, after taking the train to the other side of town where she was staying. Tired, there was not much time to do anything else but to eat and sleep so she could do it all again the next day. There was no time to think, wonder and ask questions. There was no time to get dissatisfied and look for another job.

In telling me her story, I remember thinking how important those rituals were for her team. They needed to keep their spirits up so they could do the same thing again the next day. Obviously, it was a demanding job, physically, emotionally and intellectually as they pound the streets while maintaining the strength and the energy they needed to remain witty, smiley and happy. Such is the power of rituals: It keeps people occupied, engaged, motivated and entertained.

I believe that religious rituals serve the same purpose. Religions encourage people to visit a church every weekend. Praying as often as possible is encouraged. For example, Muslims pray five times a day.

Regularly praying, reading the scriptures, saying mantras, memorising verses, all done repeatedly, helps the mind stay focussed on the teachings of religion. This helps avoid distractions and minimises the time a person has to think differently, to ask doubtful questions or to engage in acts and behaviour that may be considered 'morally wrong', 'sinful' or 'unholy' by the religion. It reduces the likelihood of entertaining a different religion, or losing faith in God altogether. To keep people hopeful and remain vigilant, they are promised the graces of God and life after death.

The Power Of Repetition

In brain science, we understand that thinking occurs through a series of interconnected network of nerve cells called neurons. The human brain contains about 10 billion neurons. On average, each neuron is connected to other neurons through about 10,000 synapses. This is why it is difficult for us to learn something because we are yet to connect the neurons in our heads that allow us to perform a certain task. Once we have learnt to do a task, however, it becomes easier to perform it again because the neurons that need to be in contact, are already in place. The more we repeat a particular task, the stronger those synaptic connections get, the easier it is for our brains to enable us to do it again and again.

Once a religious belief has configured a brain to connect its neurons in a particular way, chanting, verse recitations and singing praises help strengthen these ideas in our minds.

Given enough time and with enough repetition, religious doctrines become well ingrained in a converts' mind. The individual will begin gathering references from his life experiences to back up the ideas and beliefs espoused by his religion. As this happens, the converts' behaviour, attitude and actions towards themselves, their lives and other people, will change to reflect these invisible mental shifts.

Please understand that I am not trying to paint an evil and malicious picture of religions here. I believe that many aspects of this process are natural, and variations of them are used in many organisations.

If you are part of an Olympic team, for example, you need to eat, breathe and remain focussed on your performance. Marines also have rituals, chants and habits that help them perform well in their jobs. As a trader, I understand full well that reforming our psychology is unavoidable if we are to have any chance of succeeding in anything.

We need to be mindful, however, where we draw the line between the practices that can be considered fair, between all parties involved, from the practices that can be considered psychological coercion or brainwashing.

Brainwashing And Thought Reform

Over the decades, religious cults and sects have been known to use thought-reform, 'brainwashing' techniques, to imprint religious beliefs and doctrines in the minds of converts.

Margaret Thaler Singer and Janja Lalich write about the tactics of a though-reform program in their book, *Cults In our Midst*. The tactics of a thought-reform program are organized to:

1. Destabilize a person's sense of self.
2. Get the person to drastically reinterpret his or her life's history and radically alter his or her worldview and accept a new version of reality and causality.
3. Develop in the person a dependence on the organization, and thereby turn the person into a deployable agent of the organization.

Brainwashing includes the following:

1) Keep the person unaware of what is going on and the changes that are taking place.
2) Control the person's time and, if possible, physical environment.
3) Create a sense of powerlessness, covert fear, and dependency.
4) Suppress much of the person's old behaviour and attitudes.
5) Instil new behaviour and attitudes.
6) Put forth a closed system of logic; allow no real input or criticism.

Accurate Indoctrination (Copying Fidelity)

A religion is like a cell that continues to divide itself as it grows bigger and bigger. A religion splits itself when its doctrines are modified by individuals, who seek to reform the religion, or eventually, form new cults and sects.

Much like genes splitting into different species, denominations of religions evolved through a process of evolution through natural selection.

Islam evolved into two major 'branches':

1) Sunni
2) Shia

Judaism evolved into the following 'branches':

1) Orthodox
2) Conservative
3) Reform
4) Reconstructionist
5) Liberal
6) Karaite
7) Humanistic
8) Renewal
9) Alternative

Christianity, itself, has the following broad 'branches' and their 'twigs':

1) Roman Catholicism
    a. Anglican
    b. Eastern Catholic
    c. Independent Catholic
    d. Old Catholic
    e. Roman Catholic

2) Orthodoxy
    a. Eastern Orthodoxy
    b. Oriental Orthodoxy
    c. Syriac Christianity
3) Protestantism
    a. Lutheran
    b. Reformed
    c. Anabaptist
    d. Baptist
    e. Methodist
    f. Adventist
    g. Evangelicalism
    h. Holiness
    i. Pentecostal
4) Non-Trinitarianism
    a. Jehovah's Witnesses
    b. Latter Day Saint Movement
    c. Unitarianism
    d. Christadelphians
    e. Oneness
    f. Pentecostalism

Any organisation, splitting into many departments that do not communicate nor share resources with one another, is less effective than a congruent organisation, which has all its departments working cooperatively together. Similarly, when religions split into new religions, these new sects stop identifying with one another. Bigotry, discrimination, intolerance and hatred arise from people attaching importance to the differences they perceive to exist between their religions. When religions split, the ability of religious leaders to exert influence over a larger number of followers is divided.

In ever-changing environments, however, there are advantages for religions to have different versions. If some versions become unpopular, lose membership and go extinct, other versions of that religion may be favoured by other people. This ensures the religion will persist in the future.[pp]

Competition

Organised religions find ways to neutralise all other competing ideas and beliefs. In the past, religions have used any or all the following tactics to accomplish this objective:

1) Engage ideas through intellectual dialogue like debates and conversations.
2) Ridicule competing ideas, beliefs and religions.
3) Discredit the sources of the competing memes.
4) Shame the sources of the competing memes.
5) Silence the sources of the competing memes by using threats.
6) Destroy the minds that contain competing memes. Methods can include killing. Genocide is used to wipe out entire groups of individuals with different or opposing beliefs. In doing so, a religion can dominate the meme pool.

[pp] A similar idea exists in investing. It is called diversification. Diversification is when an investor reduces the chances of bankruptcy or loss if he spreads his risk by diversifying his investments across different markets and other types of assets.

CHAPTER 15:
THE TYRANNY OF GOD

If a religion is a true religion, it would place kindness, compassion and understanding at the top of its priorities. Why, then, do so many religious people hate, or discriminate against, people who are not like them? If religion stood for peace and harmony, why is there so much killing done in its name? In my opinion, there are far too many contradictions. It is only now that I begin to understand why.

Religions seem contradictory in many ways, but when we think of them as memetical organisms or organisations, we can explain much about their nature. The most successful religions survived not necessarily because they taught people how to be compassionate and understanding or how to build more successful societies. They are here today only because of their ability to survive.

For a religion to compete rigorously for its most precious assets – converted minds – it needs to have its memes accurately copied to as many minds as possible. Once complete, a religion must ensure that all its newly-converted minds retain much of its doctrines for as long as possible. Then, finally, an organised religion must find ways to compete with other ideas and belief systems.

As organisms of memes seeking to propagate themselves, religions undergo a series of steps to achieve dominance. Some of which include the following:

1. Establish God and His Book as authorities.
2. Demand people to take this God seriously.
3. Substitute the need for evidence with faith.
4. Instil obedience.
5. Discourage doubt and enquiry.
6. Enforce regular meetings to keep the faith.
7. Protect beliefs and silence contradictory ideas.
8. Systematically convert minds.
9. Kill people when they stop believing.
10. Coerce people to do the 'Will Of God'.
11. Hide behind other mind-friendly memes, like morality.

If my model is true, then let us apply it to the major religions that exist in the world today. Let us scour the pages of the books held to be their authority and find out how they have come to dominate the meme pool.

Note: I will be using different sources including, but not limited to, the *New International Version* of The Bible as found online http://www.biblegateway.com and The Koran as translated by M.H. Shakir and published by Tahrike Tarsile Qur'an, Inc., in 1983, found online at http://quod.lib.umich.edu/k/koran/.

Establish God And His Book As Authorities

Religions establish their god simply by declaring him as the authority over all other deities, thereby rejecting competing religions who worship other gods. After convincing people their religion came from the true almighty God, they claim that their book – made of passages and stories they have written themselves or collected from other sources – is the work of God who wrote down these stories for humanity.

They claim that they have, in their possession, the only copy of this divine book. All knowledge and information must therefore be filtered through the ideas that exist within it. Any idea or belief that contradicts it must be wrong because God, the author, is wise and all-knowing. This book becomes a tool for any of the religious leaders to modify or interpret, as they see fit.

The first of the Ten Commandments, found in the Bible: Exodus 20:2-11 and Deuteronomy 5:6–11, is used by the inventors of religion to establish their precepts. They proclaim these laws are coming directly from God, to encourage people to follow them:

> I am the Lord your God, who brought you out of Egypt, out of the land of slavery. You shall have no other gods before[139] me. You shall not make for yourself an idol in the form of anything in heaven above or on the earth beneath or in the waters below. You shall not bow down to them or worship them; for I, the Lord your God, am a jealous God, punishing the children for the sin of the fathers to the third and fourth generation of those who hate me, but showing love to a thousand generations of those who love me and keep my commandments.

The Koran also establishes its authority by declaration:

> So know that there is no god but Allah, and, ask protection for your fault and for the believing men and the believing women; and Allah knows the place of your returning and the place of your abiding.
>
> **-Koran 47:19**

Religions insist there can only be one god: theirs. By framing it this way, they justify any action or behaviour towards destroying people of other religions by any means necessary.

> Break down their altars, smash their sacred stones and cut down their Asherah poles. Do not worship any other god, for the Lord, whose name is Jealous, is a jealous God.

> Be careful not to make a treaty with those who live in the land; for when they prostitute themselves to their gods and sacrifice to them, they will invite you and you will eat their sacrifices. And when you choose some of their daughters as wives for your sons and those daughters prostitute themselves to their gods, they will lead your sons to do the same.
>
> **- Exodus 34:13-16**

Demand People To Take This God Seriously

Having a god that nobody believes in, is like installing a police force that nobody fears or respects. Religions must therefore demand people to take their god seriously. The second commandment says:

> You shall not misuse the name of the Lord your God, for the Lord will not hold anyone guiltless who misuses his name.

In the Koran:

> 'Do not subject God's name to your casual swearing, that you may appear righteous, pious, or to attain credibility among the people.'
>
> **- Koran 2:224**

So, phrases like 'God damn me' or 'God damn it', are wicked.

Substitute The Need For Evidence With Faith

After telling people that a particular religion came from an almighty, all-knowing god, it was important for the inventors of these religions for people to believe in the existence of this god. The belief in god is the only authority of a religion to influence its constituents.

Normally, however, human beings form their beliefs by references gained from their senses, experiences and logical thinking.

To overcome this difficulty, authors of religions glorify the idea of blind faith. Having faith in the existence of a mysterious God allows people to believe in Him. This bypasses people's need to corroborate claims of truth with evidence.

Instil Obedience

Religions then encourage individuals to obey the will of their god. The Bible sets the premier example of such obedience with its highly revered story of Abraham.

> Then God said, "Take your son, your only son, Isaac, whom you love, and go to the region of Moriah. Sacrifice him there as a burnt offering on one of the mountains I will tell you about."
> **- Genesis 22: 2**

When the day finally came…

> Abraham took the wood for the burnt offering and placed it on his son Isaac, and he himself carried the fire and the knife. As the two of them went on together, Isaac spoke up and said to his father Abraham, 'Father?'
> 'Yes, my son?' Abraham replied.
> 'The fire and wood are here,' Isaac said, 'but where is the lamb for the burnt offering?'
> Abraham answered, 'God himself will provide the lamb for the burnt offering, my son.' And the two of them went on together.'
> When they reached the place God had told him about, Abraham built an altar there and arranged the wood on it. He bound his son Isaac and laid him on the altar, on top of the wood. Then he reached out his hand and took the knife to slay his son.
> **- Genesis 22:6-10**

In this case, Isaac, Abraham's son, was lucky because God intervened. God told Abraham that he was merely being tested for his faith so he did not have to kill Isaac for Him.

You might have heard Isaac's story in Sunday mass. What we are not told however, is the story of Jephthah in the book of Judges. It took an atheist scientist to make me aware of his story:

> In Judges, chapter 11, the military leader Jephthah made a bargain with God that, if God would guarantee Jephthah, victory over the Ammonites, Jephthah would, without fail, sacrifice, as a burnt offering 'whatsoever cometh forth of the doors of my house to meet me, when I return'.
>
> Jephthah did indeed defeat the Ammonites 'with a very great slaughter' ... and he returned home victorious. Not surprisingly, his daughter, his only child, came out of the house to greet him with' timbrels and dances' and - alas - she was the first living thing to do so.
>
> Understandably, there was nothing Jephthah could do about it. God was obviously looking forward to the promised burnt offering, and in the circumstances, the daughter very decently agreed to be sacrificed. She asked only that she should be allowed to go into the mountains for two months to bewail her virginity. At the end of this time she meekly returned, and Jephthah cooked her. God did not see fit to intervene on this occasion.[140]

The 'moral' of these stories is this: You must love, trust and obey God to the extent that you are willing to sacrifice the most precious thing in your life for Him... even if it means butchering your beloved child.

Discourage Doubt and Enquiry

After establishing faith as an honourable trait, the inventors of religions discourage anybody from doubting the existence of their god.

Jesus said to Thomas:

> Because you have seen me, you have believed; blessed are those who have not seen and yet have believed. (John 20:29)

If you want your children to believe in Santa Claus, do not allow them to ask too many questions. They might figure out that Santa Claus does not exist.

Enforce Regular Meetings To Keep The Faith

Like we have discussed with the idea of *The Master Mind* above, religions can strengthen their doctrines, ideas and beliefs in the minds of their followers by using rituals, chants, recitation and prayer. It becomes important, therefore, that a religion sets aside a part of the week to convene and ensure their doctrines are maintained in the minds of their believers.

The third of the Ten Commandments says:

> Remember the Sabbath day by keeping it holy. Six days you shall labour and do all your work, but the seventh day is a Sabbath to the Lord your God. On it you shall not do any work, neither you, nor your son or daughter, nor your manservant or maidservant, nor your animals, nor the alien within your gates. For in six days the Lord made the heavens and the earth, the sea, and all that is in them, but he rested on the seventh day. Therefore the Lord blessed the Sabbath day and made it holy.

The Koran also has a provision for regular worship:

> O you who believe, when the Congregational Prayer (Salat Al-Jumu`ah) is announced on Friday, you shall hasten to the commemoration of GOD, and drop all business.
> - **Koran 62:9**

The Bible provides an example to true followers of its faith, commanding them what they need to do if someone does not obey this rule:

> While the Israelites were in the desert, a man was found gathering wood on the Sabbath day. Those who found him gathering wood brought him to Moses and Aaron and the whole assembly, and they kept him in custody, because it was not clear what should be done to him.
>
> Then the Lord said to Moses, "The man must die. The whole assembly must stone him outside the camp." So the assembly took him outside the camp and stoned him to death, as the Lord commanded Moses.
>
> - Numbers 15:32-36

Protect Beliefs And Silence Contradictory Ideas

Once a mind has been converted, it becomes important for the beliefs to be protected from competing beliefs and ideas. The inventors of religions made sure of this:

> **Deuteronomy 13:6-16**
>
> If your very own brother, or your son or daughter, or the wife you love, or your closest friend secretly entices you, saying, "Let us go and worship other gods" (gods that neither you nor your fathers have known, gods of the people around you, whether near or far, from one end of the land to the other), do not yield to him or listen to him. Show him no pity. Do not spare him or shield him. You must certainly put him to death. Your hand must be the first in putting him to death, and then the hands of all the people. Stone him to death, because he tried to turn you away from the Lord your God...
>
> If you hear it said about one of the towns the Lord your God is giving you to live in that wicked men have arisen among you and have led the people of their town astray, saying, "Let us go

and worship other gods" (gods you have not known), then you must inquire, probe and investigate it thoroughly. And if it is true and it has been proved that this detestable thing has been done among you, you must certainly put to the sword all who live in that town. Destroy it completely, both its people and its livestock.

Gather all the plunder of the town into the middle of the public square and completely burn the town and all its plunder as a whole burnt offering to the Lord your God. It is to remain a ruin forever, never to be rebuilt.

Considering that many of our Indian and Chinese neighbours worship and believe in a multitude of other gods. How exactly does this command help us to live in harmony with them? We better hope they do not glorify any of their gods in our conversations with them because the instructions here are clear and unequivocal for any true follower of the Bible.

Heresy, Witchcraft, Sorcery and Blasphemy

Religious leaders used to silence sources of ideas and beliefs if they contradicted their teachings, or if they went against their interests with following strategies:

1) Deem ideas that conflict with their religions to be heretical or blasphemous.
2) Heretics and blasphemers were then killed or persecuted.
3) Sometimes, if it was more convenient, other concepts, like sorcery and witchcraft, were used instead of heresy or blasphemy.

Jesus refined the practice of killing heretics and unbelievers:

"If a man abide not in me, he is cast forth as a branch, and is withered; and men gather them, and cast them into the fire, and they are burned."

- John 15:6

The Inquisition proved to be a potent tool for the Church in combating the spread of contradictory ideas and literature that went against their interests. 'Trials' of the accused heretics were conducted. These trials were often extremely biased against the defendants and there was no hope for success. It seemed, therefore, the trials were simply tools for public relations: they made the persecution and murder of the accused seem fair and justified in the eyes of the public.

The Roman Inquisition, for example, was a system of tribunals, set up during the 16th century. It was originally set up to combat the spread of Protestantism in Italy but it outlived its purpose. The Catholic Church saw its usefulness in prosecuting its 'enemies', which included scientists, philosophers and other thinkers like:

1) Franciscus Patricius (1529–1597): Philosopher and scientist.
2) Tommaso Campanella (1568–1639): Philosopher, theologian and poet.
3) Gerolamo Cardano (1501–1576): Mathematician and physician.
4) Cesare Cremonini (1550–1630): Philosopher.
5) Domenico Scandella (aka Menocchio) (1532–1599): Philosopher.

In his book, *The End of Faith*, Sam Harris included a chapter called, *In The Shadow Of God*. It pained me to read about the injustice and the brutality of what it meant to be the victim of the Inquisition. The Church captured and tortured you until you admitted you were a heretic, a blasphemer, a witch or a sorcerer.

> You are not told the names of your accusers. But their identities are of little account, for even if, at this late hour, they were to recant their charges against you, they would merely be punished as false witnesses, while their original accusations would retain their full weight as evidence of your guilt. The machinery of justice has been so well oiled by faith that it can no longer be influenced.
>
> But you have a choice, of sorts: you can concede your guilt and name your accomplices. Yes, you must have had accomplices. No confession will be accepted unless other men

and women can be implicated in your crimes. Perhaps you and three acquaintances of your choosing did change into hares and consort with the devil himself. The sight of iron boots designed to crush your feet seems to refresh your memory. Yes, Friedrich, Arthur, and Otto are sorcerers too. Their wives? Witches all.

You now face punishment proportionate to the severity of your crimes: flogging, a pilgrimage on foot to the Holy Land, forfeiture of property, or, more likely, a period of long imprisonment, probably for life. Your 'accomplices' will soon be rounded up for torture.

Or you can maintain your innocence, which is almost certainly the truth (after all, it is the rare person who can create a thunderstorm). In response, your jailers will be happy to lead you to the furthest reaches of human suffering, before burning you at the stake. You may be imprisoned in total darkness for months or years at a time, repeatedly beaten and starved, or stretched upon the rack. Thumbscrews may be applied, or toe screws, or a pear-shaped vice may be inserted into your mouth, vagina, or anus, and forced open until your misery admits of no possible increase. You may be hoisted to the ceiling on a strappado (with your arms bound behind your back and attached to a pulley, and weights tied to your feet), dislocating your shoulders. To this torment squassation might be added, which, being often sufficient to cause your death, may yet spare you the agony of the stake.

If you are unlucky enough to be in Spain, where judicial torture has achieved a transcendent level of cruelty, you may be placed in the 'Spanish chair': a throne of iron, complete with iron stocks to secure your neck and limbs. In the interest of saving your soul, a coal brazier will be placed beneath your bare feet, slowly roasting them. Because the stain of heresy runs deep, your flesh will be continually larded with fat to keep it from burning too quickly. Or you may be bound to a bench, with a cauldron filled with mice placed upside-down upon your bare abdomen. With the requisite application of heat to the iron, the mice will begin to burrow into your belly in search of an exit.

Should you, while in extremis, admit to your torturers that you are indeed a heretic, a sorcerer, or a witch, you will be made to confirm your story before a judge—and any attempt to recant, to claim that your confession has been coerced through torture, will deliver you either to your tormentors once again or directly to the stake. If, once condemned, you repent of your sins, these compassionate and learned men—whose concern for the fate of your eternal soul really knows no bounds—will do you the kindness of strangling you before lighting your pyre.

The words 'heresy' and 'blasphemy' sends shivers down people's spines because literature has attached such 'wicked' meanings to these words. But what, exactly, does it mean to be a heretic or a blasphemer?

A heretic is[141]:

- A professed believer who maintains religious opinions contrary to those accepted by his or her church or rejects doctrines prescribed by that church.
- Anyone of a faith who wilfully and persistently rejects any article of that faith.
- Anyone who does not conform to an established attitude, doctrine, or principle.

What is a blasphemer?

> A blasphemer is someone who speaks of (God or a sacred entity) in an irreverent, impious manner.[142] Irreverent means 'lacking or exhibiting a lack of reverence: disrespectful'.[143] Impious refers to irreligiousness.[144]

If this is the case, then all non-Christians are heretics to Christians and all non-Muslims are heretics to Muslims. Even the Christian belief that Jesus is the Son of God is blasphemous to Islam (Koran 5:017). Many Sunni Muslims regard Shi'as to be heretics, and vice versa. Orthodox Judaism also considers any Jew who departs from traditional Jewish principles of their faith, to be heretical.

It seems, therefore, that the concept of heresy is a strategy by one member of a religion against members of another religion, or a variant of the same religion.

Heretics and blasphemers were persecuted or killed merely because they contradicted the beliefs of the religious leaders at the time. That was their alleged crime, even if these so-called 'heresies' or 'blasphemies', in fact, turned out to be true!

To give you an example, most people believed that the Earth was at the centre of the universe. In 1610, Galileo published his work, *Sidereus Nuncius* (*Starry Messenger*) detailing the observations he made with his new telescope, which supported the proposition that the Earth was not at the centre of the universe. The Catholic Church forced Galileo to recant his heliocentrism and he spent the last years of his life under house arrest on orders of the Inquisition.

On the 31st of October 1992, three hundred and fifty years after Galileo's death, Pope John Paul II expressed regret for how the Galileo affair was handled, and officially conceded the Earth was not stationary!

Systematically Acquiring Minds

Imagine if your telecommunications company owned the business of your yet unborn children, automatically signing them up for their phone and internet services with the company as soon as they are born. What an amazing position for a company to be in! They would have a guaranteed income without spending a dollar more on advertising or selling expenses. But alas, commercial organisations can only wish for such a provision.

Religions, on the other hand, have the power to make such provisions for their benefit. What a fantastic advantage for a religion to propagate! It is an automatic stipulation that at birth, we are automatically granted our parents' religion. Furthermore, when we have children, they will also automatically inherit our religion. We become the willing agents that help propagate religious ideas and beliefs onto our children.

The Roman Catholics were quick-witted when they insisted that, when a Roman Catholic marries an Anglican, the children will be brought up as Catholic. When a Muslim man and non-Muslim woman get married, Islam insists the children be brought up as Muslims.

Another effective strategy for a religion is to prohibit or restrict people's ability to marry a member of a different religion. If a religion wants to dominate, it should install rules that minimises the chances of its believers to be converted to another religion.

If we perceive a man to be more assertive and dominant than a woman, then it might be a good strategy for a religion to allow men to marry women of other faiths but prohibit women to do the same.

This is advantageous to the propagation of the religion because males have a bigger chance of converting females than the other way around.

This is the only explanation I can think of to make sense of the fact that it is acceptable for a Muslim man to marry a non-Muslim woman, but not the other way around.

A fatwa issued in August 2007 by the secretary-general of the Assembly of Muslim Jurists in America (AMJA), Dr. Sheikh Salah Al-Sawy, states that marriage between a Muslim woman and a non-Muslim man is forbidden and invalid, and that children born of such unions are illegitimate.

Kill People Once They Stop Believing

Heretics merely reject parts of the religion they belong to. Apostates reject their religions entirely.

Religious memes that allow people to kill those who have lost their faith, are a good way of eliminating threat. An individual, who loses his or her faith in one religion and converts to another, is a dangerous agent for any religion because...

- The apostate can tell others, with credibility, about how terrible his, or her, former religion is. This reduces the potential for people of other faiths to be converted.

- The apostate might work against the interests of his or her former religion.
- The apostate will have children who may continue to act against the interests of his or her parent's old religion.

Religious leaders are aware of the damage apostasy can do to their religious interests.

On the 23rd September 1978 for example, a Fatwa committee issued a decision on a Muslim who converted to Christianity. This Fatwa describes how an Egyptian man turned apostate and the resulting punishment prescribed for him by the Al-Azhr Fatawa council.

Translation:

"This man has committed apostasy; he must be given a chance to repent and if he does not then he must be killed according to Shariah. As far as his children are concerned, as long as they are children they are considered Muslim, but after they reach the age of puberty, then if they remain with Islam they are Muslim, but if they leave Islam and they do not repent they must be killed and Allah knows best." [145]

Author: al-Azhr, the Egyptian Supreme Council for Islamic Affairs

On 3 September 1992, Sadiq Abdul Karim Malallah was publicly beheaded in Saudi Arabia after being lawfully convicted of apostasy and blasphemy.[146]

In February 2006 Abdul Rahman, an Afghan citizen was threatened with the death penalty for converting to Christianity[147], a crime punishable by death under the Afghan constitution. The Italian government offered him asylum.[148]

Today, Muslims who are speaking out against Islam, like Ayaan Hirsi Ali, Wafa Sultan and Waled Shoebat, continue to live in danger of being killed by other Muslims because they have become apostates.

Coerce People To Do The 'Will Of God'

Many of our ancestors submitted to the will of the elites who controlled them with religion. They were threatened with the idea that God would destroy them and doom them to eternal damnation if they did not believe in God. But because God does not really exist, there was no one to punish the unbelievers. Inventors of religions, therefore, wrote commands in their scriptures so that people, themselves, would fulfil the will of an imaginary god, to coerce fellow human beings to believing in God.

The holy books come with detailed instructions on how to convert or subdue non-believers:

> Prophet, make war on the unbelievers and the hypocrites and deal ' rigorously with them. Hell shall be their home: an evil fate.
>
> **- Koran 9:73**

> Believers, make war on the infidels who dwell around you. Deal firmly with them. Know that God is with the righteous.
>
> **- Koran 9:123**

We ask: What is an infidel?

An infidel is someone who does not believe in a particular faith. Therefore, for a Muslim, an infidel is anybody who is not a Muslim. Since Muslims make up 20.28% of the world's population, according to Encyclopaedia Britannica in mid-2005, 79.72% of the world's population are infidels. Similarly from a Christian's point-of-view, 66.94% of the world's population are infidels.

Religions denigrate those who are passive in spreading its memes:

> The believers who stay at home—apart from those that suffer from a grave impediment—are not the equal of those who fight for the cause of God with their goods and their persons. God has given those that fight with their goods and their persons a

higher rank than those who stay at home. God has promised all a good reward; but far richer is the recompense of those who fight for Him. He that leaves his dwelling to fight for God and His apostle and is then overtaken by death, shall be rewarded by God. . . . The unbelievers are your inveterate enemies.

- **Koran 4:95-101**

Religions then provide a reward – real or imaginary – so people can commit atrocities towards others in gusto. Blaise Pascal (1623–1662), a French mathematician, physicist, and religious philosopher once said: "**Men never commit evil so fully and joyfully as when they do it for religious convictions**"

Let those who would exchange the life of this world for the here-after, fight for the cause of God; whoever fights for the cause of God, whether he dies or triumphs, We [God] shall richly reward him.... The true believers fight for the cause of God, but the infidels fight for the devil. Fight then against the friends of Satan Say: "Trifling are the pleasures of this life. The hereafter is better for those who would keep from evil..."

- **Koran 4:74-78**

The Golden Calf

Moses' story, as an exemplar in demonstrating commitment to God, gave us a great example of how to enforce God's will. In *The Golden Calf* saga, Moses went up Mount Sinai. When his people were left alone, under the leadership of Aaron, they began gathering gold from their jewelleries to cast the gold in the shape of a calf which they could idolise. They made burnt offerings to this 'god', and afterwards they sat down to eat, drink and indulge in revelry (Exodus 32:6).

Then God sent Moses to go down the mountain because the people had become corrupt (Exodus 32:7). God threatened to kill them but Moses calmed Him down.

Moses said, "Why should your anger burn against your people, whom you brought out of Egypt with great power and a mighty hand? Turn from your fierce anger; relent and do not bring disaster on your people." (Exodus 32:11) God calmed down (Exodus 32: 14): "Then the Lord relented and did not bring on his people the disaster he had threatened."

"When Moses approached the camp and saw the calf and the dancing, his anger burned and he threw the tablets out of his hands, breaking them to pieces at the foot of the mountain. And he took the calf they had made and burned it in the fire; then he ground it to powder, scattered it on the water and made the Israelites drink it." (Exodus 32:19)

Moses then rallied the Levites and said to them:

> This is what the Lord, the God of Israel, says: 'Each man strap a sword to his side. Go back and forth through the camp from one end to the other, each killing his brother and friend and neighbour.' The Levites did as Moses commanded, and that day about three thousand of the people died. Then Moses said, 'You have been set apart to the Lord today, for you were against your own sons and brothers, and he has blessed you this day.'
>
> **- Exodus 32:27-29**

After the massacre of 3000 people, God was still not satisfied and He 'struck the people with a plague because of what they did with the calf Aaron had made' (Exodus 32:35).

Religions Struggle For Dominance

Christianity and Islam have a long history of struggle in Europe, Africa and Asia. It is beyond the scope of this book to provide a detailed analysis of these historical events in the last 2000 years but should you wish to research them, here are a few leads:

Islam's list of Jihads[149]:

- First Wave of Islamic Conquest:
    - 634 Battle of Basra
    - 635 Damascus Conquered
    - 636 Ctesiphon Conquered
    - 637 Jerusalem Conquered
    - 641 Alexandria Conquered
    - 666 Cicily Conquered
    - 670 Kabul Conquered
    - 698 Carthage Conquered
    - 711 Southern Spain
    - 720 Narbonne Conquered
    - 732 Battle of Poitiers, France

- Second Wave of Islamic Conquest:
    - 1071 Battle of Manzikert
    - 1064 Armenia Conquered
    - 1331 Nicaea Conquered
    - 1453 Constantinople Conquered
    - 1393 Bulgaria Conquered
    - 1460 Greece Conquered
    - 1389 Battle of Kosovo
    - 1521 Belgrade Conquered
    - 1683 Siege of Vienna

The Christians waged Crusades, Inquisitions and other religious enterprises[150]:

- 722 – 1249: Reconquista
- 1095 – 1099: First Crusade
- 1147 – 1149: Second Crusade
- 1155 – 1293: Swedish Crusade
- 1187 – 1192: Third Crusade
- 12th – 16th Century: Northern Crusade
- 1202 – 1204: Fourth Crusade
- 1209: Albigensian Crusade
- 1217 – 1221: Fifth Crusade
- 1228 – 1229: Sixth Crusade

- 1248 – 1254: Seventh Crusade
- 1270: Eight Crusade
- 1271 – 1272: Ninth Crusade
- 1284 – 1285: Aragonese Crusade
- 1398: Crusades against the Tatars
- 1396 – 1456: Crusades in the Balkans
- 1420 – 1434: Hussite Crusade
- 1478 – 1834: Spanish Inquisition
- 1536 – 1821: Portuguese Inquisition
- 1542 – 1860: Roman Inquisition
- 1562 – 1598: French Wars Of Religion
- 17th Century: Thirty Years War

Each of these events inflicted upon humanity unimaginable horror, suffering and loss of countless lives over religious texts. The unflinching belief in religious dogma, such as those we discussed above, makes it no longer a mystery to me why the believers of Abrahamic religions have found themselves in great conflict with one another, and with other groups of people, throughout history. With such intolerant and incompatible beliefs, it was inevitable.

On page 73 of his book, *The End Of Faith*, Sam Harris writes:

> The danger of religious faith is that it allows otherwise normal human beings to reap the fruits of madness and consider them holy. Because each new generation of children is taught that religious propositions need NOT be justified in the way that all others must, civilisation is still besieged by the armies of the preposterous. We are, even now, killing ourselves over ancient literature. Who would have thought something so tragically absurd could be possible?

The Cloak Of Morality

Nowadays, we have managed to evolve our sense of morality into one which is less oppressive and less violent. We have become more moral when we stopped organising ourselves around religion and began organising ourselves on secular ideas.

Our judicial systems, our laws and regulations were put in place not because they convey what we think God would like but because of what we think is right. Everything we do is based on our ideas of freedom, equality, independence, democracy and liberty. These enlightened ideas were fought for by many of our ancestors.

Because of our modernised morality that respects the rights and liberties of individual human beings, the memes we have in our heads are only friendly to other memes that match our modern sense of right and wrong. Therefore, for religious memes to replicate in our minds, it is necessary for our minds to welcome them.

If someone came up to you and asked you to join a religion that champions death, murder, slavery, destruction and vandalism, would you join? Your existing beliefs and ideas will make you reject this proposition. I am willing to bet that you would stop going to your church, mosque or synagogue if your priest, imam or rabbi, continued to read the brutal and cruel verses of the Scriptures.

Leaders of organised religions know this. So even though vehement verses exist in the Scriptures, they are not being read to us in our congregations. Because of this, many of us believe that religions are benign and therefore mere vehicles for peace, kindness and compassion. Religions are marketing themselves as such. This is the modern strategy for religions to survive in the morally sensitive environment that exists today.

You may not have heard about many of the intolerant, cruel verses that exist in religious scriptures and the brutality they have caused, as a result, in the past. You may have not been told to beat your children with a rod if they ever got out of line (Proverbs 13:24 / 20:30 / 23:13-14), and kill them if they became shameless enough to talk back (Exodus 21:15, Leviticus 20:9, Deuteronomy 21:18-21, Mark 7:9-13, and Matthew 15:4-7).

You may have not heard of stoning people to death for working on the Sabbath, worshipping graven images, heresy, adultery, homosexuality, practicing sorcery, and a wide variety of other imaginary crimes.[151]

Understandably, religious leaders do not talk about the madness and brutality of the Crusades, the Inquisition and the violent Jihads of the past, in Sunday Mass. They offer us a partial view of the true nature of their religions, but as a result, our perceptions of religions are also biased.

We mislead ourselves if we believe religions are vehicles for morality because religions are amoral. As much as they have been used to justify the moral actions and behaviours of certain groups and individuals, they have also been used to justify the immoral actions and behaviours of other groups and individuals.

We should be mindful of this fact when we hear proclamations that religions are more capable of leading people to a just way of life than any other invention. Let us not allow religions to hold the mantle of morality as though it is their own. As I have argued in chapter 12, we do not get our morals from religion. It is us who incorporate our own morals into our religions.

CHAPTER 16:
ESCAPE FROM RELIGIOUS DESPOTISM

Living in a secular society, it is sometimes hard for us to imagine that in the not-too-distant past, western civilisation have been gripped by religious control and authority for hundreds of years. Fortunately, humanity managed to transform its thinking to emerge and live in the world we recognise today. From my research I have come to believe that we gained the life and freedom we enjoy not because of religion, but in spite of it.

In this chapter, I would like to outline how Europe and the rest of the western civilisation escaped from the tyrannical rule of religion. It all began with the ideas of influential people, who espoused unorthodox ideas, once considered as atheistic, heretical or blasphemous. It was their ideas that freed us from the shackles of religious oppression.

The Protestant Revolution

For many people in sixteenth century Europe, life only meant worshipping God to ensure that their souls went to Heaven. Everything else was a distraction. It was a world ruled by men. The power and authority of women was limited only to the nunneries. Sex was only for reproduction. Profit was shameful and money was best donated to the Church. All art, music and literature was religious. The Church had total control over the people.

To get a picture of what it must have been like, we consult British historian Tristram Hunt in a documentary, *The Protestant Revolution*:

> The power and glory of the Catholic Church was everywhere apparent. It controlled monasteries, universities, armies and empires. For a church, it held a remarkable monopoly on authority. It could levy taxes... even wage war. For princes and paupers alike, the church dominated every stage of life: from baptism to burial. And the Church's coffers were overflowing. The Catholic Church answered the central question of medieval life: How do I save my soul? It's the question they posed when they woke in the morning and went to sleep in the evening. For a people gripped with spiritual terror, Catholicism provided the only path to salvation.

During this time, the greedy pope, Alexander II, was in power. He bolstered the papacy's riches through imprisonment, murder and seizing of his victim's property.

> In one infamous night, Alexander celebrated the *Banquet of the Chestnuts* with a grand orgy. Fifty prostitutes writhed on a floor covered with chestnuts while the Pope awarded prices for the best performances of the night.

Before the 16th century, the Bible was only available in Latin, Greek and Hebrew. This meant that only the educated elite could understand it. The Church ensured its monopoly on biblical knowledge by proclaiming it a heresy to translate the Bible in any other language. In fact, individual readings of the book were banned.

I would assume that this was their way to keep the masses dumb, since people had no way of assessing biblical information and therefore believed everything the Church would say. This allowed the Church to scare people so much that individuals were willing to do anything to save their souls from everlasting damnation.

People were told that faith alone could not guarantee man's salvation[152] but rather, salvation is achieved through active works of charity… like donating money to the church[153]. Out of fear, the populace were led to believe that for a price, they could now buy *Letters of Indulgences* that promised to absolve the vices of their sins and assure their ascent to heaven. The Church struck on a profitable money-spinner to fund their excesses. The Church's business was in full swing.

Dr Martin Treu, curator of the Luther Museum, described these mass-produced, printed letters as insurances. Instead of life insurances, however, they were afterlife insurances. These documents had blank spaces for the name of the buyer, the date to be filled in by hand, and the price for which they have been sought. Tesla, a part-preacher and part-door-to-door salesman, went around selling these documents that promised people the salvation of their souls. People gathered around and bought one for themselves, for their relatives and even for their dead relatives.

Martin Luther was born in 1483. He was a German monk and a very devout Roman Catholic during this time. Conflicted with the blatant profiteering conducted by the Church, he seized St. Paul's idea that salvation could be achieved by faith alone, not through human devices, like afterlife insurances.

According to a writing made by Philipp Melanchthon in 1546, Luther nailed a copy of *The 95 Theses on The Power of Indulgences*, to the door of the Castle Church in Wittenberg.[154] *The 95 Theses* attacked papal abuses and the sale of indulgences by church officials. It was translated into other languages, printed and quickly distributed to the rest of the population. The Church reacted slowly in containing the outbreak of Luther's heretical ideas. Europe's first printing presses were just developed and Luther exploited their power to quickly disseminate ideas to the masses. He continued writing and printing pamphlets which were sold and circulated far and wide including France, England and Italy.[155] Luther's ideas sparked a rebellion that challenged the position of the Pope as a divine authority here on Earth.

In 1521, Charles V, the Roman emperor, a Catholic, called on Luther to recant his heresies. When Luther refused, the Emperor declared, on his *Edict of Worms*, that Luther was an outlaw: a notorious heretic whose works must be banned. The Edict made it a crime to give him food or shelter and stated he could be killed without legal consequence.[156]

Afraid for Luther's safety, Frederick III, Elector of Saxony, ordered masked horsemen to kidnap him and take him to Wartburg Castle at Eisenach. There, Luther grew a beard and pretended to be a knight for the next eleven months.[157] Determined to break the Church's monopoly on salvation, he translated the New Testament into a language his people understood: German. This would empower the masses and bypass their reliance on priests and bishops by allowing them to learn and interpret the Bible for themselves. In place of a hierarchy and authority of priests, Luther envisioned a priesthood of all believers. By allowing people to meet, discuss and interpret the meaning of the Bible, a new idea emerged: the separation of Church and State.

I invoke Tristram Hunt's knowledgeable account of historical events by using quotations: "From his reading of the Bible, Luther argued the church had no claim to political authority. There was the Kingdom of God and the Kingdom of Man. And on Earth, the power of priests must never trump the power of princes. This idea nurtured a new emphasis on royal authority, answerable only to God and not Rome". The idea of secularisation – that priests should stick to theology – was seized upon and exploited by Germany's rulers who ceaselessly competed with the Church for power and authority. Luther's religious rebellion was 'mutating into a political revolution'.

Here is what I find most intriguing: Martin Luther's mind formed memes for critical thinking that said, "it is alright to challenge and protest against established religious authorities". He was convinced the Pope and many Catholics were heretics so he sought to reform Catholicism. Many, including John Wycliffe, Jan Hus, Ulrich Zwingli, John Calvin and their followers supported him. However, once he let loose the meme for critical thinking, it was hard to stop it from spreading like wildfire. It replicated itself over and over in the minds of people in towns and villages. Since no copying process is perfect, variants of this meme arose as they were transferred from one individual to another.

As the meme for protest and rebellion evolved in the minds of peasants, everything was opened for questioning. "In 1524, after years of bad harvests, persecution and heavy taxes, the German peasantry rose up in revolt. Over the next two years, mainland Europe witnessed the largest uprising prior to The French Revolution. Some hundred thousand lives [were] lost." Led mainly by self-made messianic figure named Thomas Müntzer, the peasants attacked people belonging to upper classes because of their close ties to princes of the Church.[158] Many disaffected, debt-ridden nobles supported the movement too. They burnt convents, monasteries, bishops' palaces and libraries.

Luther appealed to the peasants through his work: *Against Murderous, Thieving Hordes of Peasants* (1525) telling them that their radical approach to the Reformation was unacceptable. Most of those who resisted were crushed during the Battle of Frankenhausen on May 25, 1525, led by princes who, for their own interests of maintaining their powers, supported Luther's idea of secularism. They were the joint troops of George, Duke of Saxony; Landgraf Philipp I of Hesse; and Frederick III, Elector of Saxony.[159]

"Müntzer was captured and executed and his impaled head served as a warning to anyone else open to radicalised Reformation".

Hunt, then, said:

> Less than ten years had passed since Luther has challenged the Church and already, the Reformation has spiralled into bloodshed. Luther, had unleashed a wave of ideas over which he had no control. The nature of Protestantism is that it actively encourages dissent: Where one group finds its authority confirmed in the Bible, another finds the justification to challenge it.

Hunt's statement towards how religious groups seek confirmation from their holy books to justify their actions says a lot about how religions form.

Protestantism's attempt to reform the Catholic Church was referred to as the Protestant Reformation and is also known as the German Reformation, Protestant Revolution and in Germany, the Lutheran Reformation.

Protestantism spawned new denominations that rejected papal authority and doctrine. They include the following:

1) Adventists
2) Anabaptist
3) Anglican
4) Baptist
5) Calvinist
6) Charismatic
7) Congregational
8) Plymouth Brethren
9) Lutheran
10) Methodist / Wesleyan
11) Pentecostal
12) Presbyterian
13) Quakerism
14) Reformed
15) Restoration movement
16) Waldensians

I believe that the Protestant Revolution is one of the most important turning points in our history because it allowed us to think critically. Here is how...

1. The meme for critical thinking that formed in Luther's mind forced Luther to commit 'heresy' against the Catholic Church. From his works, he did not consider himself to be a heretic, but rather, it was the Pope and most clerics in the Church who had become heretics. Please remember that a 'heretic' is merely a person who espouses an idea or a belief that contradicts an established belief system.

2. Because such seemingly 'heretical' ideas came from a monk as devout as Luther, people gave him much credence and were prepared to take him seriously.

3. Luther advocated that the Church should hand over the political matters to their secular authority. Secular rulers and princes, who competed for power with the Church, had much to gain if they supported Luther. By allowing themselves to believe in Luther's ideas, these secular leaders could feel good about deposing the Church's position of power, and feel assured that their souls will still go to heaven.

4. Slowly, the Protestant Revolution gained increasing political and military muscle which allowed unorthodox and inquisitive ideas to mutate as memes, and spread throughout the populace.

5. Much like the early ozone layer that protected the fragile genes on Earth from the harmful effects of the sun's UV rays, the Protestant Revolution protected 'heretical' memes from the repressive 'heresy' hunts of the Roman Catholic Church which sought to destroy them.

6. With a religious movement that encouraged critical thinking, people permitted themselves to explore and act upon ideas that were once 'heretical' and still feel that such thoughts and actions did not doom them to hell.

The Age Of Reason, Enlightenment And Beyond

"Scholasticism was the dominant form of theology and philosophy in the Latin West in the Middle Ages, particularly in the 12th, 13th, and 14th centuries. It was both a method and a system which aimed to reconcile the Christian theology of the Church Fathers with the Greek philosophy of Aristotle and his commentators."[160]

By the late sixteenth and seventeenth centuries, Europe had been ravaged by religious wars. Religious zeal had left humanity in a miserable condition. There was a need for social reform. "When political stability was finally restored, notably after the Peace of Westphalia (1648) and the English Civil War (1642-1651), an intellectual upheaval overturned the accepted belief that mysticism and revelation are the primary sources of knowledge and wisdom."[161] Philosophy began to change. It started in France, Germany and Britain. Soon after, it spread through much of Europe.

We now look back at the seventeenth and the eighteenth century philosophy as *The Age of Reason* and *The Age of Enlightenment,* consecutively. Unlike before, 'reason' was advocated as the primary source and basis of authority... not God, religion or superstition.

"To understand the natural world and humankind's place in it solely on the basis of reason and without turning to religious belief was the goal of the wide-ranging intellectual movement called *The Enlightenment.*"[162]

Traditional institutions, customs and morals were questioned. Enlightenment philosophers such as Thomas Paine, Voltaire, Jean-Jacques Rousseau, and David Hume questioned and attacked the repressive institutions of aristocratic authority and the established churches.

We must recognise the courage it took to express such unorthodox ideas when it was very dangerous to do so, in a time where heretics, atheists and witches were hunted down and executed.

"*The Enlightenment* is held to be the source of critical ideas, such as the centrality of freedom, democracy and reason as primary values of society. This view argues that the establishment of a contractual basis of rights would lead to the market mechanism and capitalism, the scientific method, religious tolerance, and the organization of states into self-governing republics through democratic means.

"Applying rationality to every problem became essential. Unlike before, when religious dogma circumvented knowledge, thinkers and writers have been freed "to pursue the truth in whatever form, without the threat of sanction for violating established ideas"[163].

The Enlightenment movement "helped create the intellectual framework for the American, French, Haitian Revolutions, Poland's Constitution of 1791, Russia's 1825 Decembrist Revolt, the Latin American independence movement and the Greek national independence movement." Many historians and philosophers including Jürgen Habermas and Isaiah Berlin, credit T*he Enlightenment* with the later rise of classical liberalism, modernism, socialism, democracy, and modern capitalism.[164]

The influences of *The Age of Reason* and *The Age of Enlightenment* rippled through later centuries. Bold individuals dared to challenge the dogmatic claims of ancient scriptures, allowing us to build a world from the ruins of pitiless religious enmity. Helped by the rise of empiricist ideas and their application to political economy, government, science and systematic thinking were applied to all areas of human activity throughout the nineteenth, twentieth and twenty-first centuries.

Life Today Vs Life During Religious Dogmatism

Because of the *Protestant Revolution*, the *Age of Reason*, the *Age of Enlightenment* and scientific discoveries, human life has changed its course. Let us now contrast some aspects of today's daily life compared with the past.

Homes As Places of Worship

Before Luther, people could only worship in churches. Males and females worshipped separately. Protestant males and females began worshipping together as equals. Protestantism advocated the idea that men and women could use their homes to read the Bible and praise God with their children. As monasteries and nunneries closed down, homes became the new places of worship.

Marriage and Sex

Marriage was once seen as a mere contract between a man and a woman, secondary to the contract between man and God. Sex was only seen as an act for reproduction and was often labelled as sinful by the Catholic Church. After Martin Luther, sex could be enjoyed by couples, as a natural desire which should not be denied and suppressed. Luther, himself, regarded the family home as the 'hospital for lust'.

Divorce

Nowadays, divorce is all too common but King Henry VIII had to spawn a new religion to divorce his wife! Desperate for an heir, King Henry VIII wanted to marry a Protestant sympathiser, Anne Boleyn. "The Pope refused to annul his marriage. So in 1534, in a remarkable religious u-turn, Henry VIII split from Rome. Almost overnight, the Church in England became The Church of England...The king reaped the reward, the Catholic Church was ransacked, its monasteries stripped bare and the royal coffers, filled with riches. It was theft on a regal scale".[165]

Such was the beginning of the Anglican religion. King Henry VIII was its supreme leader. In this new religion, he kept the infrastructure of the Catholic Church, its churches, its bishops and its priests.

It is sad that many marriages do not last. It is often the women who bear the brunt of divorce. However, divorce empowers individuals by allowing them to leave abusive and irreconcilable relationships that, if maintained, would lead to more abuse, violence, desolation or unhappiness.

Literature

Reading was a primordial skill according to Martin Luther. For an individual to enable himself to steer towards his own way to God, he must be able to read the Bible himself. Books, therefore, became primordial under the influence of Protestantism.

To the most devout Christians, like the Puritans, life was an hour-by-hour struggle to lead a righteous life. In the hope of proving themselves worthy of salvation, they started writing diaries. This helped them track their chances of going to heaven and analyse where they might have gone wrong. This marks the birth of Autobiographies.

The earliest known autobiography was that of John Bunyan. From his own autobiography he wrote in prison, John Bunyan wrote what would become the first-ever novel: *The Pilgrim's Progress*. It is the second best-circulated book next to the Bible.[166]

Nowadays, novels have become detached from their original purpose. Filling our libraries, bookstores and bookshelves at home, they are now also for entertainment and education.

Liberation Of Women

The role of women in European society was largely defined by motherhood. It was only in the nunneries where women had any form of stature and power, but outside, the world was ruled by men.

Protestantism, however, encouraged women to read. This sense of equality between the sexes, later led to the empowerment of women.

Julia Ward Howe (1819 – 1910) fought for women's right to control their destiny against existing religious demands. In a speech she delivered at the Parliament of the World's Religions, at the 1893 Columbian Exposition, Chicago World's Fair, she said:

> I think nothing of a religion which puts one individual absolutely above others, and surely nothing of a religion which puts one sex above another. Religion is primarily our relation to the Supreme, to God himself. It is for Him to judge; it is for Him to say where we belong, who is highest and who is not; of that we know nothing. And any religion which will sacrifice a certain set of human beings for the enjoyment or aggrandizement or advantage of another is no religion. It is a thing which may be allowed, but it is against true religion. Any

religion which sacrifices women to the brutality of men is no religion.

- In 1908, Howe became the first woman elected to the American Academy of Arts and Letters.
- In 1920, a decade after her death, American women were finally given the right to vote.
- In the 1960s, 'the number of working women in the United States doubled… so did divorce rates. Change and choice were in the air'.[167]
- In 1963, the birth-control pill was invented and it transformed female patterns of sexual behaviour.
- Ten years later, in 1973, abortion was made legal from the *Roe v. Wade* case of the United States Supreme Court.
- By 1994, women were finally ordained as bishops in the Anglican Church.

Gay and Lesbian Relationships

Far from Luther's model of patriarchal family life, branches of Protestantism, liberal Christians, like the Metropolitan Community Churches in America, accept and recognise gay and lesbian relationships. Gays and lesbians want to be God's people too, so, as in the beginnings of most religions, holy texts were scanned for verses that supported their cause and founded their churches under those authorities.

Nowadays, the appointment of gays to positions of religious authority is headline news. In 2004, Reverend V. Gene Robinson became the first gay Diocese of New Hampshire in the Episcopal Church in the United States of America.[168]

Art

In medieval times, most art was religious in context and content. To the Protestants, the Jews and the Muslims, religious images and statues went against the Second Commandment that forbade idolatry and false worship.

Across England and Europe in the 1530s, the Protestant Reformation destroyed religious art in forms of stained glass, statues and tapestries. They believed such imagery blocked the true path to God. To them, the true path to God was through the words of the Bible.

After this grand scale vandalism of art, however, a new form of art emerged. Joseph Leo Korener of the Courtauld Institute of Art, said that people salvaged some of the artworks from the vandalised religious buildings. They took the artworks home and hung them on their walls.

In the 17th century, in Holland, a golden age of art production arose. Suddenly, art stopped being an instrument of religion and became a symbol of prestige. It became a commodity for people collect and display.[169] Art evolved from featuring only images of saints and angels to images of people living their everyday lives. These new forms of art were no longer displayed in churches. The first art museums were built, and used, instead.

Money and Wealth

The medieval Roman Catholic Church advocated that life should be devoted to worshipping God. Everything else was a distraction. "Poverty and Godliness went hand-in-hand...work was demeaning and profit was a source of shame"[170]. When one accumulates wealth, it must be distributed to the community or be given to the Church, who would allocate it for the public good.

Calvinism, the teaching of John Calvin (1509-1564), devised the idea of predestination. Predestination is a belief that God has already selected those whose souls are going to heaven. These people were referred to as the 'Elect'.

People who believed in predestination were eager to know whether they were one of the selected few. Looking for signs, it became an agreed understanding that one's prosperity was God's sign that a person is one of the Elect. This motivated Calvinists to work hard and accumulate wealth through honest and ethical means. The harder they worked, the more money they got and they felt more assured they would go to Heaven.

In their struggle for prosperity, wealth was used to make more wealth. The Calvinist belief system bred a culture that focussed on becoming productive. Time management became essential. Clocks and watches became visible and available everywhere.

In the 1640s, English Protestants fought King Charles I. Others fled to America where many, like John Winthrop (1587-1649), sought to build a country on prosperity and industry.

Benjamin Franklin, one of the Founding Fathers of the United States of America, held Puritan and Enlightenment values of thrift, hard work, education, opposition to religious or political authoritarianism, openness to scientific enquiry and tolerance for other belief systems.[171]

Max Weber, a German economist and sociologist, wrote a book called *The Protestant Ethic and the Spirit of Capitalism* between 1904 and 1905. His thesis posits that capitalism evolved when the Calvinist ethic influenced large numbers of people to work in the secular world, start their own businesses, trade and invest.

The Rise of Irreligious, Secular Ideas

Heretical and blasphemous ideas began to emerge. Some challenged the authority, power and influence of religion. Because of them, we have been allowed to progress and modernise our thinking, our society and our way of life. These ideas can be broadly classified under the following headings:

1. Non-theistic concepts of God.
2. Scientific knowledge.
3. Economic and political thoughts.

Non-Theistic Concepts Of God

Deistic Ideas

A belief system like Deism began to emerge. This belief system formed a view that there was a god who created everything. However, deists accepted nothing from religions that were 'revealed' by God to human beings or prophets. They also believed that reason, not faith, leads us to certain basic truths.[172]

Lord Herbert of Cherbury (1582, 1648), considered to be the father of English Deism, believed there are universal truths that lay in all religions which Christians and non-Christians can subscribe to. Popular deists were scientist like Isaac Newton, philosophers and economists, like David Hume and Thomas Hobbes. Deists had a desire to remodel Christianity to fit their new philosophy, while being careful not to be labelled as atheists.

Pantheistic Ideas

Pantheism is a belief system that equates God with everything: 'Gold is All' and 'All is God'. To pantheists, God is the universe. God is nature. It is an old idea discussed by ancient Greece philosophers including Thales, Parmenides and Heraclitus. It can be found even in Genesis, thus the phrase: 'acts of nature'. The word itself was first used by Irish writer John Toland in 1705 in his book *Socinianism Truly Stated By A Pantheist*.

The pantheistic concept of God is essentially a non-supernatural god. God does not exist beyond the observable domains of space and time. It falls under the domain of science.

Albert Einstein was a pantheist and he described his belief system as follows:

> I am a deeply religious non-believer. This is a somewhat a new kind of religion. I have never imputed to Nature a purpose or a goal, or anything that could be understood as anthropomorphic. What I see in Nature is a magnificent structure that we can comprehend only very imperfectly, and that must fill a thinking

person with a feeling of humility. This is a genuinely religious feeling that has nothing to do with mysticism. The idea of a person God is quite alien to me and seems even naïve.

As such, the pantheistic god is atheistic. Pantheists only use the word God to enhance the way they use language. For example when Einstein said: 'God does not play dice", he means something like "Nature does not gamble".

Atheistic Ideas

British neurologist and author, Sir Jonathan Wolfe Miller, helps us envisage the rise of early atheism from the 16th century in a documentary called *Atheism: A Rough History of Disbelief:*

> Some of the new sects [of Protestantism] introduced ideas which the Christian authorities regarded as little short of atheism. The Anabaptists, for example, were a group who, despite of their protestations to the contrary, were widely regarded as atheists. And this brings us to another group: the Unitarians, who were also viewed as atheistic.

One of them, Matthew Hammond, confirmed his atheism before being burnt at the stake for heresy:

> Christ is not God, not the saviour of the world but a mere man, a simple man and an abominable idol. All who worship him are abominable idolaters. And Christ did not rise again from death to life nor did he ascend to heaven.

It was hard for people at the time to confess their atheism, but plenty were accused of it. The rising climate of atheism was so problematic there were atheist hunters in the 16th, 17th and 18th centuries. According to Miller, many atheists might have disguised themselves as deists. It was still a very religious culture.

Cambridge historian, Simon Schaffer said, in the documentary:

> Atheism, I think, is a label lots of really clever people try to escape. And for that reason, we have this problem of looking back at the history of atheism that even folk who, surely, by any standards, should be judged atheists, do an enormous amount of work to ensure they cannot be accused of such.

Schaffer also helped paint the picture of the logical warfare that existed at the time. He said that religious people – including the most ferocious atheist hunters – denied there were atheists. Why? They wanted to give the impression that it was humanly impossible to disavow God. Despite their denials, it was obvious something was going on. They had something to fear. In 1697, the *Blasphemy Act* was imposed to combat disbelief in God.

Thomas Hobbes (1588-1679) is famous for his contributions in Western political philosophy from the perspective of the social contract theory. Although he was considered a deist, Hobbes is said to have laid the foundations for atheism:

> The universe – the whole mass of things that are – is corporeal, that is to say, body, and hath the dimensions of magnitude, length, breadth and depth. Every part of the universe is 'body' and that which is not 'body' is no part of the universe, and because the universe is all, that which is no part of it, is nothing, and consequently nowhere.

Baron d'Holbach, a Frenchman and the first avowed atheist, wrote a book called *The System of Nature* under a pseudo name. In this book, he writes the following:

> If we go back to the beginning we shall find that ignorance and fear created the gods, that fancy enthusiasm or deceit adorned them, that weakness worshipped them, that credulity preserved them and that custom respect and tyranny supported them in order to make the blindness of men serve their own interests. If the ignorance of nature gave birth to gods, the knowledge of nature is calculated to destroy them. It is only by dispelling the

clouds and phantoms of religion that we shall discover truth, reason and morality.

Thomas Paine (1737-1809) was an English radical who inspired the American revolutionaries and coined the name, *The United States of America*. After gaining their independence, the Americans gave Paine a gift: a farm in New York.

As an intellectual atheist, he made the following statements:

1) Of all the tyrannies that afflict mankind, tyranny in religion is the worst.

2) All national institutions of churches, whether Jewish, Christian or Muslim, appear to me no other than human inventions, set up to terrify and enslave mankind, and to monopolize power and profit.

3) It is from the Bible that man has learnt cruelty, rapine and murder, for the belief in a cruel god makes a cruel man. The Bible is a history of wickedness that served to corrupt and brutalize mankind.

Percy Bysshe Shelley (1792-1822), an English romantic poet, pointed out the following rhetorical questions about God in *The Necessity Of Atheism*:

1. If he is infinitely good, what reason should we have to fear him?
2. If he is infinitely wise, why should we have doubts concerning our future?
3. If he knows all, why warn him of our needs and fatigue him with our prayers?
4. If he is everywhere, why erect temples to him?
5. If he is just, why fear that he will punish the creatures that he has filled with weaknesses?
6. If he is all-powerful, how offend him, how resist him?
7. If he is reasonable, how can he be angry at the blind, to whom he has given the liberty of being unreasonable?

8. If he is immovable, by what right do we pretend to make him change his decrees?
9. If he is inconceivable, why occupy ourselves with him?
10. IF HE HAS SPOKEN, WHY IS THE UNIVERSE NOT CONVINCED?
11. If the knowledge of a God is the most necessary, why is it not the most evident and the clearest?

The Emergence And Progress Of Science

Copernicus and Heliocentrism

In 1543, Copernicus published his book: *De Revolutionibus Orbium Coelestium* (*On The Revolutions Of The Celestial Spheres*). In it, he explained the Earth was not the centre of the universe (at the time, the universe meant the solar system). People were still unaware of the grand scale of the universe we are able to observe now. Copernicus argued the sun was the centre of the solar system and the Earth revolved around it. The book caused mild controversy and it was only three years later, in 1546, when Giovanni Maria Tolosani denounced it and defended the Bible.[173] Martin Luther, himself, criticised Copernicus as a fool who went against holy writ.

Galileo Galilei Telescope Demonstration In Rome

In 1611, Galileo went to Rome to demonstrate his telescopic observations of Jupiter's moons to a group of philosophers and mathematicians called Jesuit Collegio Romano, after publishing his findings the year before.[174] It supported the idea of Copernicus and, in 1614, Father Tommaso Caccini (1574-1648) denounced Galileo's works as heretical.

"One of Galileo's most enthusiastic followers, Giordano Bruno, was imprisoned and tortured for nearly eight years. Despite denying that he held heretical views, he was burned in a Roman flower market in 1600. What remained of his body after burning was smashed by hammers and cast to the wind."[175]

Quotations by Galileo:

"In question to science, the authority of a thousand is not worth the humble reasoning of a single individual."

"To command the professors of astronomy to refute their own observations is to command them not to see what they do see and not to understand what they do understand."

Continued Scientific Progress

The Bible explained how the world came about: made by God in six days. For a long time, people believed this to be true. Without the necessary scientific tools and knowledge, they had no other alternatives.

Theologians used the Bible to calculate the age of the universe. One of them was James Ussher (1581-1656), an Anglican Archbishop of Armagh. According to his precise calculations, the process of creation began the night preceding the 23rd of October 4004 BC on the Julian calendar. On our calendar, the Gregorian calendar, this is the 21st of September 4004 BCE. This was established as truth and it was included in the authorised version of the Bible in 1701. Other exciting dates included the day when Adam and Eve were driven from Paradise: on Monday, 10th of November 4004 BC and Noah's ark touched down on Mt Ararat on Wednesday 5th of May 2348 BC.[176]

At the time, however, the newly-emerged science of Geology was getting different information from the evidence they gathered from rocks. Early geologists like William Buckland (who discovered dinosaur fossils), James Hutton and Charles Lyell, insisted the Earth existed for many millions of years.

Their findings supported the theory of an English naturalist and geologist named Charles Darwin. In 1859, Darwin published his book, *On The Origin Of Species,* based on evidence he collected and studied from a trip to the Galapagos Islands in the 1830s. In it, he explained how different species of living things evolved slowly and gradually through a process of natural selection.

Charles Darwin said:

> I cannot persuade myself that a beneficent and omnipotent God would have designedly created parasitic wasps with the express intention of their feeding within the living bodies of caterpillars...or that God would have designedly created that a cat should play with mice.

Darwin's studies and fossil evidence, found by other scientists, challenged, devastated and embarrassed religious proclamations that God created the world and everything in it. There were no accounts of dinosaurs in the Bible.

> **"Since the Bible and the church are obviously mistaken in telling us where we came from, how can we trust them to tell us where we are going?"**
>
> *- Anonymous*

Political, Economic and Philosophical Thoughts

Free to explore their thoughts, many thinkers and philosophers developed and defined ideas that offered us ways to think beyond gods, religions and superstitions. Examples of such ideas include:

1) Existentialism
2) Rationalism
3) Positivism
4) Humanism
5) Libertarianism
6) Individual Sovereignty
7) Economic Freedom

Existentialism

"Existentialism proposes that individuals create the meaning and essence of their lives, as opposed to it being created for them by deities, or authorities, or defined for them by philosophical or theological doctrines".[177] There is no god who determines right from wrong. It is up to us to decide what kind of a person we want to be. It is up to us to decide what this life should be for us. There is no God or gods who impose their will on us.

Rationalism

"Rationalism is 'any view appealing to reason as a source of knowledge or justification'.[178] In more technical terms it is a method or theory 'in which the criterion of the truth is not sensory but intellectual and deductive'.[179] Different degrees of emphasis on this method or theory lead to a range of rationalist standpoints, from the moderate position 'that reason has precedence over other ways of acquiring knowledge' to the radical position that reason is 'the unique path to knowledge'[180]."[181]

Positivism

"Positivism is the philosophy that the only authentic knowledge is knowledge that is based on actual sense experience. Such knowledge can only come from affirmation of theories through strict scientific method. Metaphysical speculation is avoided."[182]

From *The Fontana Dictionary of Modern Thought,* written by Alan Bullock and Stephen Trombley:

> Positivism is depicted as 'the view that all true knowledge is scientific' and that all things are ultimately measurable. Positivism is closely related to reductionism, in that both involve the view that 'entities of one kind... are reducible to entities of another', such as societies to numbers, or mental

events to chemical events. It also involves the contention that 'processes are reducible to physiological, physical or chemical events', and even that 'social processes are reducible to relationships between and actions of individuals', or that 'biological organisms are reducible to physical systems'.[183]

Humanism

Humanism is a broad category of ethical philosophies that determines morality from universal human qualities – particularly rationality. It rejects the dependence on beliefs without reason, the supernatural or texts of alleged divine origin.[184]

Libertarianism

According to the *Internet Encyclopedia of Philosophy,* libertarians are committed to the belief that:

1) Individuals, and not states or groups of any other kind, are both ontologically and normatively primary;
2) Individuals have rights against certain kinds of forcible interference on the part of others;
3) Liberty, understood as non-interference, is the only thing that can be legitimately demanded of others as a matter of legal or political right;
4) Robust property rights and the economic liberty that follows from their consistent recognition are of central importance in respecting individual liberty;
5) Social order is not at odds with, but develops out of, individual liberty;
6) The only proper use of coercion is defensive, or to rectify an error;
7) Governments are bound by essentially the same moral principles as individuals;

8) Most existing and historical governments have acted improperly if they have used coercion for plunder, aggression, redistribution, and other purposes beyond the protection of individual liberty.[185]

Individual Sovereignty

In their book, *The Sovereign Individual*, writers William Rees-Mogg and James Dale Davidson describe this condition in which individuals have supreme authority and sovereignty over their own choices. Individual sovereignty refers to the natural right of a person to have control over his or her own body, and life.

To summarise the important points to take from this chapter:

1) We have seen examples of how people have created religions. People got hold of an idea, they scanned the holy books for justification, then went ahead to impose that idea. In the process, they reformed their existing religion or created new religions.
2) Humanity got to where it is today NOT because it believed blindly in religious doctrines, but because people started thinking critically. They began questioning everything. They began relying more on evidence and their own reason.
3) Many revolutionary ideas were once considered atheistic, heretical or blasphemous to a god or a religion.

We must recognise that the freedom we enjoy today came from the courage of those who were imprisoned, or killed, to speak out for the ideas and values on which we build our societies today.

CHAPTER 17:
GOD'S THREAT TO DEMOCRACY

Having forgotten, or never having the inclination to learn about our history and our scriptures, many people feel that their religious beliefs do not necessarily get in the way of them believing in the ideals of modern society. I will later demonstrate, however, that because religion seeks to establish a totalitarian regime founded on its dogmatic beliefs, it undoubtedly clashes with democracy. How can it not?

If we believe that God truly exists, and his nature is as asserted by the Bible or the Koran, then it is only logical to assume that all laws must reflect God's will. By its very nature, the rule of God is totalitarian, which is the exact opposite of democracy.

Under the rule of God, freedom, equality and liberty are alien concepts. We already know what it is like to be ruled by religion in medieval Europe. We have also seen how Sharia Law oppressed its people in Afghanistan. The Taliban regime implemented the strictest form of Sharia Law ever seen in the Muslim world.[186] These societies were not the results of extreme interpretations of the Scriptures. They merely highlight that the Scriptures, themselves, are extreme when they are followed literally.

There are far too many religions. I am sure that we cannot all be so docile to allow only one to dominate us all. We now know what it is like to live in a relatively free world and I doubt many of us will ever allow our societies to fall into the trap of religious despotism again.

Therefore, it seems rather unlikely that democracy will ever be replaced by a theocracy. I hope this is true. Nevertheless, I want to emphasize the need for us to remain vigilant. Disastrous moments in our history have been merely the results of a sequence of many things going wrong simultaneously.

If we care to preserve the society we recognise and enjoy today, then we need to at least get a basic idea of why and how it works. In this section, I will outline why I believe we have created a good system to organize our societies. It is not perfect, but believing that a world can be better organised by the dictates of religion would be a terrible mistake.

Democracy

Unlike other forms of governments where only one individual or an elite class, rules the masses, democracy allows the majority to dictate how they should be ruled. It does this by giving the people, the power to vote for their own leaders.

Democracy recognises two principles, as expressed by the ancient Greek philosopher, Aristotle:

1) All citizens must have equal access to power.
2) All citizens must be able to live life as they want and be able to enjoy universally-recognised freedoms and liberties.

These two principles have the following implications:

1) The poor are more powerful than the rich because there are more of them.
2) People must not be governed by anybody, or failing that, they must govern and be governed in turns. This contributes to equalitarian liberty... to fairness.

For a democracy to work, it needs the following:

- **Separation of Powers**

    It is very important that a separation of powers exists between those who enforce the law (the executive), those who make them (the legislature) and those who interpret them (the judiciary).

- **Intelligent, well-informed voters.**

    For a society to make the right choices, it needs to have intelligent, well-informed voters. To achieve this, people need to have *Freedom of Speech*, *Freedom of Expression* and the *Freedom of the Press*. This is vital for providing voters, complete and varied perspectives on all issues.

The effectiveness of a democratic power, as well as the trust and respect afforded to it, is undermined when any of the following is caused to occur by groups with vested interests:

1) **Reduced Vote Participation**

    If many voters are prevented from voting, either through threats of violence, coercion or discouragement, democracy can fail. Vested-interest groups can argue the elected government does not have the right to rule because many of the populace did not vote for them.

2) **Lobby Groups**

    Democracy weakens when lobby groups dominate and pass laws that favour the interests of particular groups, including religious groups.

3) **Limit or Abolish Freedom of Speech/Expression/Press**

By restricting Freedom of Speech/Expression/Press, an entire voting population can be dumbed-down. Methods can include the following:

a) Deny people access to alternative views and opinions.
b) Deny people their right to express their views and opinions.
c) Distort the truth by denying and restricting the ability of the media and journalists to provide objective and balanced information.

4) **Fear and Violence**

Without good information, it becomes difficult to know right from wrong. When the intellect fails to direct us, our decisions become guided by nothing more than our emotions. Since fear is one of the strongest emotions, we become vulnerable to the will of organised groups who are able to threaten and terrorise us.

I mention the items above as a warning to us all to be critical about any group or organisation that encourages us not to vote or participate in the democratic process. Let us be suspicious when someone, or some group, denies our rights, and the rights of others to be heard.

Winding Back The Separation of Church And State

The United States was the first country to formally include the separation of Church and State in its Constitution in 1791.[187] Many countries all over the world have since adopted the concept because it worked.

From the website of American United[188]:

> Americans have more religious freedom than any people in world history. We can choose what to believe; what to teach our children; how, where and when to worship; which causes to give money to; or even whether we want to get involved with religion at all. We have the separation of church and state to thank for this broadly based freedom.
> The First Amendment to the U.S. Constitution says: "Congress shall make no law respecting an establishment of religion; or prohibiting the free exercise thereof...." The U.S. Supreme Court has interpreted this clause to mean that religion and government must stay separate for the benefit of both. The government holds no religious viewpoint and leaves all decisions about faith and religious practice to its citizens.
> ...When the government or government officials get behind one religious message, it sends the message to adherents that they are more valuable, and all others are less valuable, members of the political community. Leaving religious expression to private citizens ensures that the government will treat everyone equally.

The phrase: 'Separation of Church and State', had its beginnings after a group identified as Danbury Baptists, a denomination of Protestantism, wrote to Thomas Jefferson in 1802, seeking for the separation of Church and State. Thomas Jefferson (the third President of the United States) wrote a letter in reply on January 1, 1802:

Believing with you that religion is a matter which lies solely between man and his God, that he owes account to none other for his faith or his worship, that the legitimate powers of government reach actions only, and not opinions, I contemplate with sovereign reverence that act of the whole American people which declared that their legislature should **'make no law respecting an establishment of religion, or prohibiting the free exercise thereof,'** thus building a wall of separation between Church and State.[189]

James Madison (1751-1836), the fourth President of the United States and the principal author of the first amendment said in 1785, that no one should be coerced by government in supporting any religion, even if it means all religions. With Thomas Jefferson, James Madison stated on the Virginia Statute for Religious Freedom that:

> ...No man shall be compelled to frequent or support any religious worship, place, or ministry whatsoever, nor shall be enforced, restrained, molested, or burthened in his body or goods, nor shall otherwise suffer on account of his religious opinions or belief; but that all men shall be free to profess, and by argument to maintain, their opinion in matters of religion, and that the same shall in no wise diminish enlarge, or affect their civil capacities."

Today, the Separation of Church and State is under threat from two fronts:

- Christian Dominionism
- Islamisation

Christian Dominionism

Dominionism is the Christian tendency to influence and control the political government to apply biblical law. Its origins can be traced back from a verse in the Bible:

> And God blessed [Adam and Eve] and God said unto them, "Be fruitful, and multiply, and replenish the earth, and subdue it: and have dominion over the fish of the sea, and over the fowl of the air, and over every living thing that moveth upon the earth.
> – **Genesis 1:28 (King James Version)**

Instead of using my own words to define the problem posed by Dominion Theology, I will use the words of a subject-matter expert: Edward Tabash, a Los Angeles lawyer, chairing the

National Legal Committee of Americans United for Separation of Church and State. In a speech he gave to members of the *Center for Inquiry*, he said:

> Even though we non-believers and even liberal religionists have made great strides, the constitution of the United States means only what the Supreme Court says it means, at any given moment in time. We are now down to five-to-four bare majority for government neutrality for matters of religion.
>
> Justice Scalia, who was on the opposing side, believes that local government officials, speaking for the people, can enact religious-based laws that will be enforced by the police power of the state. We have every reason to believe that the new chief and Justice Alito agree with that.
>
> Then we have Justice Thomas. Justice Thomas goes to a radical extent. He believes that the Establishment Clause of the First Amendment does not apply to the states and each state should even be free to have their own official church.
>
> Legal scholars that are on the President's list to become federal court justices have told me personally that they believe that the atheist is not protected by the First Amendment... only religious people are.
>
> And so, even though we have made some headway in secularising American government and society, people are overly religious in overwhelming numbers that a newly reconstituted Supreme Court, opens the floodgate to religious oppression, government at all levels will enact religious-favouring laws and render the non-believer a second-class citizen. Right now we are only one justice away from the loss of sixty years of precedent requiring Church and State separation.
>
> If the current President [George Bush] replaces Justice Stevens, who is eighty-seven years old, we lose everything we have won in the past sixty years. If the next President is a Religious-Right sympathiser and replaces Justice Stevens and all the others, we will have a theocracy for maybe the balance of this century... Everything we care about in terms of a modern secular state all hinges on majorities on the US Supreme Court.

To underline what a theocracy means for Americans, it means that one religion can impose its will on its citizens. From our history, we know about the tyranny and oppression that arises when the power to rule is in the hands of religions. If you are a homosexual, a woman, a non-Christian or even non-religious, you will be a target. All areas of business, commerce, science, education and government will need to comply with God's law. Due to the powerful influence of American politics to the world at large, we have to seriously consider the possibility and the impact of such an outcome, because we will all be affected.

Islamisation (Sharia Law)

In discussing Islam, let me be clear that I do not believe all Muslims are pushing for the establishment of the Sharia Law. Many 'moderate' Muslims, I suspect, also struggle with the idea of violent Jihad. The truth, however, is that, inasmuch as many 'moderate' Christians or Muslims do not want violence, there are many 'fanatics' among them who believe that religion should rule us all. We have seen how some Christians feel justified in their idea of a theocracy based on Christianity. Let us now discuss how some Muslims may feel justified pushing for an Islamic regime.

In a documentary called *Islam: What The West Needs To Know*, Robert Spencer, author of two New York times bestsellers on Islamic jihad, including *The Truth About Muhammad* and *The Politically Incorrect Guide To Islam* said:

> Islam, from its beginnings, was both a religion and a system of government. For example, the Islamic calendar does not base Year One from the time that Muhammad was born, or the time that Muhammad received his first revelation from God – which I think, are both what westerners might expect – but from the time that Muhammad became the leader of an army and the Head of State in Medina. This is the beginning of the Islamic calendar because in the Islamic understanding, Islam is a political and social system as well as an individual faith.

Serge Trifkovic, a Serbian-American historian, journalist, political analyst and author of *The Sword Of The Prophet*, added:

> In Islam, the separation between temporal, secular and religious power is not only impossible, it is heretical. Only in the complete blending of all aspects of human activity and all aspects of political and legal functions of the state can we have the properly organised state that is pleasing to Allah.

Walid Shoebat, a former member of the Palestinian Liberation Organisation, who later converted to Christianity and authored the books *Why I Left Jihad*, *Why We Want To Kill You* and *God's War On Terror*, explains it from an Arabic perspective:

> When westerners think religion, whether it is Islam, Christianity, Judaism, Hinduism and all the isms of the world, they think it is a personal issue... So, they look at Islam with the way they understand religions. And that's the first mistake. Islam is not a religion for personal use. Islam is Sharia Law. Islam is a form of government to the world, first, then to a personal application.
>
> It is not just how you pray: you pray towards Mecca; It is how you dress: you dress in Arab culture; you speak Arabic: you can't go to heaven unless you pray in Arabic. You can't read the Qur'an in English and expect to do good deeds and go to heaven. It becomes an imperialistic system that everybody now must speak Arabic, think Arabic, practice the religion in Arabic. It's a form of law, not just in how you eat, but how you get married, how you deal with your government, how you deal with your military, how you deal with the youth, how you deal with women... Every aspect of your life becomes Islam. Everything is Islam.
>
> [From the Hadith] Muhammad said: I have been ordered to fight until everyone says that there is no god but Allah and Muhammad is the messenger of Allah. So, this is how Islam spread to North Africa, this is how Islam spread all the way to Indonesia [and] this is how Islam spread to the Middle East.

Syria was not a Muslim country. Lebanon was not Muslim. Saudi Arabia, even, was a mixed multitude... All throughout the Middle East, that's how Islam spread: by the sword. This is why you do not see any synagogues in Saudi Arabia, you do not see any churches in Saudi Arabia... Christianity virtually is non-existent. Even in my village in Bethlehem, Muslims have taken over. There's only 20% left of the Christian population. In Lebanon, Christian Lebanese are moving by the droves. Hezbollah there is very active. Lebanon used to be a Christian nation. Now, all of a sudden, it is being Islamised. Islam is moving.

Robert Spencer ties up the message:

Muslims who come to the United States and come to Western Europe with an idea that Sharia is the law of Allah, they look upon our freedom of religion, and they look upon the fact that non-Muslims are empowered in the United States and in Western Europe making laws, and making laws not in the basis of the law of Allah, but on the basis of consensus and free elections. They look upon all that, as a manifestation of *Jahiliyyah*: the pre-Islamic period of ignorance, as the times in any nations' history before it became Muslim...

Many Muslims coming into the United States and Western Europe will work to establish Islamic states here on the basis of the idea that the secular state, a state based on elections, has no legitimacy. You do not have elections over the law of Allah, you simply obey what God says.

The Noble Koran 47:4

So, when you meet (in fight Jihad in Allah's Cause), those who disbelieve smite at their necks till when you have killed and wounded many of them, then bind a bond firmly (on them, i.e. take them as captives). Thereafter (is the time) either for generosity (i.e. free them without ransom), or ransom (according to what benefits Islam), until the war lays down its burden. Thus [you are ordered by Allah to continue in carrying out Jihad against the disbelievers till they embrace Islam (i.e.

are saved from the punishment in the Hell-fire) or at least come under your protection], but if it had been Allah's Will, He Himself could certainly have punished them (without you). But (He lets you fight), in order to test you, some with others. But those who are killed in the Way of Allah, He will never let their deeds be lost.[190]

Many of us consider that, if only we changed our policies towards Israel, Iraq or Iran, we would not have this problem today. To this, Robert Spencer said:

> These ideas are based on the fundamental misunderstanding of the motives and goals of the Jihadists. This is not a conflict that was created with the creation of the State of Israel, or a conflict that was created when American armies went into Iraq, the global Jihad had gone on... since the seventh century.

Osama Bin Laden wrote to America telling them what Al-Qaeda wanted:

> The first thing that we are calling you to, is Islam. The religion of the Unification of God; of freedom from associating partners with Him, and rejection of this; of complete love of Him, the Exalted; of complete submission to His Laws; and of the discarding of all the opinions, orders, theories and religions which contradict with the religion He sent down to His Prophet Muhammad (peace be upon him).
>
> ... It is saddening to tell you that you are the worst civilization witnessed by the history of mankind: You are the nation who, rather than ruling by the Shariah of Allah in its Constitution and Laws, choose to invent your own laws as you will and desire. You separate religion from your policies, contradicting the pure nature which affirms Absolute Authority to the Lord and your Creator.[191]

According to a survey done by ICM/Sunday Telegraph, published in *The Telegraph*, show that 40% of the Muslims surveyed wanted Sharia Law in the UK.[192] In another survey done by the *Daily Telegraph*, 32% of British Muslims believe that western society is decadent and immoral and that Muslims should seek to bring it to an end. Even though these are British numbers, other countries around the world must watch such trends.

Interesting Trends In The UK

A proposed law that breaches the Separation of Church and State is recognisable when we apply this test:

> **Is it being proposed on no other basis but purely religious grounds?**

If the answer is yes, then the law may be endangering the principle of separating the Church from the State.

Relevant case studies presented themselves in the UK. In July 2008, Association of Chief Police Officers (ACPO) were drawing up guidelines to enforce the law for police sniffer dogs to wear bootees, with rubber soles, when searching the homes of Muslims so as not to cause offence, in the United Kingdom. "Where Muslims object, officers will be obliged to use sniffer dogs only in exceptional cases".[193]

In an article published by *The Sunday Times* on September 14, 2008[194], "Islamic law has been officially adopted in Britain, with Sharia courts given powers to rule on Muslim civil cases... Rulings issued by a network of five Sharia courts are enforceable with the full power of the judicial system, through the county courts or High Court". The Sharia courts are classified as arbitration tribunals, as an alternative for Muslims to resolve their disputes. The article pointed out that Jews in the UK had been using their own Jewish Beth Din courts for about a hundred years now too.

In these matters, I would like you, dear reader, to consider the following questions: If we allow communities to enclose themselves with their own laws, we will undoubtedly fail to protect those who are most vulnerable to the oppression, caused by the belief systems of these communities. For example, how can we protect the rights of homosexuals within a community that discriminates against them? How can we protect the rights of women in a community that tolerates abuse?

Further, do we have evidence proving that the nature of crime, be it theft or domestic violence, depends on the religion of the perpetrator? No. Why, then, should one criminal be punished more or less than another who committed the same crime? Do we have evidence to prove that the victims of their crimes are less wronged, depending on their religion? No. Why then should one victim be protected, supported and compensated more or less than another? Crimes should be treated similarly, regardless of whether the victim, or the perpetrator, is an atheist, a Muslim, a Christian or a Jew. Thus, I contend that we should all live under one law.

If the current system is inaccessible, too expensive, or too complex for the population, then let us work on making it simpler and more accessible. Instead of focussing our efforts on dividing our societies further along religious lines, let us think of other solutions instead. Let us educate the public on how to work with the existing system. Let us educate the lawmakers about the belief systems of new immigrants and reform our laws systematically, without compromising what works.

If certain religious beliefs are incongruent to the values upon which existing laws were built, then it must be articulated and communicated to immigrants. It is important that immigrants understand how some of their beliefs contradict and conflict with the ideals of modern society: on democracy, equality and respect for freedom.

Immigration and Assimilation

People migrate to wealthier countries mainly to improve the quality of their lives. Wealthier countries are where they are today because of the beliefs and values they chose to embrace. People in the west must be proud that they have managed to build countries conducive to the lifestyle that immigrants seek.

As an immigrant myself, it annoys me when a minority of immigrants judge the practices, the values and the people of a country that welcomed them. Immigrants are proud of their heritage, as they should. However, some can be very judgmental. To them, I ask: If your way of life and your way of thinking is so much more superior, then, why did your people fail to build a country where you, and the rest of your people, would want to live?

If you flee the poverty, the chaos, the corruption and the violence prevalent in your own country, you must consider the possibility that perhaps, the belief systems of your people has a tendency to choke any progress to be made in areas of governance, education, science, medicine and commerce.

The future peace and tranquillity of developed countries depends on how they manage to assimilate the belief systems of immigrants into their cultures. The dilemma today is that politicians who highlight these issues, expose themselves to the risks of being branded a racist or a phobic. There is nothing racist or phobic about having the courage to bring out valid concerns for discussion.

Freedom of Expression

Democracy, like any system of government, can be abused. For a democratic society to work, citizens must oblige themselves to make well-informed decisions in exercising their power to vote for their best personal interest. Therefore, it is of utmost importance that all voters be well informed, and be provided access to all information, so they can exercise their right to vote based on the best available information.

Sometimes, people and groups try to silence, ridicule or discredit other individuals in having their say. We need to recognise that, anytime we censor the rights of another person to express himself, we deny ourselves, and others, the right to hear what needs to be said. We begin making bad choices because we do not have access to information required to make well-informed voting decisions.

Centuries ago, people tried to silence scientists. The majority thought their ideas were idiotic, outlandish and senseless. They were ridiculed but as it turned out, they were merely asserting the truth.

British philosopher, John Milton (1608-1678), advanced several arguments defending Freedom of Speech which are summarised by the contributors of Wikipedia[195] as follows:

- A nation's unity is created through blending individual differences, rather than imposing homogeneity from above.
- The ability to explore the fullest range of ideas on a given issue is essential to any learning process.
- Truth cannot be arrived upon unless all points of view are first considered.
- Censorship acts to the detriment of material progress.
- If the facts are laid bare, truth will defeat falsehood in open competition, but this cannot be left for a single individual to determine. It is up to each individual to uncover their own truth; no one is wise enough to act as a censor for all individuals.

Naom Chomsky, the linguist, intellectual and political activist, said in a 1992 multi award-winning documentary film, *Manufacturing Consent: Noam Chomsky and the Media*:

> If you believe in freedom of speech, you believe in freedom of speech for views you don't like. Goebbels was in favour of freedom of speech for views he liked. So was Stalin. If you're in favour of freedom of speech, that means you're in favour of freedom of speech precisely for views you despise.

Freedom of expression is now a universal law recognised under the following statutes:

- Article 19 of the Universal Declaration of Human Rights
- Article 19 of the International Covenant on Civil and Political Rights (ICCPR)

Article 19 of the ICCPR recognises the right to freedom of speech as:

1) Everyone shall have the right to hold opinions without interference.
2) Everyone shall have the right to freedom of expression; this right shall include freedom to seek, receive and impart information and ideas of all kinds, regardless of frontiers, either orally, in writing or in print, in the form of art, or through any other media of his choice.
3) The exercise of the rights provided for in paragraph 2 of this article carries with it special duties and responsibilities. It may therefore be subject to certain restrictions, but these shall only be such as are provided by law and are necessary:
    a) For respect of the rights or reputations of others.
    b) For the protection of national security or of public order, or of public health or morals.

I will now provide you with three examples of how our right to free speech and expression is being undermined by religious beliefs.

Submission

The film, *Submission,* is a 10-minute film directed by Theo Van Gogh and written by Ayaan Hirsi Ali. It was shown on the Dutch public broadcasting network (VPRO) on August 29, 2004.

> The film tells the story of four fictional characters played by a single actress wearing a veil, but clad in a see-through chador, her naked body painted with verses from the Koran. The characters are Muslim women who have been abused in various ways. The film contains monologues of these women and dramatically highlights three verses of the Qur'an, 4:34, 2:222 and 24:2 that authorize mistreatment of women, by showing them painted on women's bodies.

Hirsi Ali, now a Muslim atheist, was motivated to make the film because of what she saw as injustice. She said:

> It is written in the Koran a woman may be slapped if she is disobedient. This is one of the evils I wish to point out in the film.[196] If you are a Muslim woman and you read the Koran, and you read in there that you should be raped if you say 'no' to your husband, that is offensive. And that is insulting.[197]

In her book, *Infidel*, Hirsi Ali tells us what happened two months after the film was released:

> Theo van Gogh got up to go to work at his film production company in Amsterdam. He took out his old black bicycle and headed down a main road. Waiting in a doorway was a Moroccan man with a handgun and two butcher knives.
>
> As Theo cycled down the Linneaeusstraat, Muhammad Bouyeri approached. He pulled out his gun and shot Theo several times. Theo fell off his bike and lurched across the road, then collapsed. Bouyeri followed. Theo begged, "Can't we talk about this?" but Bouyeri shot him four more times. Then he took out one of his butcher knives and sawed into Theo's throat. With the other knife, he stabbed a five-page letter onto Theo's chest. The letter was addressed to me.

After this incident, Hirsi Ali went into hiding. The Dutch secret service raised the level of security provided to her. Eventually, she was moved to the United States. In a letter she provided to the New York Times in May 23, 2006, her sister in Kenya warned her:

> *Your husband is looking for you... and the whole search is being coordinated by father here... Practically all the Osman Mahamud (Ali's clan) in that area are looking for you everywhere. Be warned.*

Even her father chose his religion over his daughter, in his letter he wrote[198]:

> *Dear Deceitful Fox,*
>
> *You do not need me and I do not need you. I just invoked Allah to disgrace you, as you have disgraced me. Amen!*
>
> *This is the last message you will receive from me, as your letter was the last message I will accept from you. Go to hell! And the devil be with you.*
>
> *May Allah punish you for your deception, Amen!*
>
> *Yours, The Fool*

Geert Wilders

Geert Wilders, a Dutch politician, member of the Dutch Parliament since 1998, is also another fighter for freedom of speech. In 2008, he released a short film titled *Fitna*. Fitna means 'disagreement and division among people' in Arabic. Wilders said the 15-minute film showed how verses from the Qur'an are being used today to incite modern Muslims to behave violently and antidemocratically based on those verses.

Fitna was released on the Internet on the video sharing website Liveleak, which was immediately removed because of serious threats being made to staff. After security upgrades to ensure the safety of the staff of Liveleak, *Fitna* was re-released.

Prior to the release of the film, Geert Wilders did an interview with Fox News where he made statements relevant to our discussion.

When asked why he would release a film, with all these threats of riots on the streets, he responded:

> That [threats are being made] just proves my point even more, that it is needed, a lot, to make such a movie. Indeed, only the proposition that I was going to make a movie [got] the Dutch

government panicking, talking to imams all over the country, Muslim groups threatening to go to courts to prevent the movie being published, [it is as if] we have no freedom of speech here in the Netherlands. All the reactions, even before the movie is finished, let alone broadcasted on television, prove my point that it is very needed to make [such] a movie. People should bear some criticism also in the Muslim community.

When interviewed, Geert Wilders already lived three years of his life under high security. He was asked by the interviewer whether it was more prudent for him to 'temper' what he was saying, just a little bit. Wilders response was:

If I do that, if I would moderate my voice or maybe stop talking like that, then the people who are not using democratic means, but undemocratic means – like the death threats that I am getting everyday – then, those people, would win.

In a democracy, if you are against somebody, you use your freedom of speech. Go and debate, write an article or vote for a party that thinks differently... This is civil society. This is everything that should be done in a democracy.

More than half a million people voted for my party and me personally, so I have an obligation to the voters who expect me not to stop saying what I really think. If I stop, then I would not only be playing a nasty game to my voters, I would also give a signal to everybody who says, 'If you say what we don't like, we will kill you, behead you or do terrible things to you', that they are winning.[qq]

[qq] I have paraphrased the last paragraph for clarity. The original transcript is this: "So, if I stop saying what I really think, more than half a million people my party and me personally, so I also have an obligation to the voters who expect this from me... If I do not do that, I would not only play a nasty game to my voters but I would also give a signal to everybody who says, 'If you say what we don't like, we will kill you, behead you or do terrible things to you', that they are winning."

Danish Cartoons

Perhaps, the most popular incident that most of us have heard about was that of the Danish Cartoonist, Kurt Westergaard. He created the controversial cartoon of the Muslim prophet, Muhammad, wearing a bomb as a turban.

After the publication of his cartoons, Muslims, worldwide, were enraged. In two days of heavy rioting, five people were killed in two major cities and a private property, worth millions, was torched in Pakistan.[199]

I have collected what some banners and chants said in these protests:

1) Death to Denmark.
2) Hang those who drew the insulting cartoons.
3) This is the beginning of the end for you disbelievers.
4) Denmark, go to Hell. George Bush, go to Hell. U.S.A, to Hell. Nuke, Nuke Denmark.
5) We want Danish Blood.
6) Europe, you will pay. Your annihilation is on its way.
7) UK, you obey, Bin Laden is on his way.
8) May they bomb Denmark so we can invade their country and take their wives as war booty.

Sources:

1. Times Online. 70,000 gather for violent Pakistan cartoons protest. Published February 15, 2006.
http://www.timesonline.co.uk/tol/news/world/asia/article731005.ece
(Accessed 15 August 2008)
2. CBN News. News report by Dale Hurd. Video Title: Out Of Time: Radical Islam Taking Over Europe & West.
http://www.youtube.com/watch?v=ocU5x_03MDM (Accessed: 15 August 2008).

On February 12, 2008, Danish Security and Intelligence Service, PET, arrested three people: two Tunisians and one Dane of Moroccan origin. They were planning to murder Westergaard. In a statement on Jyllands-Posten's website, Mr Westergaard said: "Of course I fear for my life when the police intelligence service say that some people have concrete plans to kill me... But I have turned fear into anger and resentment".[200]

After reading Westergaard's story, it was, again, made clear to me that religion is a tool that helps us attain peace and harmony. Religious memes work to propagate themselves with little regard to the human costs.

The publishing and drawing of the cartoons was offensive to many Muslims and they are all within their rights to protest. What is a separate issue, however, is the way most of the protests have been conducted. The slogans and the chants, themselves, were criminal. They incited and spread hate, murder and violence. Many other religions have been offended by other forms of expression, in film and in various forms of art, but none have allowed themselves to react and behave in such an outrageous manner.

What is most unacceptable for a society that values freedom of expression is that three men plotted to murder the cartoonist. Westergaard was lucky to have been protected by the Danish police. Unfortunately for Theo Van Gogh, the Dutch police was not there to save him.

Indoctrination of Children

Our children are our future. In a few decades, they will run our countries. They will make decisions for us. They will be our politicians, doctors, lawyers and military leaders. If we want to change the world, we start with our kids. If we teach them right, the future will be bright. If we teach them wrong, it will be bleak. For the sake of our children and theirs, they have the right to be taught right... but even in this, we are failing.

The Dover Trial

Some people have become so religious that they attempt to promote the biblical account of how the world came about as real science. This happened in what is now known as The Dover Trial: *Kitzmiller v. Dover Area School District* (2005). In this case, eleven parents of students in Dover, York County, Pennsylvania, sued the Dover Area School District for trying to teach creationism, disguised as Intelligent Design, as an alternative to the theory of evolution. It was concluded that Intelligent Design was not real science and should not be taught in science classes:

> Teaching intelligent design in public school biology classes violates the Establishment Clause of the First Amendment to the Constitution of the United States (and Article I, Section 3 of the Pennsylvania State Constitution) because intelligent design is not science and "cannot uncouple itself from its creationist, and thus religious, antecedents."

On this topic, here are a few interesting polls done in America by various organisations:

1) **Question**: "Which of the following statements comes closest to your views on the origin and development of human beings?"

    Results:
    - 36% said that human beings have developed over millions of years from less advanced forms of life, but God guided this process.
    - 14% said that human beings have developed over millions of years from less advanced forms of life, but God had no part in this process.
    - 44% said that God created human beings pretty much in their present form at one time within the last 10,000 years or so.
    - The rest was unsure.

    Gallup Poll: May 8-11, 2008.[201]

2) **Question**: "Would you generally favour or oppose teaching creationism along with evolution in public schools?"

   Results:
   - 58% said they favoured the teaching of creationism.
   - 35% said they opposed the teaching of creationism.

   Pew Research Center: July 6-19, 2006.[202]

Because of their parents' religious beliefs, children are now at risk of being taught what has already been proven wrong.

Jesus Camp: Indoctrination of Children

In a 2006 documentary directed by Rachel Grady and Heidi Ewing, called *Jesus Camp*, we see how parents take their children to a Pentecostal, charismatic summer camp in the United States. Becky Fisher and her ministry, *Kids In Ministry International*, runs the operation. She advocates for us to start training our kids to become an 'army of God' because, she says, our 'enemies' are focussed on training theirs.

The film follows three children: Levi, Rachael and Tory (Victoria). Levi is home schooled. He gets taught from a book that attempts to reconcile the bible with scientific principles. Detached from any outside input, he is told that global warming is a hoax. Rachel looks at other churches as 'dead churches', churches God would not like to go to. Religion breeds sectarianism at an early age.

Evolution

The evidence for the theory of Evolution is so great that even Pope John Paul II and the current Pope Benedict cannot deny it.

In 22 October 1996, Pope John Paul II addressed the Pontifical Academy of Sciences where he reaffirmed the theory of evolution is no longer just a hypothesis.

> In his encyclical Humani Generis (1950), my predecessor Pius XII has already affirmed that there is no conflict between evolution and the doctrine of the faith regarding man and his vocation, provided that we do not lose sight of certain fixed points....Today, more than a half-century after the appearance of that encyclical, some new findings lead us toward the recognition of evolution as more than an hypothesis. In fact it is remarkable that this theory has had progressively greater influence on the spirit of researchers, following a series of discoveries in different scholarly disciplines. The convergence in the results of these independent studies – which was neither planned nor sought – constitutes in itself a significant argument in favour of the theory.[203]

On 26th July 2007, Pope Benedict said there is substantial scientific proof of the theory of evolution:

> ...There is much scientific proof in favour of evolution, which appears as a reality that we must see and which enriches our understanding of life and being as such.[204]

If these two men, men who have the most to lose in admitting the accuracy of the theory of evolution, have succumbed, then surely, the pressure of mounting scientific evidence in favour of evolution must be so great that it cannot be denied. Yet, many religious people today still prefer to be ignorant and insist that the creation story, told and invented by people hundreds of years ago, is the true account of our genesis.

Faith Schools

The number of faith schools is expanding. Religious parents are segregating their kids from the rest of society. As a result, we are being fractured and divided more and more along religious lines.

This particular issue was discussed in a British television series, *The Big Debate: Sectarian Schools in Britain*. In Australia, and I'm sure in many parts of the world, there are many sectarian schools and this debate is relevant everywhere.

Professor Richard Dawkins was part of the debating panel and he said:

> I think it is important for children to learn about religion. What I am against is the labelling of children with the religion of their parents when the children are too young to know what their own views are. I am all for children being taught about a lot of different religions then making up their own minds later. What I really object to, and I think it is actually abusive to children, is to take a tiny child and say, 'You are a Christian child or you are a Muslim child'.
>
> I think it is wicked if children are told that, 'you are a member of such and such a faith simply because your parents are, because after all, every child should be able to work out for his- or herself that it is an accident of birth they just happen to be born into, say, a Catholic family or a Muslim family.
>
> As far as I can tell, by definition, a faith school is propagating one particular faith and it makes the assumption that the children in that school belong to a particular faith, which is presumably the faith of their parents.

Rabbi Dr Jonathan Romain, Minister at Maidenhead Synagogue added:

> I am a rabbi and therefore I do take faith seriously but I am worried about faith schools, their social consequences, because if you have separate Jewish, Catholic and Muslim schools, essentially you are segregating the children. They are growing up in ignorance of each other and we are going to have a whole generation who simply do not know how each other looks like. And yes, they may know about each other from books but that is not the same as interacting with each other.
>
> The same goes for parents, of course. If you separate the children, you are separating the parents who don't meet at the school gates, at school plays or summer plays and therefore, we

are cutting a huge sway through society and precisely because it is a multi-faith society. It is important that children know each other and interact together.

For me, faith should come from the home. Schools should be cross-community, where they teach about faith and you learn about each other's history and culture. The actual indoctrination should come from the home or from weekend schools. Schools should be where you build bridges, not to erect barriers and I see this from a religious point of view because I strongly believe… that you should love your neighbour as yourself. But you can only love your neighbour if you know your neighbour.

One of the most important points made in the debate was made by the Director of the Hindu Academy, Jay Lakhani:

First of all we hear the language: 'tolerate people of other religions'… [or people saying that they are] 'learning to respect people of other religions'.

This is a red herring because in reality what they mean is this:

'We are right and they are wrong but we won't make a fuss about it at the moment. They'll find out soon enough when they die'.

Faiths themselves are very exclusivist, divisive and they are something that should not be funded by public money.

In this debate, Kat Stark, NUS Women's Officer, emphasised that there is conflict between what we agree on as a democratic society versus the values advocated by religions.

For example, when a democratic society has agreed that women should have the freedom to abort a baby or not, religious schools are still allowed to insist that abortion is wrong. Likewise, we believe that homosexuals should be treated without discrimination and yet they are treated with contempt along religious grounds.

CHAPTER 18:
THE FALLACY OF RELIGIOUS MODERATION

Our sense of morality has modernised. Richard Dawkins thinks of it as an ever-changing phenomenon that changes with time: a moral zeitgeist. *Zeitgeist* is a German word meaning 'spirit of the times'.

> Slavery, which was taken for granted in the Bible and throughout most of history, was abolished in civilized countries in the nineteenth century. All civilized nations now accept what was widely denied up to the 1920s, that a woman's vote, in an election or on a jury, is the equal of a man's. In today's enlightened societies (a category that manifestly does not include, for example, Saudi Arabia), women are no longer regarded as property, as they clearly were in biblical times. Any modern legal system would have prosecuted Abraham for child abuse. And if he had actually carried through his plan to sacrifice Isaac, we would have convicted him of first-degree murder. Yet, according to the mores of his time, his conduct was entirely admirable, obeying God's commandment. Religious or not, we have all changed massively in our attitude to what is right and what is wrong.[205]

How does it work? Well, our sense of morality is formed from our analyses of events and experiences we have gained from life. When we hear or read an inspiring, or maddening, story in the news, we tell our friends, family and neighbours. We talk about I in pubs, in restaurants and other social places where we get to exchange ideas with other people.

We form our moral stance on matters and events in the world we live in, from several sources. When we read a book or an article, when we watch a movie or a TV show, we consider the dilemmas the protagonists face and the choices and decisions they need to make. We ask ourselves what we would do if we were in their place.

Another major source of our morality comes from the lead of our modern legal systems. They trial difficult cases and our judges make interpretations that act as examples and precedents to our society's idea of what is justice and fairness, right and wrong.

For most of my life, I considered myself a Christian who was adapting to the moral zeitgeist, rejecting the bad stuff from the Bible. However, when I had another look at the Bible, I came to the stark reality that my beliefs had deviated away from what it was actually saying. My idea of God no longer resembled the Christian god.

As it turns out, I am not alone in this. Many of us, who consider themselves 'moderately' religious, do this. We invent our own idea of God because our sense of morality is changing. If we look at our history, we can see that, when the Bible was written, the early concepts of God evolved. The idea of God began as one whom Abraham could have meals with, or one with whom Jacob could wrestle.

After that, people conceptualised Him to take sides between two warring factions. Thereafter, we have a mysterious three-in-one God: the Father, the Son and the Holy Spirit. During the 17th and 18th centuries, God became less personal. Suddenly, Deists believed that God created the world but was since unheard of. Then there was the Pantheistic idea of God being the same as nature or the universe. Just recently, as we became less racist and less sexist, many people started considering the possibility that perhaps God is black or that He might be female after all.

The definition of God had become so varied that perhaps He might be even one of us. In her 1995 hit song, 'What If God Was One Of Us?' Joan Osbourne sang:

> What if God was one of us,
> Just a slob like one of us,
> Just a stranger on the bus,
> Trying to make his way home,
> Back up to heaven all alone,
> Nobody calling on the phone,
> Except for the Pope maybe in Rome?

What do I mean by us inventing our own idea of God? We invent or develop our own individual concept of God when we stop reading and interpreting the Scriptures literally. It begins when we pick and choose bits and pieces of ideas and beliefs everywhere. We start incorporating ideas from the Bible as well as branches of science, philosophy, other belief systems and popular culture. In other words, we become 'moderately religious'.

We become 'moderately religious' because of...

1. Ignorance.
2. Dissonance.

Moderation From Our Ignorance

Because we do not really understand, or have not read much of the Bible or the Koran, we become 'moderately religious'. We develop our own idea of God while remaining ignorant of what our Scriptures are actually saying. So, we just make stuff up as we go through life, picking up bits and pieces of ideas everywhere and incorporate them into our own unique belief system.

Moderation From Our Dissonance

We also become 'moderately religious' because it is a way to reconcile the dissonance between the teachings of our Scriptures with other non-religious, secular ideas we adopt. We want to believe the Scriptures but we cannot deny the evidence against them and our thoughts become conflicted as we ask the following questions:

1. If God and religion are sources of morality, we ask why the Bible contains such abhorrent examples of immorality. What is so morally superior about barbequing our children, raping virgins, slaughtering thousands of people and plundering everything they owned? What is so morally superior about a God who allows and incites such atrocities towards others and is even willing to have a share of the loot?

2. If God is an all-Knowing being who wrote the Scriptures himself, with or without scribes, then why does it feel so much like it was written by a group of people from a culture that lived in the Middle East deserts thousands of years ago?

3. For a book being purported to be the 'word of God', a god who can foresee the future, the Bible flaunts lamentable limitations in its wisdom, vision and imagination. It provides plenty of instructions about making sacrifices and stoning people, but it contains no references to modern cars, dinosaur bones, planets, galaxies, DNA, tectonic plates or evolution.

Such inquiries highlight the irrationality of our beliefs but still, we are unable, or unwilling, to reject our belief in God and religion. Because of this, we experience dissonance.

To resolve this difficulty, we become 'moderately religious'. We allow ourselves to relax our interpretation of the scriptures. We say things like, 'Well, perhaps the Bible is not supposed to be read literally anyway'. You hear people say the Bible is outdated. We should only read it allegorically and metaphorically to get what we need from it.

But don't these concessions sound so much like we are seeking to believe in God despite our reasoning telling us that He may not exist, and the scriptures were written by ordinary people?

In the end, we pick and choose bits of verses of the Bible we like and cast aside the parts we do not like. This was the conclusion of A.J. Jacobs, the New York Times bestselling author and *Esquire* editor. He claims to be a human guinea pig because he has experimented on himself. He tried to live a full year of his life following all the prescriptions of the Bible. He wrote about it in his book *The Year of Living Biblically*.

He could not bring himself to follow much of the Bible's prescriptions. He found that following all the teachings of the Bible was unworkable in today's modern society. He had to disobey many aspects of living biblically. He did not stone adulterers, for example. According to Jacobs, the only way a person can live according to the Bible, was if he picked and chose only the good bits from the holy book. I suppose Jacob's conclusion echoed what many 'moderately religious' have concluded for a long time... except he did it with an actual experiment.

I am not altogether comfortable with the idea of picking and choosing from our holy books. To me, it implies that we actually do not believe the Bible was completely written by a wise, all-knowing God. By giving ourselves permission to pick and choose bits and pieces of the Scriptures, we are implying that God did not have enough foresight, writing skill or wisdom to make the context and the content of the Bible more universal and everlasting. Furthermore, by only choosing to abide by parts of the Scriptures, we are rejecting some of God's own work.

The closest idea to which I can liken 'religious moderation', is 'alcohol moderation'. In a social gathering, what do we do to moderate our alcohol intake? We do any or both of the following:

- We abstain from consuming more alcohol.
- We combat its effect by eating more food and drinking water.

In other words, to moderate our alcohol, we stop drinking it altogether for the duration of the event, or we dilute it with non-alcoholic substances by having less of it over time. Religious moderation is similar.

We moderate our religiosity by abstaining from it entirely or by replacing religious ideas with non-religious ones. To be really sober, we forgo it altogether.

As I have argued in chapter 14, the main purpose of successful religions, is to propagate. As agents for our religions, we do everything in our power to make this come true. However, even if it was once considered noble to obey all the commandments of the Bible, nowadays, we have to restrain ourselves from being carried too far. As a result, we do not go around killing infidels and unbelievers.

'Moderates' distinguish themselves from the 'Literalists', who read and interpret the Scriptures literally. Moderates claim that those who read the holy books literally are 'Extremists'. However, it seems that these so-called 'Extremists' are actually the true believers of their religions because they believe in all the following:

- God exists.
- Everything that is written in the Bible is God's word.
- Faith in God's wisdom and foresight means that they must follow his every command, no matter how cruel and unjust.
- Since God exists, He wants us to live by His book.

Because extremists are the true believers of the Scriptures, they are emboldened to carry out the instructions of their holy books. They are able to do whatever it takes to spread the 'word of God' and subdue the Earth until everyone is converted. Because they believe that God is on their side, they go around killing 'infidels', blowing themselves up, carrying out their ordained commands.

Many 'moderates' need to confront the stark fact that being a 'moderate' becomes an untenable position:

- Do you believe that God, in the form of Yahweh, exists? If not, then you are atheistic to the God of the Christians, Muslims and Jews.

- Do you believe that God wrote the Bible? If not, then you are committing heresy because such a claim is contrary to established doctrines.

- Do you obey all of God's instructions and recognise all laws must be based on God's law? If not, then you are considered as ungrateful and disobedient to the god who created you.

The 'middle' ground of 'religious moderation' is a fantasy that we entertain, because we are unwilling or unable to reconcile the totalitarian and tyrannical nature of many religious beliefs with everything else we know to be just and right.

We entertain 'moderation' at our own peril because like Sam Harris pointed out in the *End of Faith:* only in an environment of the moderately religious can extremism arise. Moderately religious people sympathise and give cover for the true believers of their faiths.

When we consider the power of today's modern weapons to destroy, we live in a dangerous climate when many of us are holding on to intolerant beliefs, from centuries gone by.

As we awaken from our slumber and confusion, however, we see that many of the real believers have been hard at work. Today, while many of us are in a fantasy land of 'religious moderation', we are under siege by extremists.

As I write this, the 2002 Bali bombers who killed 202 people in Indonesia, are in the news. Three of them are to be executed. Interviewed by the media, they threaten that other 'holy warriors' will avenge their death. In their own words, they made it clear that those 202 people died because they were infidels: non-believers of the Islam faith.

A journalist asked Mukhlas, one of the bombers, whether he was sorry for what he had done. Mukhlas said, "I've never regretted these bombings... I will not ask for forgiveness from those infidels."[206] The journalists' expectation for an apology highlights our ignorance to the true motive of extremists. Why do we expect terrorists like Mukhlas to apologise? He has successfully carried out his intention.

He said, in his trial, that westerners are "dirty animals and insects that need to be wiped out"[207]. How, exactly, are westerners such 'dirty animals and insects' and why do they need to be 'wiped out'? Well, they have already told us, haven't they? According to Osama Bin Laden, westerners fornicate, they engage in homosexuality, they drink alcohol, they gamble and they use interest rates: all of which are contrary to God's law.

Amrozi, another one of the Bali Bombers, iterates this for us. He said that the West uses six instruments for global domination: secularism, democracy, human rights, the free market, drugs and opposition to terrorism.[208]

Even after 'the true believers', themselves, have been so direct with what they want from us, even after they explain why they do what they do, we still refuse to believe them. We refuse to see how they can be against our democratic, secular ways. We presume that the 'extremists' are interpreting their religious beliefs wrongly. But, it is us who are wrong. It is the religious beliefs themselves we need to investigate.

What is happening now is the result of the conflict between ancient, but violent, religious memes, clashing against the modern ideas we have acquired after a long history of experience and experimentation.

We need to recognise that religious beliefs exist only to benefit their own progeny, not ours. In their struggle to assert themselves and dominate our minds, the memes inside our heads are commandeering us to wage war against each other. We simply become collateral damage.

The sad thing is, even if many people kill and die for these memes, they are not even alive. It is us who choose to act upon them and so they manifest themselves in our world.

CHAPTER 19:
WHY WE NEED TO JUSTIFY OUR BELIEFS

When we are born, we adopt the nationality of our parents' country. However, when we grow up, we have no reason to stay in a nation rife with violence, corruption or poverty. Likewise, we have no reason not to change religions if we feel they no longer reflect the truth. Unfortunately for others, the punishment for apostasy is death. If, however, we are fortunate enough to 'shop around' for a religion, we would like to make sure we join the authentic one.

We would not want to join a wrong religion and end up wasting our lives praising the wrong god, following the wrong rituals, observing the wrong beliefs and singing the wrong hymns.

The problem is that we have no way of knowing how to ascertain the truths of religious beliefs. In fact, when we ask organised religions for reasons and evidence attesting to their claims, they might even consider it rude to ask. It is almost as if the truth does not matter!

Douglas Adams, author of *Hitchhiker's Guide to the Galaxy*, said:

> Religion…has certain ideas at the heart of it which we call sacred or holy or whatever. What it means is, 'Here is an idea or a notion that you're not allowed to say anything bad about; you're just not. Why not? – because you're not!' If somebody votes for a party that you don't agree with, you're free to argue about it as much as you like; everybody will have an argument but nobody feels aggrieved by it. If somebody thinks taxes should go up or down, you are free to have an argument about

it. But on the other hand if somebody says 'I mustn't move a light switch on a Saturday', you say, 'I respect that'.

Why should it be that it's perfectly legitimate to support the Labour party or the Conservative party, Republicans or Democrats, this model of economics versus that, Macintosh instead of Windows – but to have an opinion about how the Universe began, about who created the Universe... no, that's holy? ... We are used to not challenging ideas... yet when you look at it rationally there is no reason why those ideas shouldn't be as open to debate as any other, except that we have agreed somehow between us that they shouldn't be.

As a society we have, somehow, accepted the notion that we are not supposed to criticise religious beliefs because it would be considered heretical or blasphemous. What is ironic to me is that religions are heretical and blasphemous to one another.

They make contradictory claims, all without evidence for us to consider. There is no compulsion for religions to provide good reasons, backed by evidence, for their beliefs. So, we have no way of proving the truthfulness of a religious claim against that of another.

I find this disconcerting especially because people, who invent and believe religious ideas, are quite capable of self-delusion. Still, we are supposed to respect religious beliefs, regardless of how much they go against everything else we know to be true.

In the modern world, we find ourselves sharing cities, living with people from many varied backgrounds and religious beliefs. In a secular society, everyone has the right to believe whatever they want.

We have to remember, however, that everything we do is based on what we believe. Our beliefs influence where we stand on many important issues like sexuality, abortion, ethics and terrorism, amongst many others. In a democratic society, we vote for leaders to whom we abrogate responsibility to make decisions that affect us all.

Since all votes are equal, the value of a well thought-out vote is the same as that of a careless one. Religious beliefs, therefore, influence the outcome of political elections and how we are all governed.

Our lives are affected by the religious beliefs of others. Here are examples:

1) If you are a woman, like Elizabeth Fritzl, who was captured, raped and impregnated, you may not abort pregnancy because someone else's religious beliefs have voted for a leader who agreed to ban abortion.[π]
2) If you are a homosexual, your rights are hindered because someone else's religious beliefs insist that homosexuality is a sin.
3) If you are a woman in the USA, suffering from the human papilloma virus (HPV), which kills five hundred thousand American women each year, you do not get the chance to live because the vaccine is withheld for public use. This is because some religious people would rather have you die of HPV, to serve as an example, in their quest to deter their daughters from having sexual intercourse before they are married.
4) In the future, when any of your loved ones, your spouse or your parents, suffer a disease, they might have to die sooner than necessary, because someone else's religious beliefs are working to hinder the progress of stem-cell research today.

[π] As I am writing this section of the book, the Australian Government, has just modified its Abortion Law Reform Bill. It requires doctors with a conscientious objection to abortion to refer their patient to another registered health practitioner who they know does not have any objection to abortion. In response, 'Catholic Archbishop Denis Hart has said the clause would force Catholic doctors and hospitals to break the law, because they would not provide referrals for the purpose of abortions'.
Source: The Age. *Abortion Clause Follows Legal Advice.*
http://news.theage.com.au/national/abortion-clause-follows-legal-advice-20080923-4m3q.html (23 Sept 2008).

What we believe, has real consequences. Our private religious beliefs affect everybody else. What we allow ourselves to believe on the basis of pure faith alone, can disadvantage, or even cause the suffering and death of other human beings, somewhere on the planet, now or in the future.

As I said before, in a secular society, we all have the right to believe in whatever we want. However, the right, the freedom and the power to believe in anything of our choosing, comes with great responsibility.

We can believe in anything we want, but we have an obligation to justify our beliefs to other people because it impacts their lives and well-being. Likewise they have a duty to justify theirs to us, because what they choose to believe in, also affects our lives and our well-being.

CHAPTER 20:
A WORLD WITHOUT GOD

In chapter 13, I argued that our religions were initially used by our ancient leaders to solve problems. They needed religion to…

1) **Understand** and explain natural phenomena.
2) **Control** and organise individuals within their societies.
3) **Inspire** the masses to achieve a common goal.

The problems our ancestors faced in the past remain to be the problems we face today. We still strive to understand ourselves and nature, we still struggle to discipline members of our societies to be good and we still want to inspire individuals to contribute and make the world a better place.

Since I have argued that religions do not really solve these problems for us, it would be fair for many readers to expect that I put forward my own thoughts. Therefore, I feel obligated to submit alternative suggestions that can lead us to possible solutions to the same problems our ancestors have sought to solve. In the next chapters, I provide my own thoughts and beliefs on the challenges we face.

This is what I will be elaborating on:

1) In our attempts to understand everything about us and the universe, we should build our knowledge on reason based on evidence.

2) Our behaviour is largely determined by our needs and wants. To get what we need and want from life, sometimes, we mistreat others. Therefore, there is a need to regulate and organise individuals and societies.

   For people to get what they want from others, we must create as many possibilities for them to give what they can, in exchange for what they need, justly and fairly. If we do not do this, people will resort to violence and we will have to rely heavily on our laws and law-enforcement organisations to maintain temporary peace and stability.

3) Our society has needs. We need individuals to step forward and contribute. We need the best and most suited in the roles they serve. Instead of coercing people to do what our religions tell us they should be doing, we should encourage them to identify what it is they are good at, and what it is they love doing. This way, we can help them live satisfying lives. Most importantly, we must reward them appropriately, in accordance to the value they provide to the community and to the planet.

CHAPTER 21:
THE POWER OF REASON

With many of the things we do not know, and cannot know, living life is like venturing inside a dark and confusing labyrinth. We can all lose our way. We need light to guide us. People have always relied on their gods and religions to act as this much-needed guide. We have seen, however, that because religions and gods are the products of our culture – products we create – they are no more able to guide us than we can guide ourselves.

In an amoral world and in the absence of clear-cut answers, philosophical questions still gnaw at us. What kind of life should we lead? What kind of world should we build? What kind of people should we be?

In answering these questions, we form ideas and beliefs. The problem is that, they are not necessarily true. The question we asked ourselves at the end of chapter 9 was: **How can we be certain that we do not choose our beliefs simply to delude ourselves in justifying and rationalising our thoughts, emotions, behaviour, attitude and actions?**

In our attempts to understand everything about us and the universe, we should build our knowledge on reason based on evidence. To believe in something, we must have good reasons to believe it. A reason is a good reason if it is based on intelligent ideas. We recognise ideas to be intelligent when they have the power to predict. This is because we can only predict after we have acquired the knowledge that is close to the truth.

To develop intelligent models, we need to use good information. Good information is based on evidence. Evidence must be understandable, relevant, reliable and verifiable.

Prediction And Intelligence

Attaching the idea of intelligence to prediction has been presented by Jeff Hawkins, inventor of the *Palm Pilot*, now working in neuroscience because of his interest in artificial intelligence. He published a book *On Intelligence* and he spoke at the 2003 TED Conferences.

The following is what I got from his talk:

- To understand something properly enables us to make successful predictions.
- Intelligence is making predictions about events.

To explain how the ability to predict is an indicator for intelligence, consider the following examples.

The Face Example

We have a database of information stored in our brain about the human face, collected throughout our lifetime of observation and experiences. We know there are two eyes on both sides of the top-third of a face, one nose in middle of the face and one mouth in the middle, bottom-third. There are also two ears jutting out of a round or circular shape connecting all the components of a human face.

How do we know that our knowledge of faces represents the truth? We know because out of the hundreds, thousands or millions of faces we have seen in our lives, all have these features.

In having this knowledge, we constantly make predictions when we look at a face or a photograph. If we look at the top-third of the face, we expect to see two eyes. However, if we see a nose instead, we get taken aback. We understand human faces and we think we are looking at a human face, but the misplacement of the nose is in direct disagreement with our expectations.

When we encounter something that goes against our predictions, we modify our model of the world. In the example above, if we see an eye where the nose should be, we make two guesses:

- We are not looking at a human face, OR
- Our understanding of human faces no longer hold true and requires modification or, it needs to be jettisoned altogether.

We then have the following options:

- We might verify whether we are, indeed, looking at a real human face. If it was a photograph, it may have been digitally modified to add a nose where the eyes are supposed to be.
- If we confirm that this face belongs to a real person, then we need to modify our model of faces. We can say that even though almost 99.9999% of faces still fit our model of faces: 1 out of 1,000,000 faces have a nose at the top.
- If we do make an exception, we can investigate why the person's nose appears where his eyes are supposed to be. We may then verify the phenomenon as the result of a deformity caused by so-and-so.

The Gravity Example

Established scientific theories are considered products of intelligence because of their ability to predict.

Take, for example, the gravitational equation:

$v = gt$

Where:
- **v** is the velocity of the object
- **g** is the gravitational constant. On Earth, this constant is 9.8 m/s² or 32 ft/s²
- **t** is the measure time of the fall (seconds)
- **gt** is the product of g times t

In English, this formula says the velocity of a falling object is equal to the gravitational constant, which is 9.8 m/s² on our planet, multiplied by how long it had been falling.

If you have never encountered this formula before and physicists tell you that it will help you predict the velocity with which an object will hit the ground, would you believe it? We should only believe it if it has the power to predict. So, we need to test it. How?

Here's one way. We would drop a ball from the top of a building. We put a huge ruler beside the wall of the building. We need a high-speed motion film camera with a time recorder. We drop the object and we film the entire event.

We take the film (or DVD or hard drive) and plug it into a computer where we can view the film in slow motion. We will see the ball falling, before hitting the ground, with the ruler beside it, and the timer ticking. From this, we can calculate to prove and satisfy ourselves that this formula is indeed true.

After realising that this formula is true, we come to appreciate that the people who developed it understood the concepts of velocity, gravity and time. They understood them so well that they were able to create tools, models and theories to help them, and the rest of us, make predictions.

When Knowledge Stops Working

We know that something has stopped working when it is giving us false predictions more often than not. If we believe in a certain proposition, say, the world is only 6,000 years old, then we need to take a look at other evidence to see if this is true. If 95% of that evidence suggests that our proposition is wrong, then clearly, we are wrong.

Once a theory stops working, once it begins to fail in its predictions, it is no longer intelligent for us to continue believing in it. After all, there is nothing intelligent about going to a doctor who keeps prescribing the wrong medicine or a lawyer who keeps giving the wrong advice.

What Constitutes Good Information?

How is it that human beings arrived to such knowledge and wisdom like the theory of gravity? They certainly did not find them in the Bible or the Koran. Since the *Ages of Reason and Enlightenment*, Europeans began breaking away from the intellectually-bankrupt regime of religion. It was no longer satisfactory to rely on religion and superstition. Instead of using more faith and more praying, they turned to reason and evidence to back their beliefs. The only guide they had was good information.

Good information often has the following qualities:

1) It is understandable.
2) It is relevant to the problem for which it has been sought.
3) It is reliable and independently verifiable.
4) It is comparable and consistent with other sources of information.

Understandable

We must make sure all information we use is understandable so those who are willing to understand it, indeed can.

In medieval Europe, the Catholic Church declared it a crime for anybody to understand the Bible. It was not allowed to be translated and everybody had to consult bishops and priests instead. People's ignorance of the Bible and their inability to interpret it has allowed priests, bishops and unscrupulous entrepreneurs to profit from expensive tickets to heaven.

When translation is not a problem, many religious doctrines remain incomprehensible because of their nature. For example, try to understand the doctrine of the Holy Trinity as provided by *The Catholic Encyclopaedia*:

> In the unity of the Godhead there are three Persons, the Father, the Son, and the Holy Spirit, these Three Persons being truly distinct one from another. Thus, in the words of the Athanasian Creed: 'the Father is God, the Son is God, and the Holy Spirit is God, and yet there are not three Gods but one God.'

The third-century theologian St Gregory, the Miracle Worker, helped clarify this for us:

> There is therefore nothing created, nothing subject to another in the Trinity: nor is there anything that has been added as though it once had not existed, but had entered afterwards: therefore the Father has never been without the Son, nor the Son without the Spirit: and this same Trinity is immutable and unalterable forever.

To other monotheists, including Muslims, this sounds like polytheism hiding under the guise of monotheism.

Relevance and Materiality

Information must be relevant to the problem for which it has been sought. It must also be material. Materiality of information refers to its significance on the outcome of a decision.

If religions and their texts are championed to help us live peaceful lives, how exactly are the stoning of people who work on the Sabbath, the hatred of homosexuals and the conversion or subjugation of infidels, relevant and material to that goal? They are not.

Reliability, Observability and Verifiability

Facts, figures and data, must be reliable. They must be as free from error as possible. If something is held to be true, it must also be universally observable and verifiable by many other independent sources.

The problem with religious beliefs is that they are justified only by their holy books or the interpretation of their holy books. Anybody can make unsubstantiated claims, write them in a book and assert that the claims are true because the book said so.

If you are shopping around for a fast computer, and a salesperson tells you that he is about to sell you the fastest computer in town, wouldn't you want to verify this claim? The least you could do is compare the computer's speed with some of the other computers in the store. You might even want to check with another salesperson, working for a competing store, because you know the information you will get will be unbiased and independent from the other salesperson.

You recognise that the salesperson has a conflict of interest, between his duty to advise you with your best interest at heart, and his financial need to close the sale immediately.

In every investment and transactions we make, we require information that is reliable and independently verifiable. Yet, when it comes to shopping around for the religious beliefs we use as a basis to live our lives, many of us are too willing to believe in unverifiable claims.

Comparability and Consistency

Information must be comparable. It must be in a form that can be corroborated with other sources of information, so decision-makers can compare 'apples with apples', not 'apples with oranges'.

Facts, methods and figures must be presented in a manner that is consistent to increase their comparability in the future. The information given by evidence is consistent.

For example, theories in algebra and chemistry are consistent and evident everywhere. Once understood, a person can use them to build planes or formulate medicine, regardless of whether they are a Muslim, an atheist or a Christian.

Science makes no claim that what it finds are literal truths. It can only assert that out of so many experiments, a certain percentage of them, prove the theory to be correct. Science does not pretend to be infallible. Religion, on the other hand, does. Its texts are claimed to be the literal word of an all-knowing God. Inconsistencies in religious texts, therefore, are very dubious.

The Inconsistencies Of The Word Of God

Anyone who reads the Old Testament and the New Testament of the Bible, can, for the most part, recognise many inconsistencies between their teachings. To many people, the New Testament seems more peaceful than the Old Testament. Interestingly enough, the opposite trend occurred in the Koran.

As explained by Robert Spencer, Walid Shoebat, Serge Trifkovic and Abdullah Al-Araby[209], in the documentary: *Islam – What The West Needs To Know*, the Koran became more and more violent and intolerant as it progressed.

The first section of the Koran is the one inspired by the Prophet Muhammad when he lived in Mecca. The second section, when he lived in Medina. While he was living in Mecca, Muhammad was 'powerless'. He had little followers. He lived peacefully with the Jews and the Christians. The first section, therefore, contains most of the peaceful verses in the Koran.

When the Prophet Muhammad moved to Medina, he had grown his congregation and had become the warlord head of a totalitarian state. He became rich, powerful and very intolerant. Many of the earlier, peaceful verses became abrogated.

The following verse is what made this possible:

> Whatever a verse (revelation) We [Allah] abrogate or cause to be forgotten, We bring a better one or similar to it. Know you not that Allah is able to do all things?
> – *The Noble Koran 2:106*

So, when there are two verses that seem to be contradictory, the one that is revealed later, chronologically, is better and thus cancels the earlier one. Many of the peaceful verses Muhammad was inspired to write, while he lived in Mecca, therefore, became null and void.

Peaceful verses like: "There is no compulsion (i.e. coercion) in religion" (Koran 2:256), became overridden with verses like: "Kill the unbelievers wherever you find them... but if they repent, accept them... then leave their way free" (Koran 9:5).

The verses in the Koran are not arranged chronologically but rather, sorted by the longest chapters at the beginning, and the shortest at the end. Most of the shorter, more peaceful verses, which were written while Muhammad was in Mecca, are therefore placed at the end of the Koran. Many of these verses have been overridden by the longer verses that Muhammad was inspired to write in Medina.

The ninth chapter of the Koran, the last chapter revealed by the prophet Muhammad, is the only chapter that does not begin with 'In the name of Allah, the compassionate, the merciful'. It contains the 'Verse of the Sword' (Koran 9:5, above) which instructs believers to kill people of the book (Christians and Jews) wherever they are found.

Reasonism

As I explained at the start of this book, I was long confused about what I believed in. I could not make the distinction whether I was an agnostic, a pantheist, a theist or an existentialist.

I thought I was agnostic because part of me held the belief that, ultimately, we will never know whether God exists or not. I then realised that I was only agnostic because of my ignorance of science and my misconception of the religion I thought I knew.

After reading several books to understand the scientific explanations of abiogenesis, evolution and natural selection, I could no longer see how there could be a god. After re-reading many passages of the Bible, I was appalled by the verses I was supposed to believe in if I still thought of myself as a Christian.

A part of me believed that if God existed, he would be in a form so complex that my mortal mind would not be able to comprehend his nature. If he existed, he would also be ubiquitous. I imagined God to be like energy, gravity, or some mathematical or physical law, held to be constant everywhere in the universe. I realise now that I was simply inventing my own concept of God, like many people do.

I also prayed because I believed in the power of prayer. But when I prayed, I imagined God to be a theistic god, someone who watched me and listened to my prayers. He empathised with my fears and acknowledged my sacrifices. I realise now, however, that I cannot continue with this type of religiosity. To continue praying without believing in God would be a betrayal of my integrity.

What has become clear to me, after writing this book, is that I am no longer an agnostic nor am I a theist. I am an atheist. I do not believe in a god or gods. Though, as simple an idea as atheism is, it is very problematic. Allow me to explain.

I do not believe in many other things either. I do not believe in racism, astrology, alchemy and superstition, to name a few. Why should I go around calling myself as an atheist, when at the same time, I have the option of calling myself an a-racist, an a-astrologer or an a-alchemist? Buddhists do not believe in God yet they see no importance in going around identifying themselves as atheists.

Besides, as Richard Dawkins pointed out: Aren't we all atheists? We are all atheists when considering other gods like Zeus, Apollo, Amon Ra, Mithras, Baal, Thor, Wotan, the Golden Calf and the Flying Spaghetti Monster.

My biggest problem with atheism is that, it is a non-word. Our way of thinking and our languages use ideas and words for what they DO represent, not for what they DO NOT represent. Atheism is a word that identifies what it DOES NOT represent.

This is difficult for us because our brains are used to thinking positively, not in terms of null. To illustrate what I mean, consider that when I ask you NOT to think of a pink elephant, the first thing you think about is a pink elephant. I may actually have wanted you to think of roses but I have led your mind to think of anything you associate with elephants. Because of these reasons, I do not like to be identified as an atheist. It is wide open to be misunderstood.

I do realise, however, that I have to identify myself somehow. So I am looking for a term that encapsulates a philosophy with which I can identify. For the reasons I have argued in this book, I seek a philosophy that does not seek to invoke religious or superstitious beliefs to explain, justify or rationalise any action, thought or behaviour.

Earlier thinkers have proposed similar philosophies like rationalism, positivism, and existentialism. However, each of them have been defined by previous thinkers and it would not be right to refer to myself as any of them, if I do not yet comprehend the subtle differences between them.

It was not the purpose of this book to formulate a philosophy. So, I might give it some more thought in later works. However, for now, I would like to submit the philosophy of '**Reasonism**'.

Reasonism can be defined as a philosophy based on the following statement:

> For us to believe in something, we must have good reasons to believe. A reason is a good reason if it is based on intelligent ideas. Ideas are intelligent if they have the power to predict. We can only predict when we acquire the knowledge we need that are close to the truth, allowing us to arrive at models and theories that help us make predictions. To do this, we need to use good information. Good information is something that is based on good evidence. Good evidence must be understandable, relevant, reliable, independently verifiable, comparable and consistent.

An individual who approaches life in this way can be called a '**Reasonist**'. Because of their reliance on reason and evidence, Reasonists depend on the scientific method.

The Scientific Method

Non-scientists loosely use the word 'theory' in place of words like a 'hunch' or 'guess'. When people hear about '*The Theory Of Evolution*', they say things like, "Well, it is just a theory".

In science, however, the word 'theory' is not an individual's hunch or guess that remains unproved or untested. Before something is recognised as a theory, it goes through a rigorous process. We need to understand the process by which scientists come to understand what they purport to know. This is referred to as '*The Scientific Method*'.

William K. Tong of the Oakton Community College, in Illinois, provides us with a good definition of The Scientific Method:

> "The scientific method attempts to explain the natural occurrences (phenomena) of the universe by using a logical, consistent, systematic method of investigation, information (data) collection, data analysis (hypothesis), testing

(experiment), and refinement to arrive at a well-tested, well-documented, explanation that is well-supported by evidence, called a theory".[210]

What we need to recognise is that scientific theories have been observed, tested and verified in many experiments, by many different, independent sources. To explain this process, let us use an example of how a theory is developed using the scientific method:

1) I make an **observation**: Every time the sun rises, it is always from the east.
2) I **hypothesise**: The sun must rise from the east.
3) I **test** this idea: I will go everywhere I can possibly go and verify that the sun is always rising from the east.
4) I **publish** it: "My research has indicated the sun always rises from the east, wherever it is observed."
5) Other people **verify** it: This research will then be corroborated by others, from all over the world to confirm that the sun indeed rises from the east.
6) We agree now that our theory has enough evidence. Out of say, 10,000, independent case studies, we are 100% sure the sun rises from the east. We now have a **theory**.
7) Maybe one day, the sun will begin rising from the west. We cannot know for sure. When it does, we will modify our theory.

As we can see, theories are far from the unproved speculations of a single scientist who just had one too many cups of coffee, late one night. Scientific method is not simply about asserting what you think is true. It may make assumptions but it does not require faith because it simply works with the evidence it has. It is a method that seeks for truth through testing ideas and conducting experiments to verify whether these ideas are true. Ideas are cross-referenced and open for widespread criticism, enquiry and debate. The scientific method requires evidence that is, understandable, relevant, reliable, observable and verifiable.

The most important aspect of a scientific theory is that it must be FALSIFIABLE. It must be clear how and when that theory is no longer valid. In our example above, the theory will remain to be true until someone makes an observation that the sun is rising from another direction. If something is not falsifiable, it is not a true scientific theory. It is a philosophy.

The contrast is clear: religions simply make up answers and assert them to be the truth. Science seeks answers based on evidence and proof and as a result, science has proven itself superior to religion in its ability to explain and understand our nature, our world and the universe. Because of this, it is able to provide us with models that can predict with great certainty of success. The reliability of these predictions has provided us with the ability to travel vast distances, cure diseases, communicate to distant friends and look beyond our horizons.

What I find most ironic is for some religious people to demand evidence and proof for scientific theories and methods, yet they have no problems accepting religious ideas on pure faith alone. A 'Reasonist' can believe in a god or anything supernatural if, and only if, there is strong scientific evidence that support their existence: evidence that is reliable, universally observable and independently verifiable.

CHAPTER 22: HUMAN NATURE

We are able to build peaceful and moral societies by understanding how to work with human nature. As we have discussed in chapter 11, there are three observable truths about us:

1. We have evolved to be social animals.
2. We have it in us to reciprocate.
3. We strive to attain our ambition of being happy.

Because we are social creatures, we can only experience the fullness of life if we are with other people. We cannot experience laughter, joy, praise, gratitude, admiration and sadness when we surround ourselves with nonliving things. So, as social creatures, we have to live in the proximity of other people.

Another reality we need to acknowledge about ourselves is that we have a tendency to treat other people the way we have been treated. It is as if we have an internal mechanism that accounts for the goodwill and generosity we receive from others. We then balance this account with the hostility and selfishness we have also received. Thereafter, we have it in us to treat people just as kindly or just as cruelly as they have treated us.

Our human nature gives each of us three modes of operation:

1. **Violence, Threats and Fear**

   We can choose to take what we want by force. We can treat other people with violence and intimidation. We can punch them, we can steal from them and we can lie to them. In return for our hostility, other people will treat us the same way. They can also lie to us, beat us or steal from us.

2. **Favours and Acts of Kindness**

   To get what we want, we can choose to exchange what we have with what others are willing to exchange with us. We come to an agreement to trade fairly and equitably.

3. **Act Honourably and Respectfully**

   We can choose to do what we think is right, by being kind and charitable to other beings, without expecting them to return our compassion and generosity. In fact, we will treat them benevolently even if we know they are unable or unwilling to ever return the favour. We choose to operate in this mode to achieve our ambition which eventually leads to our own happiness.

As a society, we do not want people exchanging threats and acts of violence ceaselessly. It can be very exhausting, wasteful and unproductive to say the least. It is very sad for human beings to make each other's lives a misery, most especially since this the only life each of us are ever going to get. We have to focus on exchanging favours and acts of kindness so we can all appreciate and be grateful for the fact that we are here, now, alive. How do we get people to do this?

Controlling Violence

To stop people from using threats and violence to get what they want, we install law and order. In the absence of law and order, we use the idea of an ethereal policeman: God. To establish God, we need religion.

The problem with religion is that it only works by instilling fear in people. The best thing a religion can ever achieve is to coerce people in being good by threatening them with the rejection of God and the eternal punishment that awaits them, should they fail.

To maintain this fear requires much indoctrination. It requires people to believe in falsehoods. Besides, a person who is only good because he or she thinks God is watching is like an employee who only gets busy when the boss is looking. I do not know about you but I seriously believe, and I hold a higher regard and expectation for you and I, to have the capacity, the motivation and the power to behave better than this.

Empower People to Exchange Favours and Acts of Kindness

Religions alone cannot solve the problems of economics: the allocation of scarce resources. There is only so much resources the Earth can provide for us all. There is only so much land, water, food, energy and oil. Economics deals with how we can allocate these resources justly and rightly. Religions are not equipped to solve any of these problems.

I believe we can build a much more robust and peaceful society if we continue to improve our systems to empower people to get what they want from each other without resorting to violence.

The key, I believe, is commerce and technology. For people to get what they want we must create possibilities for them to give what they can, in exchange for what they need, justly and fairly. In making this possible, people must be able to trust each other to fulfil their obligations when they make contractual agreements with one another.

To do this, we need to ensure free, but well-regulated, markets to be as competitive as possible. This increases their efficiency and their ability to give buyers and sellers the best prices for whatever goods and services they wish to exchange.

To ensure people make the right decisions in their transactions, they need access to high quality information. They need information to understand the implications of what they do, as well as the social and political impact of their actions. They need to concern themselves with sustainability. They have to consider whether the environment can sustain their activities. It is selfish to use up all the Earth's resources today and leave little for future generations.

To have high quality, relevant information, we need to foster studies and research in science, governance, economics and commerce. Contrary to what some religious people believe, the best form of government we have ever devised to make all this possible, is democracy.

Empower People With Their Own Ambitions

Ambition is not limited to the context of career and money. Each of us, to whatever degree, is yearning or longing to realise the achievement, or the attainment, of happiness in our lives. Ambitions vary from person to person because each of us defines happiness differently. This desire is what compels us to do what we need to do, to have what we need to have, and to be what we want to be.

I believe individuals in all levels of society must seek to inspire, support and motivate other people to find what it is they are good at and love doing, so they may contribute their skills and talents for good causes. Most importantly, all facets of society from individuals to governments, from commercial to non-profit organisations, must reward those who provide the most value to the planet or to the community.

When people have no hope, when they feel lost and defeated, their interaction with other people becomes difficult. When people see themselves as victims, they become helpless, suspicious, angry and hostile. How can they ever treat others kindly if they have nothing to be grateful for?

If we allow some of us to remain in this state, we will all incur the effect because we are all interconnected. What goes around comes around. When one person mistreats someone, that person is likely to mistreat another, and so on. Eventually, we, or our loved ones, will find ourselves mistreated, and we will continue passing the negative behaviour along. It takes extraordinary wisdom, insight and maturity for any individual to stop the cycle.

But when we have dreams, when we have hopes, when we are striving for something, we feel happy. When we are happy, we are more likely to help other people and be more generous. We are more likely to treat other people thoughtfully. And when we do this, other people begin treat us thoughtfully in return.

The irony is, after we begin treating people with dignity, honesty and integrity, we gain their respect. People will want to work with us and they will want to invest in us and in our ideas. People will support us and encourage us to do what we think is best. Surprisingly, when we begin treating people the way we want to be treated, we realise we become empowered to achieve our ambitions.

Individually, we should foster our own ambitions based on what it is we enjoy doing, and decide how our skills and talents can best serve other people and the planet, not just in our professions but in our responsibilities as parents, teachers and role models to future generations and to everyone else. In doing this, society benefits because its economy will become more efficient and more productive.

When this happens, we will be empowered. We will know what it feels like to be rewarded by the support, trust, respect and honour of other people. In control of our lives, we will be more inspired and motivated. Most importantly, we will learn to be responsible and accountable for what we do.

We will see the value of self-reliance and self-determination. No longer will we hope and depend on a god, or gods, to make us feel better about our inability or unwillingness to improve our circumstances. When we have liberated ourselves from the tyranny of our own beliefs, we will finally understand that there is only us who have the power to make our world a better place.

CHAPTER 23:
ONE LIFE

Would you live your life differently if you expected that this life, serves only as a test to determine the quality of your next life? Would you live this life differently if you expected that this life is the only one you will get? What you are inclined to believe makes all the difference.

There are those of us who want to believe that life can exist after death and so they are more likely to seek any belief system that assures them that they can – and they will – survive their death. People like me also wish for this to be true. The problem is, no good evidence has ever been advanced to support the existence of gods, nor has there been any persuasive argument made for the existence of Heaven and salvation that withstood the scrutiny of argument and enquiry.

In the process of learning about the scientific explanations of our existence, I have come to be more certain that this life is the only life we are ever going to get. Personally, this is one of the most agonising notions I had to accept. To many, this is an awful proposition. Our fear of death, our love for life, and our desire for meaning behind our existence, all contribute to our propensity to believe we can continue to live after we die. However, if we are honest in our search for what is true, we must understand that truth, when we confront it, has no obligation to comfort, nor console, us.

Regardless of how healthy a patient feels, there is nothing more threatening than seeing photographs of cancer cells growing inside his body. There is nothing more daunting for a woman than to realise the real reason her husband has been staying out late at work a little too frequently, coming home with traces of lipstick and a female scent on his clothing. There is nothing more paralysing for a retiree than to watch the value of his or her life savings decline in a market crash.

We can all choose to believe we are healthy, that our marriage is secure or that our investments are safe. But truths remain to be truths, regardless of what we want to believe. How we think the world should be, or ought to be, is different to how the world really is. Wishing, hoping, praying and engaging in self-delusions do not change our realities.

It is only when we are honest in our appraisal of our own circumstance can we be in a position to know and act in our best interest. Only when we are willing to accept evidence that our health is failing, can we take steps to rectify our problems. When we have the courage to confront our fears, we can determine the strength of our relationships. When we admit to ourselves that we have made bad decisions, our minds become free to think of how we will make things right.

It is clear to us that everything dies. Plants, including the flowers and the trees, all wilt and wither. Animals, as individuals and as species, go extinct. Even the sun ages and dies after it exhausts all its energy and meets its fate as a black hole.

Despite all of this, human beings, with our love for life and our never-ending search for meaning, want to believe that somehow, we are different. Somehow we, unlike everything else in the universe, are special.

In our refusal to accept our mortality, we delude ourselves in the world of make-believe: the world of superstition, religion and the supernatural. In our imaginations, we fantasise about a state of nirvana and the prospect of living forever in Heaven, where everything else in the universe revolves around our own happiness. We find the idea of this ethereal place to be so intoxicating that many people find comfort and solace in religions.

Karl Marx, *Critique of Hegel's Philosophy of Right*, said:

> Religion is the sigh of the oppressed creature, the heart of a heartless world, just as it is the spirit of a spiritless situation. It is the opium of the people. The abolition of religion as the illusory happiness of the people is required for their real happiness. The demand to give up the illusion about its condition is the demand to give up a condition which needs illusions.

Bear in mind that addicts say the same thing about whatever it is they are addicted to. In a sense, therefore, we inject ourselves with the comfort and solace that religion brings into our minds, much like alcoholics drink to 'wash away' their 'troubles', and overeaters eat to fill the 'emptiness' they feel inside.

In our willingness to indulge in our fantasies, we make up even more stuff to explain and justify the details of these fantasies. But our lies have grown so out of touch with reality that we need to close our senses, from evidence and reason, to believe them. We begin accepting dogmatic ideas on the basis of pure faith alone. Ironically, however, our efforts to comfort ourselves from the idea of death stop us from living our life to its fullest potential.

At some stage, in the process of our trickeries, we coerce and intimidate others to behave, think and act a certain way so they can fit our make-believe worlds. At its extremes, literal believers of Holy Scriptures are willing to die and kill the rest of us if we do not share their belief in an afterlife and in a god that favours them above others. They attach little value to this life and so, they inflict suffering to the world at large, squandering their lives and the lives of others, for the misguided ideals they hold.

The tyranny of our beliefs oppresses us into living a restricted life, forcing us to suck up to gods that do not exist, because we believe they can grant us entry for an afterlife that is real only in our imaginations.

How do we stop our delusions and our wishful thinking? How can we stop our fears from paralysing us to a point where we believe we need illusions to operate? How can we live in the Here and Now and accept that this is the only life we have?

In overcoming obstacles in our lives, we know that the courage we need, and the solace we seek, comes from within. It usually starts by changing what we choose to think about, and how we choose to think about it.

Instead of being fearful of dying, we begin being grateful of the fact we are very lucky to have had the opportunity to be alive in the first place. Richard Dawkins wrote the most beautiful appreciation of this fact when he wrote in his book, *Unweaving The Rainbow*:

> We are going to die, and that makes us the lucky ones. Most people are never going to die because they are never going to be born. The potential people who could have been here in my place but who will in fact never see the light of day outnumber the sand grains of Arabia. Certainly those unborn ghosts include greater poets than Keats, scientists greater than Newton. We know this because the set of possible people allowed by our DNA so massively exceeds the set of actual people. In the teeth of these stupefying odds it is you and I, in our ordinariness, that are here.

Someone once said that it is only when we are ready to die, do we begin to truly live. In spite of our mortality, we can still dare to make our lives more than ordinary without knowingly indulging in the addictive distraction and numbing entertainment provided by religion and superstition.

By relying less on our delusions and by learning to distinguish the make-believe worlds from the real world, we find that not much will have changed: we find that we still yearn for acceptance and belonging and we still ache for love.

Instead of agonising over having only one life to live, we confront the reality that there are no rehearsals and there will be no second chances. Each moment that passes is a moment we will never have again. We must seize every opportunity to experience what it is like to be alive.

Time is all we have and there are only so many tomorrows. In casting aside the illusions of another life, we will finally acknowledge the preciousness of this life and feel most grateful for it. Heaven is here and eternity is now.

THE END

APPENDICES

I initially wanted to include these sections in the main part of the book, however, they were not necessary in making my arguments. Furthermore, they are highly speculative. I include them here because you might find them interesting and relevant to rebuilding your belief system. I would be happy to hear about any works or studies that may or may not corroborate any of these.

(1) What Existed Before The Big Bang?

Some people accept that everything, including time and space, began with the Big Bang Theory. If you are intellectually satisfied with this, you may decide to skip this section. It is your preference.

If you are like me, however, you would not be satisfied. Accepting a proposition that says, 'Everything began with the Big Bang', seems to me, similar to accepting something dogmatic. If I accept this, I might as well add that the Big Bang was the result of God snapping his fingers for us to come into existence.

This book is about challenging dogma. It is about refusing to accept anything on faith alone. We cannot terminate our enquiry on a belief.

The 'Singularity' Problem

What existed before the Big Bang? What was this 'singularity'? The 'singularity' is commonly visualised as a little fireball appearing somewhere in space, however, this is not so. Physicists liken it to similar phenomena that exist at the core of 'black holes'.[ss]

For a long time, science was stuck[tt] because when extrapolating Einstein's *Theory of Relativity* back to the beginning, the equations 'blew up'[uu]. "The fundamental problem of cosmology is that the laws of physics, as we know them, break down at the instance of the Big Bang. Some people see nothing wrong with having the laws of physics collapse but for physicists, this is a disaster. All our lives we've dedicated to the proposition that the Universe obeys knowable laws: laws that can be written down in the language of mathematics, and here we have the centrepiece of the Universe itself, a missing piece beyond physical law".[vv]

Brilliant scientists, including the German-born theoretical physicist Albert Einstein, who has devoted the last years of his life to finding a theory that could explain and link everything that is known and understood about the nature of the universe, hope to come to an understanding of what happened before the Big Bang.

The M Theory

At this moment, the most mathematically robust theory in explaining what happened 13.7 billion years ago is *The M Theory*.[ww] The M Theory is the resulting theory arising from the works of two groups of scientists: string theorists[xx] and those

---

[ss] Black holes are areas of intense gravitational pressure where the pressure is thought to be so intense that finite matter is actually squished into infinite density.

[tt] Religion answer of course is to say that God created it all. Most of us have surrendered to the temptations and comfort of such simple, quick and easy answers. If, however, we seek intellectually satisfying answers, we need to search pass this impasse, look further and challenge our understanding.

[uu] PAUL STEINHARDT in the documentary: *Parrallel Universe,* BBC Two, 2001.

[vv] Michio Kaku, a theoretical physicist. Documentary: *Parrallel Universe,* BBC Two, 2001.

[ww] The development and history of this theory makes for very interesting and exciting research and I would refer you to two documentaries: The *Parallel Universe* (BBC, 2001) and *The Elegant Universe* (PBS, 2004).

[xx] Initially, string theorists believed that there are ten dimensions in the universe.

working on the idea of super gravity[yy]. Their tools were physics and mathematics. Specifically, they were concerned with integrating the ideas in quantum mechanics (the study of 'small things')[zz] and general relativity (the study of 'big things')[aaa]. When they finally brought their ideas together, they found that their work complemented each other.

The implications of this theory are enormous. The biggest of them all is the possibility that we are living in only one of many universes. The best way to imagine these universes would be to imagine that one as a sheet of paper, but unlike smooth, flat sheets of papers, their surfaces vibrate in waves and ripples. When two or more of these objects collide, and are forced to occupy the same space, their particles exert great force upon each other, ending up in a violent exchange of energy and momentum...like what happened in the Big Bang. "The Big Bang is the aftermath of some encounter between two parallel worlds."[bbb] The uneven surfaces of two colliding universes hit different points at different times. The ripples caused the clumps of matter we now see as stars, galaxies and quasars. With the M Theory, the idea of the 'singularity' is no longer mysterious. Now, we have a model to explain it.

What the M stands for, in the M Theory, is still open to conjecture. One of the options is 'Membrane'. I prefer to think of the M Theory as the Membrane Theory because of the way it models universes.

This idea of multiple universes is fairly new and is now being discussed in scientific circles. If it is accepted, after further experiment and enquiry, it is able to explain everything in the Universe. It is hard to accept this theory because we do not have the technological capability to test even a couple of its assertions: assertions like the existence of other dimensions and the existence

---

[yy] Scientists like Michael Duff (University of Michigan) worked on the idea that there were eleven dimensions.
[zz] Quantum Mechanics which studies electromagnetism, strong nuclear force, weak nuclear force.
[aaa] General Relativity studies gravity, space and time.
[bbb] Neil Geoffrey Turok holds the Chair of Mathematical Physics (1967) at Cambridge University.

of a particle called graviton, a tiny unit of gravity. To understand their dilemma, I need to elaborate a little more on the M theory.

Scientists have noticed one strange aspect of gravity. It is evidently one of the most powerful forces in the universe. It can pull massive heavenly bodies, like stars and galaxies, to collide with each other. Yet, we are able to defy it by our ability to lift an apple or a book upwards with our small arm muscles. We know of no other element in the universe that can be so paradoxical. To explain this, M theorists propose that everything is made up of the tiniest particles imaginable. These particles are like strings, each vibrating to a different frequency. Some of them are open and some of them are closed. We can imagine closed strings to be like rubber bands, looped with no ends. Open strings, on the other hand, have two ends, like rubber bands cut in the middle.

Most particles in the universe are open strings. Because their two ends are not stuck to each other they are free to cling, or get entangled with, other strings in our universe. On the other hand, closed strings cannot entangle themselves with other particles in the universe. They are free to float around.

To explain these ideas, I will use several explanations used by Brian Greene.

To visualise the idea of multiple universes:

Imagine that our entire observable universe is a slice of bread, existing side-by-side with other slices of bread that belongs to a loaf of bread. You can think of the loaf of bread as the multiverse which consists of other universes like ours.

To visualise open strings:

If we take a slice of bread, apply a layer of jam over it and tip it upside-down, we notice the jam does not fall off the bread. The jam is made of open strings. The jam sticks to the bread. The slice of bread is our universe. The jam represents everything that exists in our universe… except gravity.

> To visualise closed strings:

> If we take a slice of bread, pour a handful of sugar over it and tip it over, we notice that sugar particles are free to fall away from the slice of bread. Closed strings in the universe are like sugar particles on a slice of bread. They are free to flow from one slice of bread to another. Gravitons, the units of gravity, are closed strings and they can freely float from one universe to another.

To help explain the paradox of gravitational force, M theory hypothesise that the tiny particles that make up gravity – called gravitons – are thought of as closed strings. This prevents them from being tied up with other strings in one dimension.[ccc] They are free to float across other dimensions: to other universes that are parallel to ours. Because of this, the strength of gravity is weakened. It is spread thin across several universes, several dimensions.

Proving The Theory

Even if the mathematics behind the M theory add up, they are still subjected by the scientific method to provide evidence. Like Joseph Lykken[211] said: "How do you actually test string theory? If you can't test it in the way that we test normal theories, it's not science, it is philosophy, and that's a real problem."

To prove the assertions of M theory, we need to at least begin with proving the existence of other dimensions. To do this, we need a giant atom smasher. Here is how it works:

> "Scientists zap hydrogen atoms with huge amounts of electricity. Later, they strip them of their electrons and send the protons zooming around a four-mile circular tunnel... Just as

---

[ccc] This idea came after further study on why gravity is so powerful that it can pull two stars into collision and yet, it is weak enough for us to be able to resist it by say, lifting an object from the ground.

they're approaching the speed of light, they are steered into collisions with particles whizzing in the opposite direction.

Most collisions are just glancing blows, but occasionally there's a direct hit. The result is a shower of unusual subatomic particles. The hope is that among these particles will be a tiny unit of gravity, the graviton.

Gravitons, according to string theory, are closed loops, so they can float off into the extra dimensions. The grand prize would be a snapshot of a graviton at the moment of escape."[212]

M theorists are currently waiting for the completion of the largest atom smasher in CERN, a lab currently being built on the border of France and Switzerland. They are excited to test their ideas, eager to experiment on more powerful atom smashers the next few decades may bring. "Even though there's no real evidence yet, so much of string theory just makes so much sense".[213] Theorists accept the possibility they may have been wasting the last twenty years of their lives. However, the M theory is poised to rewrite much of what we know about the universe.

(2) Explaining Consciousness

One of the immortal questions was asked by my father in his own words:

> I wonder who I am or what I am. I am aware. I am conscious. When I say, 'I', or when I refer to 'me', who or what exactly am I referring to? What happens to me when I die? All my dreams… all my thoughts… where do they all go?

Philosophical questions like these crave to find the explanation for consciousness. As always, religions purport to have an answer. God gave us consciousness. Again, I am not satisfied with such an explanation so I seek another.

"Descartes [the French Philosopher, scientist, and writer who lived between 1596 and 1650] originally claimed that consciousness involves an immaterial soul, which observes a representation of the world in the pineal gland of the brain. Under this notion, the soul plays the role of a homunculus, a creature with self-directed willpower."[214]

Philosopher Daniel Dennett, author of *Consciousness Explained*, described this as the Cartesian Theatre model of consciousness. In its essence, this model suggests that inside our heads, there is a part of our brain, acting as an agent, which does the act of being conscious for us. This conscious agent sits in the Cartesian theatre of our minds, watching what we see, listening to what we hear and sensing what we feel.

If we are conscious because a little part of our brain is conscious, then what exactly makes that part of our brains conscious? Shall we also say the conscious part of our brain has a littler part that makes it conscious as well? The problem with these models is that they have not even begun explaining the true nature of consciousness. They simply create an infinite regress of littler and littler sources of consciousness.

For us to explain consciousness using the metaphor of 'Cartesian theatres', we have to open the 'pineal gland' of the brain to locate the source of our consciousness. When scientists sliced up human brains to study them, they have found no such Cartesian theatres where consciousness takes place.

Daniel Dennett said, in a lecture on consciousness[215], that it is not logically impossible that there should be a Cartesian theatre, it is just that, empirically, it is a fact there is no Cartesian theatre. To solve our problem, we have to break up the Cartesian theatre into parts that are not, themselves, conscious:

> All the work done by the imagined homunculus in the Cartesian Theatre must be distributed around to various lesser agencies in the brain that are not, themselves, conscious. Because if they are really conscious, then we have just recreated the homunculus problem and we have not made any progress at all.

There must be a better explanation than the Cartesian theatre model. To begin, allow me to use a metaphor. I would like us to consider the concept of corporations.

A corporation is a legal entity that is independent of its shareholders, directors and employees. Like a real person, a corporation has the power to make contractual agreements with individual human beings or other corporations and organisations.

A corporation is formed when one or more individuals decide to work together and form a corporation. These individuals will become employees or directors of the company. In the process of its evolution, more directors may be recruited to lead and organise the company's resources. Investors are invited to contribute their assets to the company so they can benefit from the future profits of the company as its owners. Employees are recruited to perform the roles and duties of the company's operations.

These individuals are divided to perform different roles and functions that will enable the corporation to work as a coherent entity. Depending on their functions, individuals are divided into their own particular departments: sales, marketing, accounting, operations, manufacturing, legal and human resources management. The way these individuals organise themselves will evolve depending on what type of behaviour the consumer rewards. Individuals who cannot, or are unable to, work with other individuals within the team will either quit or get asked to look for a more suited job if their work ethic or attitude is not conducive to the survival and success of the corporation.

Corporations can long outlive the life span of any of the individuals that make up its constituent. It can live to hundreds, even thousands of years, should it continue to adapt to its environment. The oldest company today is 1,430 years old. It is Kongō Gumi,[216] a Japanese construction company established in the year 578 AD. The second oldest is a 1,291 years old Japanese hotel, Ho-shi, set up in the year 717 AD. The third is a restaurant in Austria, St Peter, set up in the year 803 AD. It is 1,205 years old.

Because of many individuals, technologies and processes, systematically working together, the consciousness of a corporation is simulated. Coke, for example, recognises Pepsi as its competitor, while Time Warner and America Online – upon seeing themselves as being compatible – get married via a merger.

Let us pause now and reflect on what we know about the human body. Human beings are collections of genes working together. The human body is made up of different types of genes: genes that were once separate but now exist as part of a more intricate organism. Genes are divided into different departments: there are genes dedicated to seeing, hearing, thinking, moving, reproducing and so on. After millions of years of evolution and natural selection, genes have arranged themselves inside survival machines: organisms like us that are effective in surviving and reproducing.

The life span of an individual human being outlasts the life span of any of the cells that makes up its constituent. For example, the current world average life span of a human being is 66.12 years[217], while the life span of red blood cells has an average life span of 120 days only[218].

In studying the brain, scientists have determined that different parts of the brain specialise in different roles. Some sections of the brain concentrate on aspects of motion; others focus on locations; some focus on shapes; and others are dedicated to identifying and working with colours, and so on. In processing all this information, the brain simulates what we make out as consciousness. In his lecture, Daniel Dennett provided some examples of how different parts of the brain, by working together, may simulate consciousness.

This concept of consciousness is somewhat alarming. Like Dennett said, it gives us an eerie feeling akin to entering a factory, with all its humming machinery, and there's nobody home. There's no watchman, there's no supervisor, there's no boss. It's all just machinery.

As daunting as this may seem, however, there seems to be no other way to explaining consciousness. If we leave the watchman, the supervisor, or the boss, in our theory – the factory – then we have to explain how they get their consciousness. This puts us back to the beginning of our problem. Therefore, in our attempts to answer the origins of consciousness, we must use an explanation that does not necessitate anything to be conscious.

Many of us would probably resist this frightening explanation for consciousness. Dennett explains that this is because consciousness is like magic to us. Even if we can find the scientific, step-by-step method, of how magic tricks are performed, many of us would rather be entertained and dazzled by the illusion of magic. We want to preserve magic the way it is: as something miraculous, mystical and unexplainable. Perhaps, our consciousness is the last bit of magic many of us have in our lives. To accept such mechanical explanations to it can be devastating.

(3) The Infant Mind

In my conversations with many faithfuls, they often resort to declaring their faith similar to the following:

> Regardless of any evidence or logical arguments against the existence of God, I still want to believe in a God because the belief in Him emotionally supports and/or comforts me. I cannot accept, nor would I want to, accept there is no God.

This attitude puzzles me because I know I can be shaken out of my belief if there is good evidence and argument that God does exist. In any discussion of this nature, embracing blind faith instead of succumbing to reason might be a frustrating end to a very long and well-argued debate. Even after the faithful have conceded to the validity of the evidence and arguments against the existence of God, there can still be no victory. Some people may never be argued out of their belief in God by using logic and rationality because I believe it is more an emotional issue, not an intellectual one.

In this section, I will not argue against faith. I will simply recognise the reality that some people are willing to believe in God no matter what. I want to understand how the emotional desire to believe in God has become so strong that it persists even when it contradicts our reason.

I am interested in this matter because I personally struggle with it too. Even if I can intellectually see no way in which God can exist, I still experience the emotional effort required to accept it. I still struggle with it, but not to the extent that I reject my own reasoning. Blind faith is never a good reason to believe in anything because of our destructive and dangerous capacity to delude ourselves.

Why is the desire for a God so persistent?

The desire to believe in gods is a phenomenon that is prevalent in most cultures. Throughout all observable history, human societies have worshipped the supernatural. The proliferation of the gods we conjure up, drives me to conclude that, the belief in God is part of our make up. It seems as though we need gods, or rather, we have a natural tendency to create them.

To the religious, this is proof that God exists. According to this line of argument, religions are mere attempts to express and interpret what, to them, is the reality of God. I do not find this a satisfactory answer.

One scientific hypothesis that attempts to explain the belief in God comes from Dr Dean Hamer, the director of the Gene Structure and Regulation Unit at the U.S. National Cancer Institute. He proposed the idea that religiosity can be genetically explained. In his book, *The God Gene: How Faith Is Hardwired Into Our Genes*, identified a gene called VMAT2 to be a gene responsible for experiences that people mistakenly interpret as godly or supernatural.

What I am about to propose is similar in a sense that the cause of religion is something all human beings share in common. I conjecture that the ubiquitousness of the belief in God comes from the way our brains develop and mature in childhood. All humans share the same beginnings. Unlike other creatures that have fully-developed brains when they are born, we come out of our mother's wombs way before our brains have had time to mature. This is part of our evolution that we share with our primate cousins.

We were all born dependent, vulnerable and totally helpless. From the early years of our infancy, we depended on our parents to feed us, to keep us warm, to shelter us from the elements and guard us from pests and predators. When we were hungry, we cried, when we were cold, we cried, when we were uncomfortable, we cried. Our mother, or father, was there to ensure we were all right.

In these crucial years of brain development, our neural networks formed and fixed themselves as we slowly became aware of the world around us. We recognised ourselves from our parents who loved us, comforted us and protected us from everything else. We were all reliant and dependent on our mother, our father, or both. Without anybody to play the role of parents, we would have died. But we are here today because someone loved us enough to ensure we would live. To our small, but growing, infant mind, this being must have seemed as someone who was all-powerful, all-knowing and all-wise.

I am proposing that it is during this stage of our brain and mental development that we develop such great emotional attachment and need for beings with god-like qualities. Once formed, it becomes part of our mental reality for the rest of our lives.

After our most vulnerable years, in our childhood and teens, we may have learnt to eat on our own, communicate, and become more mobile but we still look up to our parents to provide us with everything we need to continue surviving. When we reach full mental maturity and become adults, we have already lived the first twenty years of our lives.

It is always a significant time for all of us when we move out of our parent's house for the first time. Eventually, we are able to get past the emotional struggle of severing ourselves from the great beings who once seemed like gods to us. However, our mental and emotional attachments to such beings are still ingrained in our very nature.

So, even as adults, even after our parents have long died, we still cry out for beings who love us: beings who will protect us and care for us when we are alone, hurt, isolated or scared. We may not cry for our parents as we did when we were infants, but we humble ourselves in prayer and worship for paternal or maternal gods. We hope and wish that such beings exist somewhere out there, beyond the limits of our realities… beyond the boundaries of our cribs.

This book has spawned a new website:

WWW.REASONISM.ORG

This website is dedicated to focussing on:

Religion
Superstition
Science
Ethics
Morality
The Modern World

BIBLIOGRAPHY

Boyd, Robert & Silk, Joan B. *How Humans Evolved.* (New York: Norton & Company, 2003).

Carnegie, Dale. *How To Win Friends And Influence People* (Pocket, 1998).

Carroll, Sean B. *The Making of the Fittest.* (W.W. Norton and Company, 2006).

Cowen, Richard. *History Of Life.* (Wiley-Blackwell, 1991).

Dawkins, Richard. *The Ancestor's Tale, A Pilgrimage to the Dawn of Life.* (Boston: Houghton Mifflin Company, 2004).

Dawkins, Richard. *The God Delusion* (Bantam Press, 2006).

Dawkins, Richard. *The Selfish Gene.* 3rd Edition. (Oxford University Press, 2006).

Dennett, Daniel C. *Darwin's Dangerous Idea: Evolution and the Meanings of Life.* (Simon & Schuster, 1996)

Diamond, Jared. *The Third Chimpanzee: The Evolution and Future of the Human Animal.* (New York: Harper Perennial, 2006).

Esler, Phillip F. *The Early Christian World.* (Routledge, 2004).

Esposito, John. *Islam: The Straight Path, 3rd Edition,* (Oxford University Press, 1998).

Evans, Allan S.; Riley E. Moynes, Larry Martinello. *What man Believes: A study of the World's Great Faiths.* (McGraw-Hill Ryerson, 1973).

Farah, Caesar. *Islam: Beliefs and Observances, 5th Edition,* (Barron's Educational Series, 1994).

Fortey, Richard. "Dust to Life", *Life: A Natural History of the First Four Billion Years of Life on Earth.* (New York: Vintage Books, 1999).

Gordon, Raymond G. *Ethnologue: Languages of the World, Fifteenth edition.* (SIL Publications, 2005)

Harcourt, A.H., MacKinnon, J. & Wrangham, R.W. (1984). in Macdonald, D.: *The Encyclopedia of Mammals* (Facts on File Natural Science Library, 2006).

Harris, Sam. *Letter To A Christian Nation* (Vintage Books, 2008).

Kobeisy, Ahmed Nezar. *Counseling American Muslims: Understanding the Faith and Helping the People.* (Praeger Publishers, 2004).

Rashid, Ahmed. *Taliban: Militant Islam, Oil, and Fundamentalism in Central Asia.* (Yale University Press, New Haven, 2000).

Ridgeon, Lloyd. *Major World Religions, 1st Edition*, (RoutledgeCurzon, 2003).

Robinson, George. *Essential Judaism: A Complete Guide to Beliefs, Customs and Rituals.* (New York: Pocket Books, 2000),

Rosen, Edward. *Copernicus and his Successors.* (London: Hambledon Press, 1995).

Shumaker, Robert W. & Beck, Benjamin B. *Primates in Question.* (Smithsonian Institute Press, (2003)

Tabatabae, Sayyid Mohammad Hosayn; R. Campbell (translator). *Islamic teachings: An Overview and a Glance at the Life of the Holy Prophet of Islam.* (Green Gold, 2002).

Warraq, I. *Why I Am Not A Muslim.* (New York Prometheus, 1995).

Willis, K. J.; J. C. McElwain. *The Evolution of Plants.* (Oxford: Oxford University Press, 2002).

INDEX

A

A.J. Jacobs, 237
Abraham, 233, 234
Albert Einstein, 274
Alcohol Moderation, 237
America Online, 280
Amphibia, 61
Apes, 68

B

Beast Faces. See Synapsids
Big Bang Theory, 273
Bilaterally Symmetrical Organisms, 54
Bilateria. See Bilaterally Symmetrical Organisms
Black Elk, 114
Brian Greene, 276

C

Cambrian Explosion, 52
Cartesian Theatre, 279
Cattarhini. See Downward-Pointing Nose
CERN, 278
Chordata. See Chordates
Chordates, 56
Confucius, 113
Consciousness Explained, 279
Copernicus, 288
Craniata. See Craniates
Craniates, 56

D

Daniel Dennett, 279, 281
Dean Hamer, 283
Descartes, 278
Deuterostomes, 54
Deuterostomia. *See* Deuterostomes
DNA, 236

Douglas Adams, 241
Downward-Pointing Nose, 68

E

Earth, 250, 287
Elizabeth Fritzl, 243
Epictetus, 113
Euarchontoglires. See Supraprimates
Eutheria. See Placental Mammals
Existentialist, 255

G

Gene, 283
Genes, 281, 283
Gnathostomata. *See* Jawed Vertebrates
God Delusion, The, 287
Great Apes, 69
Great Law of Peace, The, 114

H

Hitchhiker's Guide to the Galaxy, 241
Holy Trinity, The, 252
Hominidae. See Great Apes
Hominids. See Great Apes
Hominina, 70
Hominini, 69
Hominoidea. See Apes
Hominoids. See Apes
Homo Sapiens, 71
Ho-shi, 280
HPV-Human Papilloma Virus, 243

I

Islam, 254, 287, 288
Isocrates, 113

J

Jawed Vertebrates, 57
Jeff Hawkins, 248
Joan Osbourne, 234
Joseph Lykken, 277
Judaism, 288

K

Kongō Gumi, 280

L

Lizard Faces. See Sauropsids

M

M Theory, The, 274
Mammalia. *See* Mammals
Mammals, 64, 288
Metazoa, 53

O

On Intelligence, 248
Opisthokonts, 52
Osteichthye, 58

P

Pittacus of Mytilene, 113
Placental Mammals, 65
Primates, 66, 288

R

Ra, 256
Reasonism, 255, 257
Reasonist, 258, 260
Religious Moderation, 237, 239
Reptiliomorpha, 61
Richard Dawkins, 233, 256, 287
Robert Spencer, 254

S

Sam Harris, 239

Saudi Arabia, 233
Sauropsids, 62
Selfish Gene, The, 287
Serge Trifkovic, 254
Simians, 67
Simiiformes. See Simians
Singularity, 273
St Peter, Austrian Restaurant, 280
Supraprimates, 66
Synapsids, 62

T

T'ai Shang Kan Ying P'ien, 113
Tale Of The Eloquent Peasant, The, 114
Taliban, 288
Taoism, 113
Teleostomi, 58
Terrestrial Vertebrates, 59
Tetrapoda. See Tetrapods
Tetrapods, 59
Thales, 113
Thales of Miletus, 113
The Golden Rule, 113
Theory of Relativity, 274
Therapsida. See Therapsids
Therapsids, 63
Time Warner, 280

V

Vertebrata. See Vertebrates
Vertebrates, 57
VMAT2 - The God Gene, 283

W

Walid Shoebat, 254
What If God Was One Of Us?, 234

Y

Yahweh, 238
Year of Living Biblically, The, 237

Z

Zeus, 256

ENDNOTES

[1] Five-Year Wilkinson Microwave Anisotropy Probe (WMAP) Observations: Data Processing, Sky Maps, and Basic Results. nasa.gov. http://lambda.gsfc.nasa.gov/product/map/dr3/pub_papers/fiveyear/basic_results/wmap5basic.pdf. Retrieved on 2008-03-06.

[2] The National Academies Press. *The Origin Of The Universe, Earth and Life.* http://www.nap.edu/openbook.php?record_id=6024&page=3 (14 Sep 2008)

[3] All About Science: *The Big Bank Theory.* http://www.big-bang-theory.com/ (23, April 2007)

[4] The National Academies Press: *Science and Creationism: A View From The National Academy of Science.* http://www.nap.edu/openbook.php?record_id=6024&page=4 . (14 Sep 2008)

[5] "Nucleosynthesis." *Dictionary.com Unabridged (v 1.1).* Random House, Inc. 14 Sep. 2008. <Dictionary.com> http://dictionary.reference.com/browse/Nucleosynthesis>. (14 Sep 2008)

[6] Berkeley Astronomy Department, *Big Bang Nucleosynthesis.* (http://astro.berkeley.edu/~mwhite/darkmatter/bbn.html) (26 Sep 2008)

[7] "Timeline of the Big Bang." *Wikipedia, The Free Encyclopedia.* 12 Sep 2008, 15:59 UTC. 14 Sep 2008 <http://en.wikipedia.org/w/index.php?title=Timeline_of_the_Big_Bang&oldid=237954977>.

[8] The National Academies Press: *The Origin of the Universe, Earth and Life.* http://www.nap.edu/openbook.php?record_id=6024&page=4 (14 Sep 2008)

[9] AstronomyNotes.Com: *Galaxies.* http://www.astronomynotes.com/galaxy/s10.htm. (14 Sep 2008)

[10] AstronomyNotes.Com: *Galaxies.* http://www.astronomynotes.com/galaxy/s10.htm. (14 Sep 2008)

[11] AstronomyNotes.Com: *Galaxies.* http://www.astronomynotes.com/galaxy/s10.htm. (14 Sep 2008)

[12] Christian, Eric. *How large is the Milky Way?,* http://imagine.gsfc.nasa.gov/docs/ask_astro/answers/980317b.html. (2008-04-30).

[13] Sanders, Robert. "Milky Way galaxy is warped and vibrating like a drum", UCBerkeley News, January 9, 2006. http://www.berkeley.edu/news/media/releases/2006/01/09_warp.shtml. Retrieved on 2008-04-30.

[14] Montmerle, Thierry; Augereau, Jean-Charles; Chaussidon, Marc et.al (2006). "Solar System Formation and Early Evolution: the First 100 Million Years". Earth, Moon, and Planets 98: 39–95. Spinger. doi:10.1007/s11038-006-9087-5.

[15] In 2006, Pluto was declassified as a planet after the discovery of two other celestial bodies called Ceres and Eris. These three are now classified as 'dwarf planets'.
[16] *Dalrymple, G.B. (1991). The Age of the Earth. California: Stanford University Press. ISBN 0-8047-1569-6.*
[17] Jörn Müller, Harald Lesch (2003): Woher kommt das Wasser der Erde? - Urgaswolke oder Meteoriten. Chemie in unserer Zeit 37(4), pg. 242 – 246, ISSN 0009-2851
[18] According to A. Morbidelli et al. (Meteoritics & Planetary Science 35, 2000, S. 1309–1329).
[19] Richard Dawkins, *The Selfish Gene* p. 12.
[20] *Wilde, Simon A.; et al. (2001). "Evidence from detrital zircons for the existence of continental crust and oceans on the Earth 4.4 Gyr ago". Nature* **409***: 175–178. doi:10.1038/35051550.*
[21] *Miller S. L. (1953). "Production of Amino Acids Under Possible Primitive Earth Conditions". http://www.issol.org/miller/miller1953.pdf Science* **117***: 528.* doi:10.1126/science.117.3046.528.
[22] *Archer, Corey; Vance, Derek (2006). "Coupled Fe and S isotope evidence for Archean microbial Fe(III) and sulfate reduction". Geology* **34** *(3): 153–156. doi:10.1130/G22067.1.*
[23] Including HD 70642, HD 154345 or Gliese 849
[24] From gslc.genetics.utah.edu (http://learn.genetics.utah.edu/units/basics/tour/) May 20, 2008.
[25] From gslc.genetics.utah.edu (http://learn.genetics.utah.edu/units/basics/tour) May 20, 2008.
[26] Chromosomes are duplicated before cells divide when DNA molecules replicate.
[27] *Pearson H (2006). "Genetics: what is a gene?". Nature* **441** *(7092): 398–401, http://dx.doi.org/10.1038%2F441398a*
[28] *Peaston AE, Whitelaw E (2006). "Epigenetics and phenotypic variation in mammals". Mamm. Genome* **17** *(5): 365–74.* doi:10.1007/s00335-005-0180-2. PMID 16688527
[29] http://learn.genetics.utah.edu/units/basics/tour/ (22 may 2008)
[30] Wyhe, John van (2002). Charles Darwin: gentleman naturalist. *The Complete Work of Charles Darwin Online.* University of Cambridge. http://darwin-online.org.uk/darwin.html. Retrieved on 2008-01-16.
[31] See: http://tolweb.org
[32] *The Selfish Gene* by Richard Dawkins p17.
[33] *Darwin's Dangerous Idea* by Dan Dennett p86.
[34] Adenoisne Triphosphate (ATP)
[35] Fortey, Richard [1997] (September 1999). "Dust to Life", *Life: A Natural History of the First Four Billion Years of Life on Earth.* New York: Vintage Books, 50–51. ISBN 0-375-70261-X.
[36] Chaisson, Eric J. (2005). *Early Cells. Cosmic Evolution. Tufts University.* Retrieved on 2006-03-29.

[37] The existence of Columbia was first proposed by J.J.W. Rogers and M. Santosh (Rogers, J.J.W. and Santosh, M., 2002, Configuration of Columbia, a Mesoproterozoic supercontinent. Gondwana Research, v. 5, pp. 5-22).
[38] Ancient supercontinent proposed, article: http://news.bbc.co.uk/2/hi/science/nature/1892869.stm. 29 May 2008.
[39] Chaisson, Eric J. (2005). Ancient Fossils. Cosmic Evolution. Tufts University. http://www.tufts.edu/as/wright_center/cosmic_evolution/docs/text/text_bio_2.html; Retrieved on 2006-03-31.
[40] Bhattacharya, Debashish; Linda Medlin (1998). "Algal Phylogeny and the Origin of Land Plants". *Plant Physiology* **116**: 9–15. (PDF). http://www.iib.unsam.edu.ar/IIB-INTECH/html/docencia/BioVegetal/Evolucion03.pdf
[41] Torsvik, Trond H. *(*May 30, 2003*).* " *The Rodinia Jigsaw Puzzle* ".http://www.sciencemag.org/cgi/content/full/300/5624/1379?ijkey=fYKdlXStamWxU&keytype=ref&siteid=sci Science **300** *(5624): 1379–1381.* doi:10.1126/science.1083469.
[42] Jennifer Bergman. Heterotrophs (English). http://www.windows.ucar.edu/tour/link=/earth/Life/heterotrophs.html&edu=high (Retrieved on September 30, 2007)
[43] Richard Dawkins, *The Ancestor's Tale* p 314.
[44] Fortey, Richard *[1997] (September 1999).* "Landwards", Life: A Natural History of the First Four Billion Years of Life on Earth. New York: Vintage Books, 138–140. ISBN 0-375-70261-X.
[45] Heckman, D. S.; D. M. Geiser, B. R. Eidell, R. L. Stauffer, N. L. Kardos, & S. B. Hedges (August 10, 2001). "Molecular evidence for the early colonization of land by fungi and plants". http://www.ncbi.nlm.nih.gov/entrez/query.fcgi?cmd=Retrieve&db=PubMed&dopt=Abstract&list_uids=11498589 Science **10** *(293): 1129–1133.* PMID 11498589, doi:10.1126/science.1061457.
[46] Johnson, E. W.; D. E. G. Briggs, R. J. Suthren, J. L. Wright, & S. P. Tunnicliff (May 1994). "Non-marine arthropod traces from the subaereal Ordivician Borrowdale volcanic group, English Lake District". *Geological Magazine* **131** *(3): 395–406.* (abstract)
[47] http://evolution.berkeley.edu/evolibrary/article/0_0_0/arthropods_intro_01 (29 May 2008)
[48] *Kuraku et al. (December 1445 B.C.). "Monophyly of Lampreys and Hagfishes Supported by Nuclear DNA–Coded Genes". Journal of Molecular Evolution* doi:10.1007/PL00006595**49**: 729.
[49] http://www.tolweb.org/Gnathostomata/148436/6/08.
[50] *Erdmann, Mark V. (April 1999).* "An Account of the First Living Coelacanth known to Scientists from Indonesian Waters". *Environmental Biology of Fishes* **Volume 54** *(#4): 439-443. Springer Netherlands.* doi:10.1023/A:1007584227315. 0378-1909 (Print) 1573-5133 (Online). Retrieved on2007-05-18.

[51] The Tree of Life Project. *Terrestrial Vertebrates.* http://www.tolweb.org/Terrestrial_Vertebrates/14952 (Accessed 11 September 2008).
[52] Willis, K. J.; J. C. McElwain (2002). *The Evolution of Plants.* Oxford: Oxford University Press, 93. ISBN 0-19-850065-3 and Plant Evolution (http://sci.waikato.ac.nz/evolution/plantEvolution.shtml). University of Waikato. Retrieved on 2006-04-07.
[53] Dawkins, Richard *(2004). "Amphibians", The Ancestor's Tale: A Pilgrimage to the Dawn of Life. Boston: Houghton Mifflin Company, 293–296.* ISBN 0-618-00583-8.
[54] http://icb.oxfordjournals.org/cgi/reprint/37/4/428.pdf (29 May 08)
[55] Richard Cowen, History Of Life, p 147.
[56] Carroll, R.L. (1969). "Problems of the origin of reptiles." *Biological Reviews,* **44**: 393-432.
[57] "placenta." *The American Heritage® Science Dictionary*. Houghton Mifflin Company. 05 Jun. 2008. <Dictionary.com http://dictionary.reference.com/browse/placenta>.
[58] *Palæos Vertebrates 480.400 Archonta Primates* http://www.palaeos.com/Vertebrates/Units/480Archonta/480.400.html#Primates (2006-01-08).
[59] *Robert W. Shumaker & Benjamin B. Beck (2003). Primates in Question. Smithsonian Institute Press.* ISBN 1-58834-176-3.
[60] Richard Dawkins, *The Ancestors Tale,* p 121.
[61] *Jacobs, G. H.; Neitz, M., Deegan, J. F., & Neitz, J. (1996). "Trichromatic colour vision in New World monkeys". Nature (382): 156-158.*
[62] *Sean B. Carroll (2006). The Making of the Fittest. W.W. Norton and Company. ISBN* 978-0-393-06163-5.
[63] Andrew Lock, Charles R Peters, Handbook of Human Symbolic Evolution. P 169.
[64] Richard Dawkins, *The Ancestor's Tale* p 124.
[65] Richard Dawkins, *The Ancestor's Tale* p 121.
[66] Richard Dawkins, *The Ancestor's Tale* p 104.
[67] *Harcourt, A.H., MacKinnon, J. & Wrangham, R.W. (1984). in Macdonald, D.: The Encyclopedia of Mammals. New York: Facts on File, 422-439.* ISBN 0-87196-871-1.
[68] *Goren-Inbar, Naama; Nira Alperson, Mordechai E. Kislev, Orit Simchoni, Yoel Melamed, Adi Ben-Nun, & Ella Werker (2004-04-30). "Evidence of Hominin Control of Fire at Gesher Benot Ya`aqov, Israel". Science* **304** *(5671): 725–727. doi:10.1126/science.1095443.* (abstract)
[69] "Homo (genus)." *Wikipedia, The Free Encyclopedia.* 19 May 2008, 23:06 UTC. Wikimedia Foundation, Inc. 6 Jun 2008 <http://en.wikipedia.org/w/index.php?title=Homo_%28genus%29&oldid=213579403>.
[70] Boyd, Robert & Silk, Joan B. (2003). *How Humans Evolved.* New York: Norton & Company. ISBN 0-393-97854-0.
[71] See www.smgf.org for more information.

[72] Dawkins, Richard *(2004). The Ancestor's Tale, A Pilgrimage to the Dawn of Life.Boston: Houghton Mifflin Company.* ISBN 0-618-00583-8.
[73] See works of evolutionary biologist, Alan Templeton and geneticist Spencer Wells, amongst others.
[74] Wolman, David (2008). "Fossil Feces Is Earliest Evidence of N. America Humans" (http://news.nationalgeographic.com/news/2008/04/080403-first-americans.html) National Geographic
[75] http://news.bbc.co.uk/2/hi/health/5219752.stm. Dark skin 'does not block skin cancer'.
[76] "Abrahamic religion." *Wikipedia, The Free Encyclopedia.* 7 Jul 2008, 08:08 UTC. Wikimedia Foundation, Inc. 11 Jul 2008 <http://en.wikipedia.org/w/index.php?title=Abrahamic_religion&oldid=224095932 >.
[77] Mencken, "*Aftermath*," The Baltimore Evening Sun, September 14, 1925.
[78] Diamond, Jared *(1992, 2006). The Third Chimpanzee: The Evolution and Future of the Human Animal. New York: Harper Perennial, 141-167.* ISBN 0060183071.
[79] Sanskrit Literature (http://dsal.uchicago.edu/reference/gazetteer/pager.html?objectid=DS405.1.I34_V02_298.gif) The Imperial Gazetteer of India (http://en.wikipedia.org/wiki/The_Imperial_Gazetteer_of_India), v. 2, p. 263.
[80] "*Ethnologue: Languages of the World, Fifteenth edition*", accessed 28 June 2007, ISBN 1 55671 159 X
[81] (http://www.ned.univie.ac.at/Publicaties/taalgeschiedenis/en/dial.htm (Accessed Sat 21 June 08)
[82] http://www.cognitivebehavior.com/theory/languageandthinking.html (20 June 08) Jerome R. Gardner.
[83] http://www.cognitivebehavior.com/theory/languageandthinking.html (20 June 08) Jerome R. Gardner.
[84] "Judaism." *Wikipedia, The Free Encyclopedia.* 15 Jul 2008, 16:01 UTC. Wikimedia Foundation, Inc. 23 Jul 2008 <http://en.wikipedia.org/w/index.php?title=Judaism&oldid=225825076 >.
[85] "Talmud." *Wikipedia, The Free Encyclopedia.* 22 Jul 2008, 15:53 UTC. Wikimedia Foundation, Inc. 23 Jul 2008 <http://en.wikipedia.org/w/index.php?title=Talmud&oldid=227223937>.
[86] Robinson, George. *Essential Judaism: A Complete Guide to Beliefs, Customs and Rituals.* New York: Pocket Books, 2000, p. 229. and Esler, Phillip F. *The Early Christian World.* Routledge (2004), p. 157-158.
[87] "Our Common Heritage as Christians". (http://archives.umc.org/interior.asp?mid=1806)The United Methodist Church. Retrieved on 2007-12-31.
[88] "Nicene Creed." *Wikipedia, The Free Encyclopedia.* 22 Jul 2008, 14:03 UTC. Wikimedia Foundation, Inc. 23 Jul 2008 <http://en.wikipedia.org/w/index.php?title=Nicene_Creed&oldid=227206838>.
[89] "It is our desire that all the various nations which are subject to our clemency and moderation should continue to the profession of that religion which was

delivered to the Romans by the divine Apostle Peter, as it has been preserved by faithful tradition and which is now professed by the Pontiff Damasus and by Peter, Bishop of Alexandria, a man of apostolic holiness. ... We authorize the followers of this law to assume the title Catholic Christians; but as for the others, since in our judgment they are foolish madmen, we decree that they shall be branded with the ignominious name of heretics, and shall not presume to give their conventicles the name of churches." Halsall, Paul (June 1997). "Theodosian Code XVI.i.2". *Medieval Sourcebook: Banning of Other Religions*. Fordham University. Retrieved on 2006-09-19.

[90] "Christianity." *Wikipedia, The Free Encyclopedia*. 21 Jul 2008, 20:04 UTC. Wikimedia Foundation, Inc. 23 Jul 2008 <http://en.wikipedia.org/w/index.php?title=Christianity&oldid=227060950>.

[91] "Islam." *Wikipedia, The Free Encyclopedia*. 21 Oct 2008, 20:01 UTC. 22 Oct 2008 <http://en.wikipedia.org/w/index.php?title=Islam&oldid=246790821>.

[92] See: Accad (2003): According to Ibn Taymiya, although only some Muslims accept the textual veracity of the entire Bible, most Muslims will grant the veracity of most of it. Also: Esposito (1998), pp.6,12; Esposito (2002b), pp.4–5; F. E. Peters (2003), p.9; F. Buhl; A. T. Welch "Muhammad". Encyclopaedia of Islam Online. Retrieved on 2007-05-02 and Hava Lazarus-Yafeh "Tahrif". Encyclopaedia of Islam Online. Retrieved on 2007-05-02.

[93] Article: *"Fritzl blames Nazis and speaks of mother love"*. The Age. May 10, 2008. Andreas Sam, Vienna.

[94] *How To Win Friends And Influence People* by Dale Carnegie

[95] According to a presentation made during the 50th Anniversary of the Holy Rosary High School entitled: "Kayan Mission: A Brief History". Source: My Igorotness – A Glimpse on the History of Christian Igorots. http://peiqianlong.blogspot.com/ (Accessed 14 September 2008).

[96] Ms Weygan is the executive director of the Upland Development Institute and the Association of Young Igorot Professionals

[97] My Igorotness – *Religion In The Igorot and Japanese Culture.* http://peiqianlong.blogspot.com/2007/04/religion-in-igorot-and-japanese-culture.html (Accessed 14 Sep 2008).

[98] Wenner, Sara. "Basic Beliefs of Animism". *Emuseum*. 2001. Minnesota State University. 10 July 2008 <http://www.mnsu.edu/emuseum/cultural/religion/animism/beliefs.html>

[99] The Analects XV.24, tr. David Hinton

[100] Pittacus, Fragm. 10.3

[101] Diogenes Laërtius, "The Lives and Opinions of Eminent Philosophers", I,36

[102] Isocrates, "Nicocles",6

[103] Epictetus, "Encheiridion"

[104] Scientist Finds the Beginnings of Morality in Primate Behavior. The New York Times. March 20, 2007. Scientist Finds the Beginnings of Morality in Primate Behavior http://www.nytimes.com/2007/03/20/science/20moral.html?pagewanted=2&_r=2&ref=science (Accessed: 9 August 2008).

[105] Reciprocal Food Sharing In the Vampire Bat
http://www.life.umd.edu/faculty/wilkinson/Wilkinson84.pdf (Accessed: 09 August 2008)
[106] The Practice of Human Sacrifice.
http://www.bbc.co.uk/history/ancient/british_prehistory/human_sacrifice_04.shtml (13 August 2008)
[107] http://www.speedylook.com/Original_account.html (26 June 2008)
[108] http://users.erols.com/bcccsbs/africa/maasai.htm (26 June 08)
[109] http://www.speedylook.com/Original_account.html (26 June 2008)
[110] http://www.speedylook.com/Original_account.html (26 June 2008)
[111] http://san-shin.org/dan-gun-2.html (26 June 2008)
[112] "Creation myth." *Wikipedia, The Free Encyclopedia*. 24 Jun 2008, 11:59 UTC. Wikimedia Foundation, Inc. 26 Jun 2008
<http://en.wikipedia.org/w/index.php?title=Creation_myth&oldid=221415330>.
[113] Myths and Legends of China, E.T.C Werner, http://www.gutenberg.org/files/15250/15250.txt Ebook.
[114] "Creation myth." *Wikipedia, The Free Encyclopedia*. 24 Jun 2008, 11:59 UTC. Wikimedia Foundation, Inc. 26 Jun 2008
<http://en.wikipedia.org/w/index.php?title=Creation_myth&oldid=221415330>.
[115] "Norse mythology." *Wikipedia, The Free Encyclopedia*. 23 Jun 2008, 01:46 UTC. Wikimedia Foundation, Inc. 26 Jun 2008
<http://en.wikipedia.org/w/index.php?title=Norse_mythology&oldid=221102290>.
[116] "Creation myth." *Wikipedia, The Free Encyclopedia*. 24 Jun 2008, 11:59 UTC. Wikimedia Foundation, Inc. 26 Jun 2008
<http://en.wikipedia.org/w/index.php?title=Creation_myth&oldid=221415330>. Also: http://www.egyptianmyths.net/ennead.htm, http://www.egyptianmyths.net/ogdoad.htm
[117] http://www.yale.edu/ynhti/curriculum/units/1994/3/94.03.03.x.html, *Title: Aztec Mythology* by Lorna Dils
[118] "Maya mythology." *Wikipedia, The Free Encyclopedia*. 20 Sep 2008, 17:43 UTC. 30 Sep 2008
<http://en.wikipedia.org/w/index.php?title=Maya_mythology&oldid=239821354>.
[119] Genesis 1:28, King James Version.
[120] Esposito (2002b), p.17
[121] "Five Pillars of Islam." *Wikipedia, The Free Encyclopedia*. 23 Jul 2008, 10:52 UTC. Wikimedia Foundation, Inc. 23 Jul 2008
<http://en.wikipedia.org/w/index.php?title=Five_Pillars_of_Islam&oldid=227388158 >.
[122] Farah, Caesar (1994). *Islam: Beliefs and Observances, 5th, Barron's Educational Series*. ISBN 978-0812018530, p.135
[123] Kobeisy, Ahmed Nezar (2004). *Counseling American Muslims: Understanding the Faith and Helping the People*. Praeger Publishers. ISBN 978-0313324727, pp.22-34

[124] Ridgeon, Lloyd (2003). *Major World Religions*, 1st, RoutledgeCurzon. ISBN 978-0415297967. p.258
[125] "Zakah", *Encyclopaedia of Islam Online*
[126] Farah, Caesar (1994). *Islam: Beliefs and Observances*, 5th, Barron's Educational Series. ISBN 978-0812018530, pp.144-145
[127] Esposito, John (1998). *Islam: The Straight Path*, 3rd, Oxford University Press. ISBN 978-0195112344, pp.90,91
[128] Tabatabae, Sayyid Mohammad Hosayn; R. Campbell (translator) (2002). *Islamic teachings: An Overview and a Glance at the Life of the Holy Prophet of Islam. Green Gold*. ISBN 0-922817-00-6, pp. 211,213.
[129] Farah, Caesar (1994). *Islam: Beliefs and Observances*, 5th, Barron's Educational Series. ISBN 978-0812018530, pp.145-147
[130] Esposito, John (1998). *Islam: The Straight Path*, 3rd, Oxford University Press. ISBN 978-0195112344, pp.111,112,118 and "Shari'ah". Encyclopaedia Britannica Online. Retrieved on 2007-05-02.
[131] "Islam." *Wikipedia, The Free Encyclopedia*. 22 Jul 2008, 13:26 UTC. Wikimedia Foundation, Inc. 23 Jul 2008 <http://en.wikipedia.org/w/index.php?title=Islam&oldid=227201513 >.
[132] http://www.theage.com.au/opinion/the-future-of-the-planet-is-in-our-hands-20080603-2l48.html?page=-1, 3 June 2008
[133] The Age http://www.theage.com.au/opinion/the-future-of-the-planet-is-in-our-hands-20080603-2l48.html?page=2 June 3, 2008.
[134] Daniel Dennett, Breaking The Spell, p4.
[135] "The Root of All Evil?." *Wikipedia, The Free Encyclopedia*. 17 Jul 2008, 09:29 UTC. Wikimedia Foundation, Inc. 18 Jul 2008 <http://en.wikipedia.org/w/index.php?title=The_Root_of_All_Evil%3F&oldid=226205417 >.
[136] Evans, Allan S.; Riley E. Moynes, Larry Martinello (1973). What man Believes: A study of the World's Great Faiths. McGraw-Hill Ryerson, 424. ISBN 0-07-077440-4.
[137] Infallibility means more than exemption from actual error; it means exemption from the possibility of error," P. J. Toner, Infallibility < http://www.newadvent.org/cathen/07790a.htm (20 Sep 2008)> , Catholic Encyclopedia, 1910
[138] The Watchtower. *A Business With A Long History*. http://www.watchtower.org/e/20010222/article_01.htm (5 July 2008).
[139] According to Exodus 20:3 'Or' means 'besides'.
[140] Richard Dawkins, *The God Delusion*, p 243.
[141] "heretic." *Dictionary.com Unabridged (v 1.1)*. Random House, Inc. 31 Jul. 2008. <Dictionary.com http://dictionary.reference.com/browse/heretic>.
[142] "blasphemer." *The American Heritage® Dictionary of the English Language, Fourth Edition*. Houghton Mifflin Company, 2004. 31 Jul. 2008. <Dictionary.com http://dictionary.reference.com/browse/blasphemer>.
[143] "irreverent." *The American Heritage® Dictionary of the English Language, Fourth Edition*. Houghton Mifflin Company, 2004. 31 Jul. 2008. <Dictionary.com http://dictionary.reference.com/browse/irreverent>.

[144] "impious." *Dictionary.com Unabridged (v 1.1)*. Random House, Inc. 31 Jul. 2008. <Dictionary.com http://dictionary.reference.com/browse/impious>.
[145] Image:Rechtsgutachten betr Apostasie im Islam.jpg , Wikipedia. http://en.wikipedia.org/wiki/Image:Rechtsgutachten_betr_Apostasie_im_Islam.jpg (Last Accessed: 22 October 2008)
[146] I. Warraq (1995). Why I Am Not A Muslim. New York Prometheus. p175
[147] http://english.aljazeera.net/archive/2006/04/20084101323236719 34.html Afghan clerics want convert sent back. (25 July 2008)
[148] Afghan convert arrives in Italy for asylum. http://www.cnn.com/2006/WORLD/asiapcf/03/29/christian.convert/index.html (25 July 2008)
[149] Quixotic Media, Documentary: *"Islam – What The West Needs To Know"* (2006).
[150] "Religious war." *Wikipedia, The Free Encyclopedia*. 13 Jul 2008, 19:59 UTC. Wikimedia Foundation, Inc. 25 Jul 2008 <http://en.wikipedia.org/w/index.php?title=Religious_war&oldid=225455262 >.
[151] *Letter To A Christian Nation* by Sam Harris, p5.
[152] (Trent, l. c., can. xii: "Si quis dixerit, fidem justificantem nihil aliud esse quam fiduciam divinae misericordiae, peccata remittentis propter Christum, vel eam fiduciam solam esse, qua justificamur, a.s.")
[153] (cf. Trent, Sess. VI, cap. iv, xiv)
[154] "Luther's lavatory thrills experts", http://news.bbc.co.uk/2/hi/europe/3944549.stm, BBC News, October 22, 2004.
[155] Macauley Jackson, Samuel and Gilmore, George William. (eds.) "Martin Luther", *The New Schaff-Herzog Encyclopedia of Religious Knowledge*, New York, London, Funk and Wagnalls Co., 1908–1914; Grand Rapids, Michigan: Baker Book House, 1951), 71. http://www.ccel.org/ccel/schaff/encyc07/Page_71.html (5 August 2008)
[156] Bratcher, Dennis. "The Edict of Worms (1521)," in *The Voice: Biblical and Theological Resources for Growing Christians*. http://www.crivoice.org/creededictworms.html (05 Aug 2008).
[157] Schaff-Herzog, "Luther, Martin," 72. http://www.ccel.org/ccel/schaff/encyc07/Page_72.html (5 Aug 08).
[158] Schaff, Philip, History of the Christian Church, Vol VII, Ch IV. http://www.ccel.org/s/schaff/history/7_ch04.htm (5 August 2008)
[159] "Battle of Frankenhausen." *Wikipedia, The Free Encyclopedia*. 31 Jul 2008, 11:36 UTC. Wikimedia Foundation, Inc. 5 Aug 2008 <http://en.wikipedia.org/w/index.php?title=Battle_of_Frankenhausen&oldid=228997109 >.
[160] "Scholasticism." *Wikipedia, The Free Encyclopedia*. 27 Jul 2008, 23:48 UTC. Wikimedia Foundation, Inc. 30 Jul 2008 <http://en.wikipedia.org/w/index.php?title=Scholasticism&oldid=228282886>.
[161] "Age of Enlightenment." *Wikipedia, The Free Encyclopedia*. 26 Jul 2008, 21:57 UTC. Wikimedia Foundation, Inc. 30 Jul 2008 <http://en.wikipedia.org/w/index.php?title=Age_of_Enlightenment&oldid=228078136 >.

[162] http://history-world.org/age_of_enlightenment.htm. 31 July 2008
[163] "Age of Enlightenment." *Wikipedia, The Free Encyclopedia*. 26 Jul 2008, 21:57 UTC. Wikimedia Foundation, Inc. 30 Jul 2008 <http://en.wikipedia.org/w/index.php?title=Age_of_Enlightenment&oldid=228078136 >.
[164] "Age of Enlightenment." *Wikipedia, The Free Encyclopedia*. 26 Jul 2008, 21:57 UTC. Wikimedia Foundation, Inc. 30 Jul 2008 <http://en.wikipedia.org/w/index.php?title=Age_of_Enlightenment&oldid=228078136 >.
[165] BBC Four. Documentary: *The Protestant Revolution* by Tristam Hunt (2007).
[166] John Mullan, Professor of English University College London. BBC Four. Documentary: *The Protestant Revolution* by Tristam Hunt (2007). Part 3 of 4.
[167] BBC Four. Documentary: *The Protestant Revolution* by Tristam Hunt. Part 2 of 4. (2007).
[168] "The Diocese of New Hampshire: The Rt. Rev. V. Gene Robinson: Bishop of New Hampshire", Diocese of New Hampshire. http://www.nhepiscopal.org/bishop/bishop.html (Accessed 7 August 2008).
[169] BBC Four. Documentary: *The Protestant Revolution* by Tristam Hunt (2007). Part 3 of 4.
[170] BBC Four. Documentary: *The Protestant Revolution* by Tristam Hunt (2007). Part 4 of 4.
[171] Walter Isaacson. *Benjamin Franklin: An American Life* p 491 (2003).
[172] Sir Leslie Stephen's *English Thought in the Eighteenth Century*
[173] *Rosen, Edward (1995). Copernicus and his Successors. London: Hambledon Press. ISBN 1 85285 071 X. (1995, pp.151–59)*
[174] *Gebler, Karl von (1879). Galileo Galilei and the Roman Curia. London: C.K. Paul & Co. (1879, pp. 22-35).*
[175] *Atheism: A Rough History of Disbelief a documentary by Jonathan Miller (BBC Four TV. 2004.)*
[176] http://www.lhup.edu/~dsimanek/ussher.htm. Lock Haven University of Pennsylvania. Bishop Ussher Dates The World: 4004 BC (accessed 8 August 2008).
[177] "Existentialism." Wikipedia, The Free Encyclopedia. 26 Aug 2008, 20:25 UTC. 28 Aug 2008 <http://en.wikipedia.org/w/index.php?title=Existentialism&oldid=234425542>.
[178] Lacey, A.R. (1996), A Dictionary of Philosophy, 1st edition, Routledge and Kegan Paul, 1976. 2nd edition, 1986. 3rd edition, Routledge, London, UK, 1996. p286.
[179] Bourke, Vernon J. (1962), "Rationalism", p. 263 in Runes (1962).
[180] Audi, Robert (ed., 1999), *The Cambridge Dictionary of Philosophy*, Cambridge University Press, Cambridge, UK, 1995. 2nd edition, 1999. p. 771.
[181] "Rationalism." *Wikipedia, The Free Encyclopedia*. 28 Aug 2008, 01:31 UTC. 28 Aug 2008 <http://en.wikipedia.org/w/index.php?title=Rationalism&oldid=234694019>.

[182] "Positivism." *Wikipedia, The Free Encyclopedia*. 18 Aug 2008, 12:32 UTC. 28 Aug 2008
<http://en.wikipedia.org/w/index.php?title=Positivism&oldid=232674817 >.
[183] "Positivism." *Wikipedia, The Free Encyclopedia*. 18 Aug 2008, 12:32 UTC. 28 Aug 2008
<http://en.wikipedia.org/w/index.php?title=Positivism&oldid=232674817 >.
[184] "Humanism." *Wikipedia, The Free Encyclopedia*. 28 Aug 2008, 13:29 UTC. 28 Aug 2008
<http://en.wikipedia.org/w/index.php?title=Humanism&oldid=234777867 >.
[185] *Zwolinski, Matt, "Libertarianism", Internet Encyclopedia of Philosophy, <http://www.iep.utm.edu/l/libertar.htm>. Retrieved on* 29 August 2008
[186] Rashid, Ahmed (2000). Taliban: Militant Islam, Oil, and Fundamentalism in Central Asia. Yale University Press, New Haven, CT. ISBN 0-300-08340-8., republished by Pan Books with the title Taliban: The story of the Afghan warlords: including a new foreword following the terrorist attacks of 11 September 2001, ISBN 0-330-49221-7. Page 29, on the Pan Books edition.
[187] Feldman, Noah (2005). *Divided by God*. Farrar, Straus and Giroux, pg. 10 ("For the first time in recorded history, they designed a government with no established religion at all.")
[188] http://www.au.org (Accessed 14 August 2008)
[189] Jefferson, Thomas (1802-01-01). "Jefferson's Letter to the Danbury Baptists". http://www.loc.gov/loc/lcib/9806/danpre.html, U.S. Library of Congress. Retrieved on 2008-07-31.
[190] http://www.ummah.net/what-is-islam/quran/noble/nobe047.htm, The Noble Koran: Surat 47 (Accessed 15 August 2008)
[191] The Guardian. *Full Text: Bin Laden's 'Letter To America'*. http://www.guardian.co.uk/world/2002/nov/24/theobserver, Published 24 November 2002. (Accessed 3 October 2008)
[192] Telegraph. Polls reveals 40pc of Muslims want sharia law in UK. http://www.telegraph.co.uk/news/uknews/1510866/Poll-reveals-40pc-of-Muslims-want-sharia-law-in-UK.html. (Accessed: 15 August 2008)
[193] Times Online. Sniffer Dogs To Wear 'Muslim' Bootees. http://www.timesonline.co.uk/tol/news/uk/article4276489.ece. (Accessed 17 Sept 2008).
[194] Times Online. Revealed: UK's First Official Sharia Courts. http://143.252.148.161/tol/comment/faith/article4749183.ece (Accessed 17 Sept 2008).
[195] "Freedom of speech." *Wikipedia, The Free Encyclopedia*. 9 Sep 2008, 04:00 UTC. 10 Sep 2008
<http://en.wikipedia.org/w/index.php?title=Freedom_of_speech&oldid=237210061>.
[196] Dutch News Digest: Hirsi Ali on Film over Position of Women in Koran, http://www.dnd.nl/showarticle.php3?newsID=15018 (Accessed 15 August 2008).

[197] CBS News: Slaughter and Submission, http://www.cbsnews.com/stories/2005/03/11/60minutes/main679609.shtml. (Accessed 15 August 2008).

[198] The New York Times, Somali in The Hague Faces a More Personal Attack. http://query.nytimes.com/gst/fullpage.html?res=9501E7D7103EF937A15756C0A9609C8B63&sec=&spon=&pagewanted=2 (Accessed 15 August 2008).

[199] BBC News: Hidden Motives Behind Cartoon Riots. http://news.bbc.co.uk/2/hi/south_asia/4716762.stm (Accessed: 15 August 2008).

[200] BBC News: Danish Cartoons 'Plotters' Held. http://news.bbc.co.uk/2/hi/europe/7240481.stm (Accessed: 15 August 2008).

[201] PollingReport.Com. Science And Nature. http://www.pollingreport.com/science.htm (Accessed 5 September 2008)

[202] Pew Research Center for the People & the Press and Pew Forum on Religion & Public Life survey conducted by Schulman, Ronca & Bucuvalas (SRBI). July 6-19, 2006. (http://www.pollingreport.com/science.htm) Accessed 5 September 2008).

[203] Eternal Word Television Network. Pope John Paul II 22 October 1996 To Pontifical Academy of Sciences. http://www.ewtn.com/library/PAPALDOC/JP961022.HTM (Accessed 20 August 2008).

[204] Herald Sun. Pope Benedict Admits Evidence For Evolution. 26 July 2007. http://www.news.com.au/heraldsun/story/0,21985,22136550-5002700,00.html (Accessed 20 August 2008).

[205] *The God Delusion* by Richard Dawkins. p265.

[206] *The Age* newspaper. *"Bali Trio On Death Row Promise Revenge"*. Published 1st October 2008 (Accessed 3 October 2008).

[207] The Hudson Institute. Radical Islamist Ideologies in Southeast Asia. (http://www.futureofmuslimworld.com/research/pubID.31/pub_detail.asp) Published 19 May 2005 (Accessed 3 October 2008).

[208] *The Herald Sun* Newspaper, 19 May 2003. Page 1 to 5.

[209] Director of *The Pen Vs The Sword Publications*.

[210] "The Scientific Method: Hypothesis to Theory." http://servercc.oakton.edu/~billtong/eas100/scientificmethod.htm (20th Apr. 2008).

[211] Joseph Lykken is a theoretical physicist at the Fermi National Accelerator Laboratory.

[212] Brian Greene in the documentary *The Elegant Universe,* PBS, 2004.

[213] Brian Greene in the documentary *The Elegant Universe,* PBS, 2004.

[214] "Cartesian theater." Wikipedia, The Free Encyclopedia. 23 Jul 2008, 19:50 UTC. 9 Sep 2008 <http://en.wikipedia.org/w/index.php?title=Cartesian_theater&oldid=227477743>.

[215] YouTube.com. *The Magic Of Consciousness*. By Daniel Dennett. http://video.google.com/videoplay?docid=-8084768678469239623 (Accessed September 2008).

[216] http://www.kongogumi.co.jp/

[217] CIA. CIA- The World Factbook – Rank Order – Life Expectancy at birth. https://www.cia.gov/library/publications/the-world-factbook/rankorder/2102rank.html (Accessed 10 September 2008).
[218] Utah State Office Of Education. *"Life Span Of Cells And Organisms."* http://www.schools.utah.gov/curr/Science/sciber00/7th/genetics/sciber/life.htm (Accessed 10 September 2008).

[END OF BOOK]

www.ingramcontent.com/pod-product-compliance
Lightning Source LLC
Chambersburg PA
CBHW031251230426
4367OCB00005B/127